Boko Haram and Its Suicide Squad

(The Confession of a Jihadist)

Adrian Davieson

DEDICATION

Dedicated to the 300 school girls abducted by Boko Haram from Chibok Government Girls Secondary School; and to the memory of the slain in the hands of Boko Haram, Al-Qaeda and terrorist cells across the world.

The evil that men do lives after them — William Shakespeare in Julius Caesar: Act 3, Scene 2, Page 4

THE INTENT OF THE DEVIL

The devil came, masquerading with evil intent, and before the onlookers knew what was happening, they became victims of the evil machination of the devil!

Chapter 1

As a journalist, my news sources usually include official records, publications, broadcasts, government functionaries, competitive corporate executives, witnesses of crimes, whistleblowers, accident victims and bystanders or chanced spectators. Of all the various sources, the latter source is often the most factual and honest. Bystanders will give you their names and tell you the truth of what happened. Though each bystander will give a different account of what happened, at least you could piece the rest together, to get a story. In journalism, we piece information together often. With most government functionaries, it is different as they often prefer to give information anonymously. Getting the news from the people involved and or affected in an incident is a rarity. In my over three decades in journalism, I have never had an occasion to witness a remorseful and compelling confession, given by someone involved, as the one I am about to tell.

It was a rainy day in Maiduguri, the capital of Borno State, in northeast Nigeria, and the atmosphere had a look of gloom to it. Dubbed the city of fear, gloom had become the norm in this once peaceful city, formerly called the *home of peace*. It didn't help that five westerners were being held hostage by a terrorist network called Ansaru, in the city's suburb. I had arrived the night before in a chartered Cessna flight, having flown in from Abuja, the capital of Nigeria, where I was based as the West African Bureau Chief, of Central News Broadcast, to cover the kidnapping and possible rescue of the five westerners who were being held hostage by a new terrorist group called Ansaru, an offshoot, and a splinter group of Boko Haram, an Islamic jihadist militant terrorist sect.

I was in my hotel in Abuja, enjoying a rare peace in my overpriced hotel suite, when I got a call that the M15 and the CIA operatives, along with their Nigerian counterparts, were planning to rescue the kidnapped hostages, in a clandestine operation that was reminiscent of the CIA-led operation, code-named Operation Neptune Spear of the U.S. Naval Special Warfare Development Group, called DEGRU or Seal Team, that included U.S. Army special operations command's 160th special operation aviation regiment (airborne), in Abbottabad, Pakistan that led to the killing of Osama Bin Laden, the founder and head of the Islamist militant group, Al Qaeda.

I had arrived in Maiduguri, as the rain got heavier and fog started to set in, and the condition of the atmosphere began to get murky. The roads were in mud and waterlogged which made traveling in the ancient city difficult. The potholes, the unpaved and unmaintained roads, did not make traveling in the city easy, as we often had to stop our Land Rover, each time to allow the water to subside, to get to our destination. A thirty minute trip from the local airport became a four hour trip. When one adds the traffic congestions, compounded by Okada (bike riders who use their bikes to transport people for fares), and old, smoke-puffing vehicles, an already bad situation often becomes worse, as was the case on that day in Maiduguri.

Having travelled to every part of Nigeria, bad roads were nothing new to me, and the north was not an exception to what has become a substantial evidence of Nigeria as a failed state. Bad roads, lack of drinkable, treated, or treatable pipe-borne water, and irregular electricity (where they exist), were proof of Nigeria's failure as a country.

For some weird lucky reason, the little Cessna plane made it safely to Maiduguri without any incident. If I had flown in a commercial plane, the pilot would have refused to fly in that godforsaken weather. But we flew and made it safely to the ancient Kanem Borno Empire that was once the envy of smaller empires in sub-Saharan Africa, Africa, and the Arab world, in general.

Arriving at the hotel, six hours later, tired and jetlagged, I was looking forward to a good rest. The flight from Abuja had been bumpy and rough, even though it had been a safe flight, it had been filled with apprehensive moments, as the pilot constantly kept us updated about the gloomy weather condition. But he had reassured us that there would be no problem, and we had believed him. We had to, under the circumstances, since all we had left was hope. But he did deliver on his word to get us to Maiduguri safely, and he did.

Before leaving Abuja, I had asked my fellow journalists if they knew of any decent hotel in Maiduguri, that was safe to stay in, from Ansaru and Boko Haram kidnappers, and I was told the New Haven Hotel was a good bet. Over the years, I have learned that the best way to get reliable information was through your colleagues, because they were the ears of the streets; and they had their ears to the ground. Though I was more concerned about safety than luxury, I did not expect the hotel to be as dingy, shabby and squalid, as it turned out to be. Looking at the hotel, I could understand why it was safe. It was the last place any would-be kidnapper would expect a westerner to stay. I was given instructions on how to stay alive by my colleagues. I was to shave and cover my head with turban, and wear Muslim attire, from head to toe. And I was told to wear dark glasses at all time, to conceal my blue eyes.

Before boarding the Cessna plane with six other journalists, I had put on my turban and Muslim attire that I had purchased earlier. They included a set of dishdasha, jalabiya, shalwar, kameez, shemagh, igal, and several other outfits, in black, with hats to match. I had jettisoned my western clothes in Abuja, by leaving them with a trusted friend. I did not want to make the mistake of accidentally wearing them in Maiduguri, as the city had become a hotbed for Boko Haram operatives.

Years before, it would have been unnecessary for a westerner to disguise himself in Maiduguri, but things are different now, than the peaceful days of the pre-Boko Haram formation in 2001, by Mohammed Yusuf, when westerners could openly play golf and drink Guinness Extra Stout beer, in any bar or hotel, in the city. With Boko Haram having been responsible for over 10,000 deaths of mostly innocent Nigerians, which includes children, women, Muslims, and Christians, the days of freedom for westerners, were long gone. It was suicidal for any westerner to expose himself in the streets of Maiduguri or any part of Borno State now, or the three states the sect call its strongholds. Not when Boko Haram perceives western culture as a sin.

As soon as I settled down in my hotel, I called a number I was given by the U.S. embassy, for a guide. I suspected that the guide would be a CIA operative, an Arab, of northern Nigerian descent. I was right. It was my encounter with my embassy appointed guide, that I stumbled on the story that I am about to tell you.

My guide, a tall, light-skinned Nigerian, of Fulani descent, looked like a regular Arab of Middle Eastern descent, at first glance, but the twenty six years old was born and raised in northeastern Nigeria. His Fulani background spreads across twenty countries and generations, in Africa, which stretched from

Mauritania, Liberia, Ethiopia, Sudan, and several African countries.

My guide told me his father's bloodline included a French father and a Fulani mother, which explains his lighter skin color. He further told me that the majority of the Fulani people had lighter skin colors because of their nomadic lifestyle and settlements in various countries, which may have led to interracial marriages over the years.

Having satisfied my curiosity about the ethnicity of my guide, with his generous explanation, I settled down to the business at hand. I often did not go about questioning the people that I meet, about their racial backgrounds, but in northern Nigeria, especially in Borno State, and in Maiduguri, one had to know who he was associating and dealing with. I was not especially worried about my guide since he worked for the embassy but it was still necessary to know if he was a middle easterner or an African. Not that it mattered but I like to know things that I don't know. Funny I said that, but it is true. Since my guide speaks fluent Arabic and several other Middle Eastern languages, including the Hausa language, I got curious. As we talked, it became clear why he works for the CIA, if he does. But my experience with U.S. embassy staffs was that most of them were usually CIA operatives. I could be wrong. But as a journalist you knew these things. And I knew a lot.

Though I had been informed by the embassy that his name was Mohammed Musa, I wanted a formal introduction, as a form of punctilious sense of propriety, since I was going to be entrusting my life to the hand of this total stranger. I told him my name, and we shook hands to cement our new friendship, if you want to call it that. For good measure, I also told him about myself. I told him I have duo nationalities as my father was American and my mother British. I told him how they had met and how I became a journalist. "But your name is American," Musa said, wondering why I didn't have a British name. I started to explain and then it occurred to me that he wouldn't understand.

Not that Musa was unintelligent or uneducated. He was well educated, with a master's degree from one of the local universities. And on top of that, he speaks nine languages, which, I suspected, was one of the reasons he was employed by the U.S. embassy. Another reason that I was beginning to suspect, was that the man could fit into any Arab or Islamic speaking country with ease. People with his training and ethnic background of multilingual fluency, were highly sought by the CIA, M15 and the Mossad, to infiltrate terrorist cells in Muslim and Arab countries. And if he works for the CIA, I wouldn't be surprised if he was a double agent. Most people with his backgrounds were double agents. As a journalist, I knew these things.

Musa told me to get rid of any western clothing I have and when I told him I did not have any with me, he was relieved, surprised and impressed. "It is too dangerous for westerners in these parts of Nigeria. The north has become a danger zone for westerners, especially Americans and Europeans," Musa explained unnecessarily, as if I was new to the game. Like a good pupil, I listened and nodded my head as he talked. From experience, I knew it was always a good idea to let people talk so that knowledge can be gained, if there was knowledge to be gained. My training as a journalist required me to be patient and to be a good listener. Over the years, I have learned to be a very good listener, and it has paid off, on numerous occasions.

"About the hostages, when do you think the rescue is going to take place?" I asked, realizing that we have not made any mention of the reason I was in this terrorist hotbed. At first, he ignored my question and I was beginning to think he didn't hear me. And I was about to repeat myself when he looked at me straight in the eye and said. "This is going to be a very dangerous assignment, and I want you to know that lives could be lost, which may include yours or mine," he said with a very somber look that made me stiffen. But this was not my first foray into enemy territories. But I listened as he began to explain what was at stake.

"Now to answer your question, the rescue should take place tonight or tomorrow night. I don't know the exact time. We have to wait by the phone. The U.S. commander of the operation is a very strict man and he does not believe in taking chances. I think we will either get a phone call immediately before or after the operation. I don't think they will tell us the exact time, because so many lives are at stake," Musa said, as if talking to one of his lieutenants. As he began to talk, it occurred to me that I will need to be very careful around him.

When he did not get any response from me, he nodded his head as if it was a reassurance that I understood what he had said. I did understand but something else was bothering me. At first I had not thought of it, but as I started to listen to him, a feeling began to gnaw and nibble inside me. Why did the U.S. embassy send this man to be my guide? There was nothing special about me or my mission. I was just a journalist. Though I was a U.S. citizen, I didn't think my assignment was that important to warrant me to have the privilege of an embassy staff. Since curiosity always takes the better part of me, I asked. "Why did the embassy send you to guide me? I could manage on my own. This is really not my first visit to Borno State," I told him. He had that look in his eyes again that seemed to be both soulful and somber.

"I understand how you feel but then again I don't understand. I am not a journalist. I was only sent to assist and protect you. Boko Haram is very active in these parts of the north, and the embassy thinks it is important to protect you since you are an American journalist. You have to understand that it is the responsibility of the embassy to protect Americans in any country, but to answer your question we don't want to add you to the number of hostages currently in the possession of Boko Haram and Ansaru. These terrorist groups are deadly and have been known to behead the heads of westerners to make a statement, and the embassy wants to make sure you do not become a part of that statistics," he said, with smirk on his face that I immediately disliked and distrusted.

"I appreciate the embassy's concern for my welfare and safety but I have been in battle fronts before and survived. I was in Iraq during the desert storm in 1991 when Iraq had invaded and annexed Kuwait. I also covered Operation Iraqi Freedom in 2003, when Saddam Hussein was suspected of having weapons of mass destruction; that led to the toppling of the dictator. I have covered raids by U.S. Special Forces in Tora Bora, a cave in the white mountains of Afghanistan, known to be insurgents' hideouts," I told him. He looked at me as if I was talking gibberish. "I know about your background as a war correspondent but this is not a war. With Boko Haram, Ansaru, al-Shabab and al-Qaeda, you are dealing with invisible enemies, and that is what makes them more dangerous than battlefields and warfronts. These terrorists ride in motorcycles and sometimes look like regular people. In a country whose popular mode of transportation is motorcycle, we have our work cut out for us because motorcycles are everywhere, and one of them could be a suicide bomber, or an assassin," he said almost annoyingly.

I realized he was right. Though I already knew what he was talking about, it made more sense as he explained it. In warfronts in Iraq, Afghanistan and Syria, I didn't have the need to disguise myself. But here, in northern Nigeria, Somalia and Mali, and lately, Algeria, it was very dangerous to walk around and be visible as a westerner. So, listening to Musa, I realized he was sincere but I still had the nagging feeling that he was not entirely being honest about the reason he was sent by the embassy to serve as my guide.

Chapter 2

The next day, we were still waiting for a phone call about the planned rescue operation but the call never came. It became clear to us that something had gone awry. I went into the streets for sightseeing, dressed like a Muslim adherent, going from one mosque to another, to pretend to pray and to listen to the grapevine in the mosques. Since mosques were everywhere, I could go to any mosque unnoticed as a westerner. Being a practicing catholic, and worshipping with other Catholics, the very few times I do attend church, I was always visible as members often pray together, either holding hands to pray or shaking hands and wishing each other peace. With Muslims, there was no such interaction with other worshippers. The only time any modicum of interaction appeared visible was when the imam preaches.

Imams do not preach like pastors in churches. Most of the time, they condemn the unbelievers and extol the virtues of Allah and Muhammad. As the prayer leader of a mosque, imams pray while the worshippers simply pay obeisance to Allah as the prayer goes on.

In Islam, the Muslim leader or imam was a very important figure. Imams were said to be divinely appointed by Allah, and held in high esteem. They were said to be sinless and infallible successors of the holy prophet Muhammad. And because of the divine appointment of the imam, he was seen and looked upon as a spiritual and temporal leader.

Unlike the celestial hierarchy in Christendom where a traditional hierarchy of angels ranked from lowest to highest, there was no such thing in Islam. In Christendom for instance, the celestial hierarchy exists in nine orders: angels, archangels, principalities, powers, virtues, dominions, thrones, cherubim, and seraphim. In Islam, there is the all encompassing Allah, with Muhammad who is held in high esteem as the holy prophet.

When one becomes a Muslim, he begins to see the imam at the mosque as a supreme figure whose words were divine with spiritual authority. His actions are considered sacred and ecclesiastical rather than lay or temporal. The imam can also wield some sort of supernatural influence among worshippers and those who lean on his every word. His religiosity was often emulative and often deeply emotional, especially when he condemns those who did not believe in the Koran or Islam. Explaining the sacred writings in the Koran to fellow Muslims to whom he reigns supreme, the imam often speaks of the revelations made to Muhammad by Allah through the angel Gabriel, pretty much like the bible with a few twists and turns in the writings.

Based on everything I have explained so far, you will soon begin to understand where the story that I will be narrating emanated, and how the jihadist became radicalized. But before you meet the confessor in this story, I will like to further explain that the Koran is similar in so many ways to the bible except that the Koran is accepted by Muslims as a book of revelations made known to Muhammad by Allah; while the bible contains sacred scriptures of Christians that comprise the new and old testament, which was a covenant between God and human beings.

The testament is a visible and tangible proof of tributes, revelations, prophetic missions, creed, an expression of religious conviction and God's commands, concerning the human race. The testament is a very powerful aspect of the bible, because of the various testimonies in the sacred book.

In the streets of Maiduguri, I visited several mosques before going to the central mosque, where gunmen, suspected to be members of the Boko Haram radical Islamist group, had gruesomely slashed the throats of nine Christian workers at a construction site near the uncompleted central mosque. It was at the site of the same central mosque that a suicide bomber blew himself up, killing five people, in an assassination attempt against the deputy governor of the state, Zannah Mustaphar, and the Shehu of Borno, Abubakar Kyari.

Though the mosque was under construction, several Muslim worshippers were already praying there, on Fridays, when workmen were not at the site. I walked around and quickly left the place. With several deaths already marking the landmark of the central mosque, it was gradually attaining a dangerous ground to be in, as the uncompleted mosque has been the site of so many deaths carried out by Boko Haram. The deaths in and around the central mosque were not coincidental as Boko Haram continues to wage a separate war against prominent Muslim figures in the north. The slashing of the throats of worshippers at the mosque, and suicide bombings, were attempts to turn worshippers away from the mosque, and to derail its construction. But despite the deaths and the threats to the lives of the construction crew, work still continued at the site.

I quickly left the arena of the central mosque and headed back to the hotel. On the way, I decided I should snoop around. In these parts of northern Nigeria, everything appears newsworthy. The sight of the beggars and paupers in the streets of Maiduguri was newsworthy itself but not enough to convince my editor that it was worth reporting on. In these parts, poverty and beggary were a common sight.

It was hard to understand the existence of poverty in a country like Nigeria with its enormous oil wealth. The enormity of Nigeria's oil wealth and resources should be enough to reduce the poverty and misery in the streets of Nigeria to a significant minimum, but not so when corruption was rife and endemic in the country. Corruption appears to have reduced most Nigerians to beggary as years of embezzlement and stealing by government functionaries have beggared the country with such an enormous economic promise. Looking at the squalid condition of the capital, Maiduguri, which bespeaks of the cities, streets and towns of Nigeria, one begins to see how the situation beggars belief that government functionaries can be so cruel to reduce the country to what it is, a country where unemployment and underemployment beats statistical imagination and compilation.

After hours upon hours of trying to discreetly collect information about Boko Haram and Ansaru, the so-called vanguard for the protection of Muslims in black lands, I decided it was time to go back to the hotel. To maintain invisibility and low profile, I took a bike ride to the hotel. As a journalist, I have learned that the reason that westerners were targets in places like northern Nigeria and elsewhere in terrorist hotbeds was because of the lifestyles they kept. I have always prided myself on being able to mingle with indigenes anywhere. And another thing that works in my favor was that I speak fluent Arabic and Hausa, without an accent. And because of my fluency in the language, I have never had any problem, except for my western look. I had learnt the Hausa language during my years in Nigeria.

Another language I have learnt was the Yoruba language. I picked up a little bit of the Ibo language as well, though not as fluent. Though I speak fluent native languages and dialects, I kept this a secret from Musa. I have learned from past experience to keep aces up my sleeve in case I needed them later on, in an emergency. And when Musa had told me he speaks several of the native dialects and languages, I had remained quiet, not wanting to give him the impression that I knew anything.

I was still thinking about Musa when my phone rang. In these parts, there were no worries of phones being bugged. The technology was simply not there, or if it was, no one uses it or there was not enough power grid, or adequate electrode to maintain an electron tube and a network of conductors to distribute electric power.

I answered the phone, not recognizing the number. It didn't matter. I didn't have to check the number before answering. In these parts, SIM cards can be purchased anytime, and inserted in any of the disposable Nokia phones being hawked in the streets. It was always futile to memorize numbers as numbers come and go. Not when SIM cards can be purchased for next to nothing in the streets. "It is me, Musa," he said, when I said hello into the mouthpiece of the cell phone. As usual, when talking to him, I would say as little as possible. As a journalist, it was always good to be a listener as one never knows when a news-scoop might be in progress.

"I think I know what is happening. Words got out that there was going to be a rescue and the kidnappers moved the hostages to a different location. But the beauty of it was that we already had information about the new possible location. I will keep you informed. Let me know if you need to go somewhere. Remember what we talked about maintaining a low profile. Try as much as possible to stay in the hotel. If you need anything, just call me," he said. I said I will call him if I needed him, and the call ended.

I was not looking forward to hanging out with Musa, as I did not particularly like his mien. There was something about him that I couldn't really put my fingers on, but it was there and I could feel it every time he was around me. Anyway, he had left the hotel to go and attend to some personal matters, after we had waited for hours on end, for a phone call that never came. I was glad that he had left as that gave me the opportunity to leave the hotel and do my sightseeing. Even with that, I had the eerie feeling that he was having me watched. If my experience with dealing with secret agents was anything to go by, I would say he had someone else posted around the hotel to watch me.

At around 8am, the next day, he came back to the hotel, brimming with news and happiness as if he had won the lotto or come into some inheritance. Though I was not particularly thrilled with his presence, I pretended to be glad to see him again. As a journalist, acting comes natural to me because, believe it or not, it is an integral part of the trade. Not that all journalists are in the business of acting or lying, but in times of trouble a journalist must act to survive. Acting, in case you are wondering, is not the same acting actors engage in. This type of acting is of a different nature.

As I waited for Musa to tell me the reason for his excitement, it gradually dawned on me that he may have received the long awaited phone call about the rescue the CIA and the M15 were planning, to free the hostages. I patiently waited but I could see he was determined to leave me in suspense. Not willing to be lured and pushed into anxiousness, I waited, and soon my patience paid off, as he opened up and started to speak, like a torrential rainfall. "The rescue happened last night! Three of the hostages were killed. Most of the kidnappers were killed but one escaped into the bush, and he is believed to be seriously wounded."

As he talked, I could tell he was holding something back. I knew he was not being honest with me. My instinct told me he knew more than he was letting me on. I also had the gut feeling that he was part of the raid, the night before, but chose not to tell me about it, for reasons best known to him. But I was worried. I came to this dangerous city to cover a rescue and I have been prevented from the action. But I kept my frustration to myself, not wanting to make the situation worse than it already was.

"So, when can you take me to the place?" I asked, concerned that other news reporters may have beaten me to the news. I don't like being fed with second-hand news or hearsays. I like to get it firsthand. "Sure, my friend, that is why I am here, to take you there. And don't worry you will be the first journalist at the scene. I said the rescue took place last night, by that I mean in the wee hours of this morning, after 2am, which you could refer to as last night, if you like," he said, as if reading my mind.

I realized what he meant. After all, this was Nigeria. Media houses do not have hotlines for citizens to report incidents, news or unusual things. In the States, and in the U.K., citizens feed news to media outlets 24/7, which makes news reporting easy. But in Africa, that type of process and service was limited by the lack of technology and wherewithal to do so.

I quickly got ready, even though I was already dressed, with my materials handy and ready to go. I noticed he was ready too, already moving towards the door. "I have brought a bulletproof vest for you, in case we run into trouble, while out there. The place is cordoned off by the CIA, and there is no need to worry, but with militants and terrorists, you never know," he said, as he checked his two handguns for bullets, and gave me the bulletproof vest. He gave me one of the guns, not bothering to ask me if I knew how to use it or not. I quickly realized that he already knew about my military background, about me having served in the marines, after my high school education.

I put the 9mm in my waistband, not letting him know that I have another gun, a .38 police special, in my shoulder holster. I had purchased the gun from an old friend, on Gombe road, when I had arrived the day before. My old friend was a retired journalist who had retired from the Nigeria Television Authority, after 35 years. If anyone knew where to get odds and ends, he knew because he was familiar with the area. I guess you could call a gun a member of the odds and ends family.

We walked to his old jeep wrangler, and entered. We drove for several minutes on Maiduguri road, before suddenly veering onto Kashim Ibrahim road, as if we were being chased. We rode on the road for several minutes, before entering a dirt road. We drove on the dirt bushy road for almost an hour, before coming to a small town that looked deserted. I wanted to ask about the town, why most of the huts were burnt down, and why the town looked like the site of a nuclear disaster. As the words formed in my lips, and as I looked, the place did remind me of the Chernobyl nuclear plant accident, in Ukraine, in 1986.

"So, what happened to this town?" I asked when I couldn't hold it in, any longer. As a journalist, I always had to know, and knowing helps me with my news gathering. Musa looked at me, and with a sad look on his face, said: "that village was once inhabited by over 500 villagers. The Nigerian army came around and burnt down the village because they suspected the villagers of providing a hideout to the members of the Boko Harm militants." I looked at him, confused, and he saw the confusion on my face. "Some of the villagers were burnt along with their huts. You see, according to reports from the neighboring villages, the soldiers came at night and touched the huts, roasting alive the inhabitants who were asleep at that time of night. Those who managed to escape the inferno were shot and killed by the soldiers. A few that managed to escape ran to the nearby villages," he said, as if incidents like that was a norm in those parts of Nigeria.

"When did this happen?" I asked, trying to see why the incident did not get to the media. "This happened the week before. And In case you are wondering why the media did not cover the incident, it was probably because a bigger incident involving Boko Haram and Ansaru overshadowed the incident. The way things go here, Boko Haram is more newsworthy than news about soldiers burning down villages." I jotted down the information on my shorthand notepad, and took pictures with my shoulder camera, which also had a video camera. I would have preferred a cameraman but the place was too dangerous to take a cameraman.

With modern technology and the prevalent of miniature video cameras, that sometimes come installed in ballpoint pens, like the HD Spy Pen Camera, sometimes it was not even necessary to take a cameraman to a warzone, or if you like, a terrorist warzone. So, with my pen and camera handy, I discreetly recorded what I could, while pretending to take pictures. A video editor would make it look professional later, but my main goal was to record as much as I could. And I did.

We drove on, and as we drove, I began to think that we were never going to reach our destination, when all of a sudden Musa turned the car into another bushy road, where a small bungalow was tucked inside what looked like a Kirikiri maximum prison, in Lagos. At the top of the high walls were barbed wires. The barbed wires had sharp edges with points arranged at intervals, along the strands at the top. The top of the barbed wires were complete with metal staples that looked as if it had been electrified. Whoever built the place must have thought of every security measure that was available in these parts of northern Nigeria. The bungalow was heavily fortified to wade off intruders.

But the huge wrought iron gate was wide open as we approached it. There were police and army vehicles everywhere, and from the look of things, it appears local law enforcement agents had just being informed about the rescue, possibly the same time I was informed about it, too. We pulled up behind a military lorry that appeared to have seen more wars than it was originally planned for.

I waited for Musa to leave the jeep before stepping out of the vehicle. In these areas, soldiers and police were often trigger-happy, and it was always a smart idea to wait before coming out of the vehicle. After I was sure that Musa had familiarized and made introductions with the local law enforcement agents and soldiers, I stepped out of the vehicle and shook hands with the only American in the place, who appears to be a senior CIA operative. I was expecting more CIA and M15 agents, but only one CIA, as far as I could tell, was present.

"This is Commander Branson, an attaché of the U.S. consulate in Kano," Musa said, as he introduced us. I shook hands with the Commander, and I could see by his cold demeanor and eyes that I was right about him. The man was as detached and as cold in manner and attitude, as a KGB operative of old. I knew I couldn't trust the man more than I could throw him. And from the look of him, I knew he didn't expect me to. I knew what the man was. He was a CIA operative and I could tell he was a secret agent and a government licensed killer.

In places like this, one cannot openly reveal himself, except to those that matters. Before arriving at the bungalow, I had removed most of my disguises. I didn't want to look too Muslim where these trigger-happy soldiers were, as they appeared on the hunt for anyone resembling a Muslim radical or a Boko Haram operative. I knew the reputation of these soldiers, and I have seen them operate under the full glare of a television camera. I have seen them pick up innocent people that looked like Muslim radicals, round them up, and shoot them facedown. They call it waging war against terrorism in these parts. With them, it was eye for an eye, but sometimes, and more often than not, they kill more innocent Muslims than they do Boko Haram operatives.

I was ushered into the building by a Nigerian secret service agent who looked out of place in his rumpled and tousled, oversized brown suit. His hair looked disheveled and I could tell he had not had a bath in days and that he had not been home in days. Despite his unkempt appearance and wrinkled clothes, the man was actually very courteous and professional.

He greeted me as if we were old colleagues. I immediately liked him. He gave me as much information about the rescue as he could. "I lost a couple of my men here today. They were good family men," he said, as he shook his head, with sadness and a hint of tears in his eyes. I wanted to comfort him but I didn't know how to. I was not very good in the business of comforting aggrieved people. Instead, I patted him on the shoulder.

The Nigerian secret service agent explained what had happened and how the militants had surprised them, with reinforcements from nowhere. "They came from everywhere in the compound, with AK47s, M16s, Heckler & Koch G3s, FN FALs, Tavor TAR-21s, Stgw 90s, FAMAS G2s, FN SCAR-Ls, Steyr AUGs, and hand grenades. If we hadn't anticipated that they had good weapons, we would have suffered more casualties than we did. But thank God we only lost a few good men," he said. As he talked, I took pictures of the dead bodies that were still strewn everywhere in the building. I must have counted over 30 bodies in the bungalow. Some of the bodies were torsos with the heads brutally and grisly severed off, obviously blown away by the weapons or bombs used by the rescuers.

One dead body was so gruesome and grisly that I immediately threw up. I have seen grisly dead bodies in warfronts and battlefields during my years in the marines and as a journalist, but nothing compared to the gory sights that I saw in that bungalow.

In Nigeria, the authorities appeared to have less respect for the dead than most countries in the west. During my years of covering the West African sub-region, I had seen dead bodies lie in the streets for days on end, sometimes weeks before getting picked up for burial in a mass grave. I was not surprised that the dead bodies of the militants and secret service agents were still on the floor of the bungalow, six hours after the botched rescue operation.

I took as much pictures as I needed, and secretly recorded the whole ghastly sight, and afterward, I asked the Nigerian secret service agent if I could look around the grounds of the bungalow.

He said it was up to Musa, since the place was still considered very dangerous. "Boko Haram militants like to fight to the end. I will not be surprised if they are reinforcing to try to reclaim the bungalow," the Nigerian secret service agent said. I looked at him, confused, and he saw the look on my face and quickly explained. "The reason I said that is because they will try to come back for the bodies of their fallen colleagues. Jihadists don't like to leave their dead behind. We have to identify the bodies first, before burying them in a secret mass grave. We want to make sure some of the wanted leaders and operatives of the Islamic extremist sect were not among the dead," he said.

I understood what he meant. In the war against terrorism, the dead always had to be double checked to make sure they were not among the wanted. If they were among the wanted terrorists, the names of the wanted among the dead would be deleted from the list. But Boko Haram likes to take the bodies with them, to make the fallen terrorists, martyrs. I have seen it happen in Iraq and Afghanistan. And even in Yemen, where the Al Qaeda in the Arabian Peninsula now control the entire terrorist network that Osama Bin Laden once controlled, from his hideout in the Pakistani border with Afghanistan.

Musa agreed to go with me to check out the grounds of the bungalow. But before going, he wanted to check the place for landmines. Boko Haram, like al Qaeda, likes to set booby traps and to use landmines to fight the infidels or enemies. Of course, those who do not believe in the Koran or Allah, as the almighty, were considered infidels and enemies of Islam. As a journalist, working in Muslim territories, I know.

Musa used a bomb detector to sweep the compound for landmines. Satisfied there were none, he said it was okay for me to check the grounds, which I readily acquiesced to. It was while checking the grounds that I met the wounded terrorist, on the throes of agony and death. Meeting him and his eagerness to confess to the crimes he had committed against humanity was what led to this story, and what this story is about.

If I hadn't been looking for something newsworthy, I probably would have missed him as he crouched on the brink of death, huddled between the flowerbeds. I didn't want Musa to know at first that I had seen the dying man but it was already too late as he had also seen the man. He immediately brought out his weapon and was ready to shoot when he realized that the man was harmless and dying. I was glad he did because if he had killed the man, I wouldn't have this story that I am about to tell you.

Musa told me to cover him with my gun, in case the man suddenly became a threat or tries to shoot him. I said okay and pulled out the gun he had given me earlier. From what I could see of the man, he didn't appear to pose any threat to anyone. I saw bullet holes in his clothes. I counted five bullet holes, besides the fatal wounds on his body. I don't know how the man had managed to remain alive with that many bullet holes and wounds. I figured Allah or whoever he believes in, must actually be looking out for him.

He was in a pool of dried and oozing fresh blood which I assumed to be his own blood, since he was among several dead bodies. Immediately we got closer with our guns drawn, he asked for a cup of water. I immediately pulled out a flask of cold water from my small valise that I carry around with me, and gave him some water. He drank it thirstily as if it was the succor that would heal his bullet wounds. When he was finished drinking, he said thanks, and I nodded my head.

The water must have given him strength as he smiled and mumbled something. At first I couldn't hear what he said, and Musa warned me not to get closer as the man might still be dangerous. "A dying man has nothing to lose," Musa said, as he told the man to get up. The man tried to get up but he couldn't. Musa told him to bring out his hands to where he could see them, and the man complied, albeit weakly.

"I am no danger to anyone no more," he said in accented English. "I will like you to finish me off because I know my chance of survival is very slim. Even if I can get a very good medical attention right now, I will still not make it. I used to be a medical doctor in another life, so I know," the man said weakly but still audibly. I wondered how a man with so much education and learning got himself involved in a worthless cause like jihad. It didn't surprise me much. As a journalist covering the war on terror in Iraq and Afghanistan, I had noticed that educated people still get brainwashed with the promise of paradise after death, just like the naïve and gullible.

I remember an incident in Afghanistan where a medical doctor blew himself up to kill five American soldiers he was supposedly working with, in Kabul. When it comes to jihadists nothing surprises me. After all, the current leader of Al Qaeda, Ayman al-Zawahiri, who took over the leadership of Al Qaeda, when Osama Bin Laden was killed, is an eye surgeon.

I have long done away with the theory that only the naïve and uneducated get brainwashed to believe in the paradise that exists hereafter when the ultimate sacrifice was made to promote jihad. When it comes to getting brainwashed, no level of education was enough to shield the gullible and naïve. The naivety of men who are brainwashed into some kind of utopian belief has always baffled me. History is full of such men as al-Zawahiri who gave up saving lives to taking lives.

In the 1970s, Dr. George Habbash, was a Marxist-Leninist terrorist who led a terrorist organization called the Popular Front for the Liberation of Palestine. Though Dr. Habbash believed he was fighting a cause, he was still labeled a terrorist by those he fought against, because he was a terrorist. Every terrorist believes he is fighting for a cause. What differentiates a terrorist fighting for a cause and a genuine freedom fighter is how the world accepts and perceives such a cause. For a while, Nelson Mandela was branded a terrorist, by the then apartheid South African government, until the world recognized the injustice of apartheid and what Mandela was fighting for. Overnight, Mandela became a hero instead of a terrorist, in the eyes of the world. He would later be awarded a Noble Prize for peace and become the first black South African president.

Mandela and the ruling ANC remained in the terrorist watch-list, in the U.S., until 2008 when Congress removed it. Reagan had placed ANC and Mandela in the watch-list in the 1980s. Mandela would later die at the age of 95 in December 2013, and celebrated by world leaders as a freedom fighter and first black South African President.

Going back in time, before the 19th century's jihadist terrorism, the first known terrorists, before Al Qaeda, Al Shabab, Chechnya separatists, and terrorist groups like Boko Haram, Ansaru, and many others, were the Russian nihilists, who were medical doctors and students. It is evidentially hard to really say what prompts and continues to attract a disproportionate number of the medical fraternity to terrorism. Doctors are supposedly hardworking, and intelligent by trade, and that is why it defies logic to understand why such an organized and intelligent group of professionals would be involved in terrorism. But they have, from time immemorial.

Back to the story, I listened to the man as he talked, and I could feel Musa's impatience and readiness to finish the man off, and move on. But I was curious and wanted to hear the man, who appears to be in a talking mood. My journalistic instinct told me the man was trying to say something useful and newsworthy. Usually, human beings have the urge to cleanse their souls and confess at the sunsets of their lives, when they knew they were transitioning to the world beyond.

In journalism, a typical and serious journalist is always on the hunt for a story because story sells, especially a good story. A good story brings in the big bucks as high ratings draw advertisers who are always looking for opportunities to showcase their products. So the more audience a story brings the more bucks it begets.

I have covered lots of stories but I have never been face to face with a terrorist who appears ready to spill his guts to the world. With a little empathy left in my emotional arsenal, I listened to what the terrorist had to say. But before continuing, I had the urge to make the man as comfortable as possible so that I could get as much information as necessary from him, before he passes on. I asked Musa if we could get the man some modicum of succor but I could tell by the look on Musa's face that he would say no. So I put on my journalistic shoe, the way I knew how, to convince Musa.

"I think the man wants to confess or tell me something. Maybe what he has to say could help you with your investigation," I told Musa, who didn't look convinced that the terrorist had anything useful to say. "Look, Johnny Cameron, this man is a terrorist. What I need is to finish him off and go back to work. He is a terrorist with Boko Haram and Al Qaeda. He has nothing useful to say to me," he said.

"I know that, but I am a journalist and he may have something that could be useful to me. I really want to hear his story or whatever he has to say. And as you can see, he does not have a lot of time left," I said, trying to convince Musa to allow me to talk to the jihadist. I could tell his facial features had relaxed a little, and I could also see that it was against his better judgment to allow me to talk to the jihadist. I didn't care. I was on the hunt for a good story and this man appears to have the story I wanted to listen to. This could be a news scoop, I told myself, as I brought out an ultra sensitive digital recorder to record the jihadist, who I had now suspected, really wanted to talk about something.

Chapter 3

After a few minutes of haggling with Musa, he agreed to give a reprieve to the dying man. I was elated that he allowed it. Musa was not the easiest man to appeal to. The next step was even more difficult. I wanted to get the dying jihadist into the bungalow to make him comfortable but that was immediately turned down by Musa. "It will be against protocol to even think about it," he said but quickly changed his mind and agreed. I figured he must have realized something which I did not bother to ask. I was only too glad that he would allow the dying jihadist to be brought into the bungalow.

I had wanted to go back to the bungalow to get assistance to get the jihadist back into the bungalow but quickly decided against it, as I still did not trust Musa. I thought my absence would give Musa an ample opportunity to finish off the dying jihadist, which would put an end to my story. So, I did the next best thing and asked Musa to go and get help from the medics in the building. He went reluctantly. As Musa turned to leave, I could see the lips of the dying jihadist mumble something.

I bent down to listen but I needn't have as the words came out more clearly. "Thanks for not letting that man stay with me," the jihadist said with a clear and understandable voice. I nodded my head with understanding. "I don't mind him killing me but I want to talk to you because I know you are a journalist. I have heard about you. Confession is good for the soul, and I need to confess my atrocities before I pass on," he said as he started to cough. I gave him some more water.

A question started to form in my mind, and after a while I couldn't hold it back any longer. I had to ask the jihadist, and I did. "Why do you think your actions are atrocious? I thought jihadists believe that there is a paradise hereafter if they die while fighting for Allah," I said, looking at him and waiting for his response. "Yes, we all believe that because that is what we have been brought up to believe. Our imams often preach that to us, that if we fight to death in the name of Allah that paradise await us, with everything we have ever dreamed of," he said, as he started to cough again. I waited for him to stop coughing before asking again.

"If that is the case why do you need to confess to clear your

22

conscience?" I asked, trying to get him to say what I already suspected he would say. I didn't have to wait too long to hear it, as he explained with a little hesitation in his voice. "Um, it is different when a person is at the point of death, when he is between life and death. There is always the urge to clear your conscience when death spares you for a moment to do so. It is different while you are still whole and not half dead as I am. If death had taken me totally, I wouldn't have had the need to clear my conscience. But when the urge grips you, it is often not by your own volition. There is usually an urgent inner voice that demands a confession. I think it is the soul in me that is asking for a confession. Because left to me, I wouldn't. The soul needs cleansing before it can transition to the beyond," he said.

I was glad that I had my digital recorder at hand to hear his explanation of death and confession. So, I urged him to continue, in my most humble journalistic prodding. "I am glad that you trust me enough to confide in me," I said, as I waited for him to continue. "This is not about trust, my friend. It is about my need to rest in peace afterward. I feel I need to get out my words to the world. I thank Allah that you are here to help me with that. It was as if Allah has finally given my final wish, when He brought you to me," he said with reverence, and with a tremendous effort, with eyes looking above, as if he could see Allah to whom he was paying obeisance.

Not wanting to rush him, I let him talk, hoping he would say what he had on his mind that was heavy on his soul and mind. "In my fight against infidels, I have killed many. I have even killed fellow Muslims. But Christians have been the target of my atrocities throughout my life. At first, I was taught to hate infidels who did not believe in Islam, especially those who did not believe in Allah as the sole deity, and in Muhammad, as his prophet. We were told to spread the word amongst unbelievers that Islam is the dominant religion that they should believe in. Those who refused to adhere to the religious faith of Muslims were to be executed as such acts would open the door to paradise in heaven for the jihadists who fight the holy war," he said, as I handed him more water, which he gratefully accepted.

"When and how did you become radicalized to kill and maim people, especially Christians?" I asked, hoping he would continue.

23

He waited a few seconds, to rest. I could tell by his demeanor that he was not doing very good as he had lost a lot of blood. I knew that I had to make him talk before he gave up the ghost. I looked back, hoping that Musa would bring a gurney to take him to the bungalow. I figured that Musa must be having a hard time convincing the commander to bring the jihadist to the bungalow. Just as I was thinking he wasn't coming, I saw him with two medics, with a gurney, and I felt an instant sigh of relief.

Musa arrived with an expression I could not fathom or read. It was not that I could always read his expressions. I have never known him not to be expressionless and stoic and he was even more so at that moment, as I watched him approach me and the dying jihadist. "The CIA commander did not like it one bit but he was willing to go for it after I convinced him that the man was ready to talk to you. He had wanted whatever the man had to say to be classified for further investigation. I told him you were already getting confession from the jihadist on tape. He did not like that. He thought the confession should be withheld from general circulation and publication for reasons of national security. I told him the jihadist only wanted to talk to you. Like I said, he did not like it at all," he said, with a hint of anger. I couldn't tell whether the commander meant the national security of Nigeria or of the United States. But I had an idea what he meant.

I kept quiet. In situations like this, you want to say as little as possible, not to worsen the situation. So, I stood there, listening, while maintaining my own deadpan expression. After he had finished expressing his frustration, he relaxed and I could tell he wanted to get that out of his mind. It occurred to me he wanted me to know he made a sacrifice on my behalf to enable me get the story. Rather than say thank you to him, I kept my silence. In moments like this, the most sensible thing to do was to always be quiet. So I remained quiet.

While Musa had been talking, the jihadist had been listening. As if in solidarity, he offered to hold my hand as they put him in the gurney as if to let them know he was only doing it because of me. He wanted his confessions out in the media, for reasons best known to him. The commander thought it was part of a terrorist propaganda, Musa had said, but I disagreed. I had told Musa that a dying man has no need for propaganda. I do know for a fact that people who are at the throes of death usually want to confess to a clergyman or a priest, to clear their conscience. So I didn't think the jihadist was any different, even though he knew I was not a clergyman or a priest.

Another thing that began to bother me was how the jihadist had recognized me as a journalist. Though I had gotten rid of most of my disguise before arriving here, I still had on my Muslim outfit and turban. I figured he must have recognized me by my eyes. In these parts, some Arabs, especially those of Middle Eastern descent, were hard to differentiate from Caucasians, except by their accents and eyes. Caucasians were discernible through the color of their eyes, which often comes in gray, blue or hazel. I once spoke with an eye doctor about the color of different eyes, and he attributed the light eyes, like the blue, green and gray, as peculiar to Europeans. His explanation was a little confusing. It was confusing because I have seen some middle easterners with blue eyes.

He had told me that the eye color was a polygenic phenotypic character determined by a couple of distinct factors, which included the pigmentation of the eye's iris and the frequency of the dependence of the scattering of light by the turbid medium in the stroma of the iris. I didn't buy the explanation as I put it down as gibberish or technical jargon. Eyes come in different peculiarities, according to race, period. For blacks the color of the eyes was usually brown. For whites it was usually blue, gray or hazel, which was usually light greenish or grayish brown. I could be wrong but that is my layman's perception of the different color of eyes.

The jihadist must have been a fan to instantly recognize me the way he did, especially in his dying moment. Anyway, I am glad that he did as it meant that my journey to Maiduguri hadn't been a wasted trip. I had come to cover the rescue of the hostages, and even if I couldn't be there at the moment of the attempted rescue, I could still get a story out of it, even though it was a story that was well beyond my expectation.

We got to the bungalow, fifteen minutes later, and as the medics were pushing the gurney to the bungalow, I kept on talking to the dying jihadist, trying to keep him alive. I didn't probe him hard so as not to lose him. I knew he was making a huge effort to remain conscious and I helped by talking to him. He told me about his parents. His mother's name was Amina, while his father's name was Shehu Gambari. He said he was named after his father, because he was the first son. It surprised me that even in these parts where the light of civilization was still very dim, that the first son was still named after the father. It was a rarity in the Muslim world, and in Africa, as far as I knew and had seen.

I gave the dying jihadist some more water, and the medics saw that and quickly fixed a drip on him to keep his body fluid ongoing. It temporarily helped him, as he seemed to have regained some vitality. The relief in his eyes was almost instant. He smiled weakly, as he continued. "My father and mother were devout Muslims. I grew up believing in Allah. At the age of six, I could read the Koran and speak fluent Arabic. As I grew older, I began to attend mosques on a regular basis.

On my 16th birthday, my father took me to Mecca for the holy pilgrimage; during the Hajj period, which was often held in the twelfth Muslim lunar month of Dhu al-Hijjah. It was there I totally metamorphosed into a devout Muslim. My radicalization must have started from there. Before you begin to wonder how that could have happened, let me explain something about Mecca, and its spirituality in the life of a Muslim," he said, still maintaining the same vitality. I could see he was making an effort to stay conscious. To make sure he did not drift into unconsciousness, I kept talking to him. Conversations, I learnt a long time ago, was very important to a dying man. The more you hold him in a conversation, the better for him. He continued after a short racking of coughing spasms.

"Mecca is a very important holy ground for every Muslim, for several reasons. As the birthplace of Muhammad and the site of Muhammad's first revelation of the Quran, Mecca is regarded as the holiest city in Islam. The Hajj pilgrimage is mandatory for all devout Muslims. Another reason Mecca is a crucial holy ground is because it is home to the Kaaba, Islam's holiest site, as well as the center of the Islamic universe.

While in Mecca, I attended several mosques, went to holy grounds and listened to the various preaching and lectures given by Muslim scholars and clerics. Some of the preaching and lectures were radical in nature but not extreme. In every lecture I attended I began to see a pattern of how Muslim scholars see the west, especially America, which they all perceived as a country of infidels that wants to destroy Muslims. I did not understand most of the condemnations, as I was still too naïve to understand. It was as we were preparing to leave Mecca to go back home that my father took me to visit an imam who showed us videos of the atrocities committed against Muslims by the west. There were bombings and shootings of Muslim women and children. The gory sight of these killings did something to me, even though it did not radicalize me," he said, as he rested to take a deep breath.

I wanted to get as much information from him as possible. I knew he had more to tell and waited. I could see his chest heaving, which was good because if it stops, then it means he was dead and couldn't talk anymore. The fact that I could see his chest moving up and down was an encouraging sign. As if reading my mind, he opened his eyes, and continued.

"After the hajj operation, we went back home," he said, as I raised my index finger to interrupt him. "Yes, Mr. Cameron," he said. "When you said home, where exactly was home?" I asked, and at that point, he smiled, and for the first time, I saw his teeth. They were the most perfect and whitest set of teeth I have ever seen. He wiped away a tear from his face but I could see he was not crying. "To answer your question, I was born in Jos, in Plateau State," he said.

I knew of Jos. Jos was a terrorist hotbed, in the Middle Belt of Nigeria. Until recently, it was a somewhat peaceful city that attracted migrants from other parts of Nigeria and Europe, because of the commercial, mining and tourism that the city was once reputed for. As the population grew, the city became a melting pot for what would herald future clashes among the different religious groups. The diversity of the ethnically polarized population was still manageable until the formation of Boko Haram in 2001. For a while, in the far distant past, Jos was an important economic hub, known for tin mining.

Since the beginning of the millennial, Jos has suffered religious clashes between its Christian and Muslim residents, which lately has featured Boko Haram and Ansaru, as the major perpetrators of such clashes.

Looking at the dying jihadist, I could tell the drip was helping him a great deal. I also knew that if I didn't keep him talking that he wasn't going to be around much longer. So I probed harder. "So, both your parents were from Jos?" I asked needlessly. "He nodded his head. My father was a big time trader and farmer. We had cows, goats, and chickens that my father would raise and sell in Sabon Gari Market, formerly called Abubakar Rimi Market. Abubakar Rimi was a former governor of Kano State," he added as if that was something that I should know. I nodded my head, urging him to continue. I did not want to say anything that would stop him from continuing.

"My father was a very successful farmer and trader. He had Fulani herders working for him as well as other laborers who helped him to manage his big farm. The crops in my father's farm included Irish potatoes, apples, grapes, wheat, barley, and vegetables. To keep growing our crops, my father built wells to retain water during the rainy seasons, to use during the dry season. With the help of the irrigation water from the dams and old mine ponds, we were able to maintain regular water supply to the farm. As I got older, I started helping my father in the farm," he said, as he took time to cough, which lasted for several seconds. I almost panicked, as the coughing seemed to rack him with spasms.

Luckily he regained himself, and started talking again. "I went to an Islamic school for young Muslims where I learned to read and write in Arabic. I was a very good student. I grew up like most of the students in northern Nigeria, without any hatred for those who practiced the Christian religion. Most of my playmates were Christian children. During the Ramadan months, we would fast together, as children, even though they were Christians. It didn't matter, we were all having fun, fasting! As I grew older, and approached my fifteenth birthday, I began to spend more time at the mosque, upon my father's urging, as he wanted me to be a devout Muslim.

At the central mosque, I began to learn more and more about the sharia law, which had many dos and don'ts for Muslims. Personal matters like sexual intercourse, hygiene, diet, prayer, and fasting were strictly adhered to, by all Muslims. As I began to know more about the sharia law, based on the precepts set forth in the Koran, and the example set by Prophet Muhammad, I began to understand the many topics addressed by sharia law, in areas such as crime, politics and economics. I began to see the sins of the west and how such sins were contaminating the sharia law and Muslim adherents.

In 2001, a new Muslim outfit called Congregation and People Tradition for Proselytism and Jihad was attracting the youth in my area. In Hausa, Congregation and People Tradition for Proselytism and Jihad means Boko Haram, which literally means western education is sinful. And because I was educated in Islam and the Sharia mindset, I began to understand what it meant. My father saw that I was quickly changing and sent me to a western college system, where I furthered my education at the University of Maiduguri and later became a medical doctor. But I never gave up my belief in the sharia law and in Islam.

I was a noncommittal member of Boko Haram at the outset but that would later change as I continued to attend meetings at the mosque, organized by the imam. One summer holiday, I told my father I would like to travel, and since I had always been a responsible boy, he said it was okay for me to travel with my friend as long as I did not get into trouble. I told him I was going to Dubai with a friend, whose father lives there, and he agreed. My friend and I went to Yemen instead.

In Yemen, we stayed in Sannaa, the capital, where we moved around a lot, trying to fit in, with the local community of Muslims. We did not have any particular purpose for going to Yemen other than to know more about Al Qaeda in the Arabian Peninsula. We had heard about their recruitment drive of young Muslims and wanted to see what it was all about. Again, mind you, we were just having fun without any particular purpose in mind, other than curiosity.

In Sanaa it was easy to hang out without any place in mind. The food was cheap and the hotels were inexpensive. We visited the Saleh Mosque which was built in 2008, by President Ali Abdullah Saleh. The mosque was immensely huge and had distinctive features which made it a tourist attraction. I fell in love with the mosque immediately. It was just beautiful, the type that Allah and Muhammad would approve of. The mosque had six minarets that were 100 meters, with several beautiful domes that were about 28 meters in diameter, and 22 meters high.

The sign on the building said the mosque occupied 27300 square meters, and 24 meters high. The sign also said the mosque had a capacity of 44,000 worshippers, with a separate women's section. The main hall of the mosque had a diameter of 13,596 square. When I said it was huge, I was not exaggerating," he said, as he waited to take a deep breath, as if having a flashback. I was tempted to give him water but because of the drip that the medics had fixed on his arm, I did not want to disrupt the fluid in his system.

As if reading my mind, he said he was okay. And I was glad that he felt okay. Though he had been talking, he had not really said a lot. Most of what he had said was already known to me. I did know about the Saleh mosque he was talking about. It was the controversial mosque built by the corrupt and authoritative former President of Yemen. I had visited the mosque myself when I was in Yemen in 2010 to cover the drone killing of five militants by the CIA. The mosque was indeed immense. I remember it had 10 doors on both the eastern and western sides of the building, while it had five doors in the southern side that led to the rear courtyard, which was huge itself. The courtyard was aptly named the Islamic Sharia College courtyard, with an ablution area for the washing of one's body or parts of it, as a Muslim religious-rite.

I remember, marveling at the roof's five domes and how beautiful and distinctive they were. Four of the domes were 15.6 meter in diameters, with a height of 20.35 meters above the rooftop. If I remember correctly, the central dome itself was 27.4 meters in diameter, with a height of 39.6 meters above the rooftop of the mosque. The mosque was equipped with a powerful central air conditioning system, and fire extinguishers that made it unique in that part of the world, in the Arabian Peninsula. The walls were inscribed with Quran verses, adding to the spirituality of the edifice.

I was jolted back to reality as the dying jihadist started to say something, which got my attention. "It was at the mosque that I met a Muslim brother who totally changed my perceptions about Islam. My friend and I were walking around the mosque, reading the Quran verses on the wall, when the man approached us. 'Allahu akbar! Allah is great! It is good to see young Muslims reading the Quran,' said a heavyset Muslim, who was wearing a white Muslim v-neck stroma robe, and a cap that seemed to be too small for his dome-like head.

He was fully bearded, like a cleric, and his presence was very reverential. Salam, we greeted. But he shook his head. 'My young brothers, you never say Salam to a cleric. Instead you say As-salam-o-alaikum, or as some choose to say these days, as-salamu alaykum, but you never say Salam as that is disrespectful. Among your friends you could say Salam, but to an elder Muslim leader, you don't say that,' he said. He was so inspiring that we listened to every word he said. He had this hypnotic command about him that made you want to listen to him," the dying jihadist said. "So how old was this man," I asked, trying to see if the man fits the description of Anwar al-Awlaki, the American born Al Qaeda leader who was killed on September 30, 2011 by a CIA-led U.S. drone strike.

"I don't know how old the man was, but I think he must have been in his late 30s, or early 40s. He wore eyeglasses and looks like a Muslim scholar," he said. In my mind, I did some quick calculations. Awlaki was born in 1971. That means, the Al Qaeda leader fits the description of the man the jihadist was describing, especially with the eyeglasses, even though most of the known Al Qaeda leaders wore eye glasses, as well.

The jihadist looked at me, as if waiting for me to urge him to continue. I saw the sign and nodded my head as if it was an agreed indication for him to continue with his story. "The bearded cleric spoke to us at length, after which he invited us to a lecture he said he was having for other young Muslims, at his place. The way he spoke made us want to attend the lecture. Everything he said about Islam made sense and was consistent with what we already knew about the religion. He told us that it was a shame that Muslims were facing the same persecution that Jews faced under Hitler.

The cleric said today's *Hitler* was the west, especially the U.S. which looks at every Muslim with suspicion, for simply believing in Islam. That part of his comment resonated very well with me as I have read newspaper accounts of Muslims being harassed and profiled because of their Muslim faiths. The cleric gave us some pamphlets to read which contained stories of how Israel was trying to push the Palestinians out of their homelands, by annexing almost all the lands previously owned and occupied by the Palestinians.

The Pamphlet went on to narrate the historical background of

Palestine, describing the region as being in western Asia, between the Mediterranean Sea and the Jordan River. According to the pamphlet, several attempts had been made to change the course of history by giving the region different names to steal it from the original Palestinian dwellers. The first name given to the region was Syria Palaestina, when it was a Roman province between 135 and 390, when it was split up and merged as Roman Syria and Roman Judaea, following the Bar Kokhba Revolt in 135. Later on, it became Byzantine Palaestina Prima. It was opined in the pamphlet that it was an injustice for a land that was located between Egypt, Syria, and Arabia, to be renamed the birthplace of Judaism and Christianity. The contention in the pamphlet was that renaming it as the land of Israel was an attempt to steal the land that historically belonged to Palestinians," the jihadist said, as if recalling everything from memory.

I listened, wanting to change the direction of his story to something else. I knew he might think I was part of the problem if I tried to switch him to the story about his radicalization. I waited for him to get back to the subject of terrorism and how he became a part of it. But to do that, I had to wait for him to get back to the subject, since the topic at hand was a very sensitive topic to him.

Rather than switch to a new topic, he continued. "The Palestinians have been controlled throughout history. The pamphlet opened my eyes to a lot of things I did not know. Through the pamphlet, I learned that the region of Palestine had been controlled by ancient Egyptians, Canaanites, Israelites, Assyrians, Babylonians, Persians, Ancient Greeks, Romans, Byzantines, Sunni Arab Caliphates, Shia Fatimid Caliphate, Ayyubids, Mameluks, Ottmans, British, and now modern Israel. Just about every nation in the Arab world and Middle East, and in the west, has had a share in controlling the region, even those who now claimed to be on the side of the Palestinians," he said, telling me something I already knew. But I listened.

I figured it was time to steer him back to the topic of his confession. I was not interested in ancient history, even though I knew he was trying to give me a background of the genesis of his jihad and radicalization. I knew if I did not get him back to the confession that he would not live long enough to finish the story that was more important to me than the history of the problems in the Middle East. As far as I know, the region of Palestine has had a tumultuous history due to the different religions, culture, and politics in the area. It was nothing new. So I felt it was time to put on my journalistic shoe. And I did.

"So, did the cleric in Yemen help in transforming you into a jihadist?" I asked, trying to get him back to the story he had digressed from earlier. He nodded. "That little pamphlet did the transformation, more than anything else. When we left the Saleh mosque we went back to our little hotel, and ate, showered and went sightseeing. As we visited shrines and tombs, in Sanaa, we went to the al Ja'dani shrine in Al Tareyyah that was partly destroyed by members of Ansar al Sharia. We also visited the villages of Al Darjaj and Sayhan near Jaar in Abyan Province.

It was in Jaar that we met several radicals who took us in their homes and treated us like family members, even though we were strangers. We felt a kinship with the Muslims in Jaar who refused to accept payment from us for the hospitality we received. When it came time for us to leave, we felt sad and promised to go back.

Our entire time in Yemen was so educational that we left the country with different mindsets. We had fun, and enjoyed the freedom of being free to think and act the way we wanted. For the first time, we began to understand what it felt like to be Muslims. Not that we did not understand this at first, but our visit to Yemen totally changed our perception," he said, as he took a deep breath.

I wanted to know more about his training in Yemen and the specific thing that made a difference in his life. So I asked him. "I know I am asking too many questions, but can you tell me the specific event that changed your thought process in Yemen? And by the way, did you attend that meeting that the cleric invited you to?" He looked at me with eyes full of hidden meanings and wisdom as he said. "Yes, the next day, we went to visit the cleric in his house. We were well received as if we were long lost relatives. There were fifteen of us in the meeting, mostly young men my age and six young women. We sat down on a deep Persian rug, and were each provided with a small, time-worn Koran.

The cleric preached and spoke at length about infidels and the sufferings of Muslims in the hands of unbelievers in the Islamic faith. He condemned the U.S. support of Israel and the complicity of some Arab countries to destroy Muslims. He condemned Arab countries that support the west in its persecution of Muslims. He said it was the duty of every Muslim to fight to protect Islam. He referred us to several passages in the Koran to make his point, saying any Muslim that makes the ultimate sacrifice for Allah, on behalf of Prophet Muhammad would go to paradise. The cleric said paradise was for believers who make sacrifices on behalf of Allah.

Later on that evening, after we had left the home of the cleric, we went to see a movie, at the recommendation of the cleric, about a war unjustly waged against Muslims by unbelievers and infidels in the west and in the Arab world. The movie was a very educational one that further opened my eyes to the persecutions of Muslims. We also saw the desecration of the Koran by unbelievers who disrespected the Koran by burning it. It angered me that anyone would choose to burn a holy book. Despite the unprovoked burning of the Koran it was still not enough to transform me into an extremist. Like I said earlier, the pamphlet had a lot to do with what changed me into a radical and a jihadist," he said, as tears welled up his eyes.

I could not understand the tears. For a man who wanted to clear his soul and who believed he had done wrong to mankind, it would be ironical that he would tear up at the mere mention of the burning of the Koran. Maybe for him burning the Koran was an emotional issue. Or maybe the tears had nothing to do with the confession or story, if you like. I did not say anything. I merely made a face of sympathy to commiserate with him on whatever it was that was aggrieving his mind. I am not a very religious person and wouldn't know what it felt like to have one's religious book trashed and burnt by unbelievers. Though a catholic I hardly took things to the extreme. I held my tongue. With extremists, albeit a repentant one, it can be dangerous or, in my own case, counterproductive to hold a contrarian view.

I needed to get as much story out of him, and because of my desire to make him talk, I decided it was time to ask a question that would lure him to the confession he had voluntarily offered to give. So I asked the first thing that came to my mind. "If the burning of the Koran did not turn you into an extremist and if the pamphlet did not entirely do it for you, what did it?" He looked at me, with the tears in his eyes, as if I had said something that added to his pain, but there was no anger in his eyes. The tears were from a previous flashback that he had had when he narrated his experience at watching the video about the burning of the Koran.

"When we got back from Yemen, we still had a month before our summer vacation would end. Since we did not have much to do and since we wanted to learn more about Islam and the Sharia, we went to Sokoto, in the northwest of Nigeria. Sokoto is considered the most important seat of Islamic learning in Nigeria. Every young Muslim had studied there, and my yearning for more knowledge about the Koran, Islam, and the Sharia, took my friend and I, to the state," he said as another spasms of coughing took hold of him. I thought he was going to die, but thank God he survived the coughing ordeal.

His mention of Sokoto brought back my own memories of the state. I had visited the state a few years back, when the Sultan was holding a meeting with northern leaders to find ways to curb the violence that was destroying the economy of the region. Sokoto, to my recollection, was the seat of the Sokoto Caliphate, and the sultan was considered the head of the Caliphate. The sultan was also said to be the spiritual leader of Nigerian Muslims. I have been to the sultan's palace, which is luxuriously furnished, with western features and fixtures, something that has angered Boko Haram militants who see the sultan as having been adulterated, tainted, and infiltrated by western influence.

As my mind went on a nostalgic journey of my visit to Sokoto, I remember attending a Kokawa (wrestling) and Dembe (boxing) events, at the urging of the guide who had traveled with me, to help me, as a form of entertainment. At the time of my visit, the northern Nigeria was a very peaceful region, and there were no religious violence like the ones that has been brought to the region by Boko Haram and Ansaru. I had fun, and enjoyed the throng, bustling and hustling of the 3.5 million population of the state as they went about their daily activities and livelihoods.

I was still having a nostalgic rewind, when I caught the eye of the jihadist, as if he was ready to go on. I nodded as if I could read his mind. The flashback of my visit to Sokoto totally took me by surprise. For a westerner, you would think my recollection of the city would be one of disdain, disgust and snobbishness. Not so with me. I really enjoyed my visit to the state and city. My old friend, who had worked for the NTA, now retired, had been my guide, and I even remember going with him to his farm where he cultivated millet, maize, rice and beans. Though the region was generally dried, it was covered with alluvial soil, which included particles of silt and clay. Silt has a mineral origin of quartz and feldspar, which makes the soil very rich, my friend had told me.

Seeing the distant look in my eyes, the jihadist continued with the confession. He must have thought I was having some kind of epiphany of some sort, or maybe he thought his story was having an effect on me. In a way it was, as his story evoked memories of the past. But his words jolted me back to the present.

"I was in Sokoto when violence erupted, following the calls for an Islamic Sharia Law, in the state. The violence broke out around midday as my friend and I were leaving a local restaurant where we had just finished eating rice in an upscale indigenous restaurant. Businesses and offices had hurriedly closed as people were being killed and beaten. I saw several students from Usman Dan Fodio University, demanding the introduction of Sharia Law. Following the demonstration, the riot police immediately closed down the university. It didn't affect a lot of activities as most students were still on summer vacation. In the crowd, I recognized most of the students. I was impressed by the demand. As a Muslim, the demand for a Sharia Law was a welcomed request. I joined the demonstration.

We were in the midst of a huge violence that quickly became a religious violence between Muslims and Christians. Within minutes, people were being killed and strewn everywhere in the streets. I had to defend myself, and to do so involved killing someone or getting killed.

Cars, buildings and shops were vandalized, and riot police and soldiers pounced on the crowd, arresting anyone that looked like a demonstrator. What really angered me was the manner the police and soldiers were picking up innocent women and children, especially Muslims. I saw innocent people being shot by police and soldiers as if they were animals. The victims in that riot were mostly Muslims, young Muslims.

I was in the midst of the violence, fighting my way out of trouble, when I was arrested. I was surprised that they chose to arrest me rather than kill me, as I had seen them kill innocent women and children. I was put in a police lorry that was already full of people who were arrested. Lots of women and children were among those who were arrested. I later heard that the same demonstration had broken out in Kaduna, about the Sharia Law. For some weird reason, I felt glad that I was caught in the riot because it made me feel as if I belonged to something important, a cause that was worth fighting for.

There was no trial, as we were tossed into a makeshift prison, where I met a man who would further push me into the road of radicalism and extremism, or jihad if you like. The man said his name was Ibrahim, that he was doing something very important for Allah. He talked about the duty of a devout Muslim, and how most Muslims do not like to make any sacrifice for their faith. He also said some Muslims loved being Muslim, but lacked the desire to fight for Allah. I listened to him as he talked to me and other young Muslims in the place, about what was required of a Muslim. It was while he was talking to us, that a fight broke out between the inmates and the police who were guarding the makeshift prison."

I gave him a few minutes to rest before asking the next question that was bothering me. When I saw that he had somewhat recovered, I asked. "When you said a fight broke out between the inmates and police, what did you mean?" I asked.

"What I meant was that the Muslim extremists in the makeshift cell suddenly started screaming *Allahu Akbar! Allahu Akbar!* The police tried to make them stop, but rather than stop they got louder, and then one of the inmates seized the baton from one of the police officers, while several other inmates somehow got hold of cudgels, and truncheons, that they used on the police. Out of the ten police officers guarding the inmates, only two of them had handguns. With eight of the officers overpowered, the two with guns started firing, trying to find their way out of the makeshift prison. The diehard jihadists in the makeshift prison fought back and overpowered the police officers with guns and got out of the makeshift prison.

Out of the ten police officers, only two survived the attack, and they were the two with guns. At the time reinforcement came, several inmates were dead, along with eight police officers. But the violence did not stop there, we went into town, and headed for the police station. At the time we got to the police station, most of the officers had abandoned their duty posts and ran. We quickly broke into the arsenal in the police station, which had very few outdated guns, but they were enough for us. We took more cudgels, batons, and any weapon we could find. Some of us took police uniforms, and disguised ourselves as police officers.

We started with homes that belonged to Christians in the area. How and when the idea first started that we should go after Christians in the area, I don't know. I have never hated Christians. Most of my childhood friends were Christians, and I have never had any reason to hate them. I had more love for them than the Muslims I grew up with. But on that day, we went to homes that belonged to Christians and started burning them down when we could not find anyone in them. We figured the Christian occupants in the homes had abandoned them. We did not care, and still vandalized and burnt the homes.

It was while this was going on that one of the ring leaders amongst us said we should head to the churches. We all thronged there, shouting *Allahu Akbar!* With the weapons that we had with us, we went to several of the churches, were worshippers thought they would find refuge in the sanctuaries. But they were wrong. We bludgeoned the heads of the men, women and children we met in the sanctuaries. There was blood everywhere, lots of blood. After each kill, we would cry *Allahu Akbar!*

Since we had been taught that there was a reward of paradise when a Muslim kills an unbeliever, we felt we were doing the wish of Allah by killing infidels and unbelievers in our faith. As I am talking to you, I can still recall the cries of mercies of the children and women as they begged us, but the cries and appeal for mercies fell on deaf ears. I remember the face of one boy of about ten years old, who as I cut off his head with a machete, cried and begged for mercy. His head had rolled away from his torso, with his lips still moving and pleading! That image haunted me for a long time, despite my belief that it was part of my religious sacrifice," the jihadist said, as he stopped to gather his strength.

I almost threw up at the gory picture he was painting. In my mind's eyes, I could picture the bloodcurdling screams. I shuddered convulsively. I continued to shiver and quiver at the same time, as the thoughts to strangle this son of Lucifer, who lay, dying in the gurney, went through my mind. I could not understand how anyone would believe that it was his god-given right to take another man's life, a life created in God's image, by God. If there was a religion that permits the killing of others as a sacrifice, then something is fundamentally wrong with that religion.

As I said earlier, I am not a religious person or pretend to be one, even though I claim to be a catholic. It sometimes baffles me that people who claim to be religious in their own rights, often do things that would make Lucifer flinch, cringe and wince. Killing innocent children and women is one of such devilish acts.

As a journalist who has travelled to several troubled parts of the world, I have never seen anything like the type of atrocities committed by Boko Haram, in Nigeria, and Taliban in Afghanistan and Pakistan, against women and children, which I think Allah wouldn't approve or sanction. Though Muslim extremists and jihadists often say that paradise awaits them for every killing carried out on behalf of Allah, I think it is hogwash and nonsense. I don't think Allah would approve of such things as killing innocent people. I have interviewed lots of peaceful Muslims who said Allah does not condone violence or the killing of innocent people who believe in other religion.

As I looked at the jihadist who now believes he must confess to clear his soul, in order to transition to the world beyond, I began to think how he could have been so gullible and naïve to believe such balderdash as killing in the name of Allah in order to go to paradise. If anything, killing, according to the Hebrew bible, in the books of Exodus 20: 2-7 and Deuteronomy 5: 6-21, is against the Ten Commandments, which said thou shall not kill. And the Koran, in so many ways, is like the Hebrew bible.

I realized I must be objective, and must preclude my personal feelings and prejudices. As a seasoned journalist, etiquette calls for objective judgment in order to avoid distortions that could be the byproduct of personal feelings. A good journalist, I was once told by my editor, handles facts or stories without distortion and presuppositions, and I wholeheartedly agreed with that notion. I see myself as a good journalist, and for that same reason, I controlled my emotion and forced myself to look at the son of Lucifer, whom I had referred to as the jihadist in this story, and smiled what I called a smile of tolerance.

Having succeeded in controlling my emotions, I asked him the next question, trying to tactfully lead him away from the bloodcurdling narration, even though I knew in my heart of hearts that such narration will be inevitable in the course of the confession, which I had sworn to listen to in its entirety.

"Was that experience the crucible that finally tipped you over into the realms of radicalism?" I asked, doing everything I could to be as professional as possible. He must have sensed that his confession of the killing of innocent women and children in churches had affected me. His next words threw me by surprise.

"Looking back, I can now say I am not proud of what I did. In the twilight of my life, I can see now that it was all wrong. It is funny that I realize that now, after all the lives that I have taken. I can see clearly now that there will be no paradise in the afterlife for me. It was all a gimmick to entice us, naïve Muslims, to action, to commit all these crimes against humanity. If I had known what I know now, I would have remained as I was, as a child, playing in that sand, with other Christian children," he said. I couldn't tell if he was sincere or playing with my emotion.

Something inside me must have kicked my emotion, and I felt tears streaming down my cheeks, as if I was grieving for the murdered children and women in his confession. He must have mistaken my tears for something else, because what he said next swayed me a little.

"There is something I want you to know. I had ten children from four wives, and they were all murdered by soldiers when they found out about me. The killing of my family by soldiers, to be honest with you, did not affect me much. The reason it did not affect me was that I knew I would meet them soon enough in the paradise, that Allah had prepared for me. I felt it was the wish of Allah that they should die, that Allah was preparing a way for my exit to meet them, so we could all be together. To me, their deaths meant a celebration, rather than a loss, because I saw it as a passageway for me; that it was Allah blessing me for all the sacrifices I had made in his name."

It took a full minute for me to recover from what he had said. At first it spooked me that he would speak of the murder of his family as a part of the reward for the sacrifice of killing innocent people on behalf of his Allah. I quickly regained my composure and poise, realizing that his brainwash must have been very effective. He was full of discrepancies but I kept my opinion to myself. One moment he did not believe he would go to paradise, the next he was extolling the idea of going to paradise.

Despite all he had said about his confessions, I realized he had not really said anything that I did not already know. I knew Al Shabab, Boko Haram, Ansaru, Taliban, and lots of Islamic militants kill women and children without qualms, and I had covered incidents in Abuja, Sokoto, Kano, Maiduguri, Jos, and many villages in northern Nigeria, where families had been beheaded and hacked to death in their sleeps, in their huts or homes, in northern Nigerian villages and towns. Thinking of the atrocities of the Islamic militants brought me to the next question.

That is the beauty of journalism; one question always leads to another. In this case, one thought leads to a question. So I asked the jihadist where and when he started receiving his militant trainings. Even though this was not an interview of any form or shape, I had often asked him questions to make sure his confessions were relevant enough to report. I was digging for relevance in his confessions, and I did not want to give him the privilege of spilling his guts without me guiding him. So I asked him what I thought would lead him to what I really wanted to hear.

"Tell me about your initial training and membership in Boko Haram or any of the Islamic militant groups you were affiliated with?" He looked up, as if in a trance, or lost in space. I let him do his thing. I did not want to rush him. I wanted to make sure he gave me the best recollection as much as possible.

"One thing I did not finish telling you earlier was about the man I met in the makeshift prison, during the Sharia Law riot in Sokoto and Kaduna. I met a powerful Muslim cleric, whose name you are familiar with: Ustaz Mohammed Yusuf. Mohammed Yusuf told me about Boko Haram and the supports the sect was getting, and how young Muslims in Niger, Nigeria, and neighboring countries, were joining, in order to protect Muslims in the world.

He spoke passionately about the Sharia law, and how sins and crimes had destroyed peoples' lives in the world because of the influence of the sins of the west. A lot of young Muslims gathered to listen to him while we were in that makeshift prison.

At first I did not realize how really powerful the man was until I heard in the news, later that day, that he was being sought by law enforcement agents in Nigeria, for inciting violence and religious riots. After we broke out and unleashed terror in towns and cities, we were invited to a camp for training, by Yusuf.

We were sent to a training camp with Malian militants for six months in Timbuktu where we learned to use Kalashnikovs, shoulder-fired weapons, and several handguns and rifles. We were also taken to the desert to train under the scorching desert sun without water, for hours to test our resistance. Those who did not pass the training were given different tasks that did not involve fighting.

We trained with a local al-Qaeda offshoot called Ansar Dine, whose members came from Mali, Niger and other countries. They spoke deep Arabic and other languages I could not understand, even though I spoke Arabic very well. Even with that, we all had one thing in common, which was our disdain for anything western.

Each day, while we were in the training camp in the desert, several young Muslims would come to register to train. I didn't know where they came from. It was as if there was an advertisement placed in the media for recruitments, for jihadists somewhere. I identified young Muslims who came from as far as Somalia, Sudan, Kenya, Togo, Chad, and Nigeria. But I could not place a lot of the trainees who looked like Arabs from Tunisia, Egypt, Algeria, and Libya, or even from the Middle East.

The trainers came from Yemen, Pakistan, India, and Afghanistan. The training camp must have had about 500 wannabe militants who were there to train. The excitement to train to fight for Allah was so overwhelming that no one questioned the rationale behind what we were training for. There were dusty cars and trucks of different makes and models, in the desert, and several black flags of al-Qaeda stood in every tent, as if to inform us that we were all members of one militant group.

I made several friends in that training camp during the six months I was in that camp. I would later meet those friends again when I was sent to another training camp in South Sudan, after the south became a separate country, in 2011," the jihadist said. I had allowed him to talk for a long time since he was in a talking mood without interrupting him. Now, as he rested for a few minutes before resuming, I decided it was time to ask him a question that had formed in my mind as he was talking.

"What type of training did you guys undergo and how many of the trainees were al-Qaeda militants?" I asked him after I had made sure he had rested enough. He did his usual gazing and staring, as if something was reassuring him to go on. After a while, he looked in my direction without actually focusing on me, before answering.

"Our day would usually start before dawn, to pray and read the Koran. We would run eight laps around the several sand dunes and sand choked-desert, which was an equivalent of five hundred meters in diameter. We would do several exercises in the sand which included jumping, pushups, and martial arts. After three hours of exercises, we would all sit in the sand to eat breakfasts which often consisted of bread and powdered milk.

Light breakfasts were recommended for training, to make sure we did not become lazy, during training. We had IT people among the trainers who were always busy working in their laptops. There was a videographer who was videoing the exercises. There were two trainers who kept telling us how to breathe steadily to avoid fatigue. I suspected they must have been senior members of al-Qaeda because of the superior way they were talking and walking around, as if supervising the trainees.

I knew there were lots of people who associated with Boko Haram in the camp, but there were militants from Al Shabab, Ansaru, and al-Qaeda, everywhere. I also saw militants from an Islamic group in Algeria and Tunisia that I could not place," he said as he was trying to recollect some more details. I noticed he was repeating himself, and quickly thought of other questions to steer him away to a different topic.

"Earlier, you said young Muslims were coming from everywhere for training. Was there anything motivating them, like money or something? Or was it just the mere fallacy of going to paradise?" I asked, trying to understand the incentive for anyone to subject himself to such barbaric fallacies. He answered right away without even gazing upward to think of an answer.

"I do remember the commanders of Boko Haram, al-Qaeda, Ansaru, Ansar Dine, giving out money to the young Muslims that came to enlist. I think I remember being given about 4,000 CFA or

N1200, which was about $80. For a lot of those new recruits who were mostly unemployed, it was their first real paychecks, since there were no jobs in their various countries. One could tell that a lot of those young Muslims who came to the camp had never been employed in their young lives. Most of them were uneducated, and only understood Arabic," he said, as he stopped to stare at a fly that perched on his wounded arm. He did not bother to scare the fly away or to kill the fly. Since he left the fly alone, I did the same.

His comment led me to the next question that came immediately to my mind. "I know you said earlier that you were in school. How did you manage to attend school and attend these training camps in Timbuktu and elsewhere?"

"There is something that you should understand about university education, or any education in Nigeria. Half of the semester, either the lecturers will be on strike or the students will be on strike. There was always something going on. When we were not on strike, I would be in school, studying hard. I would take my books with me everywhere. To make sure I did not lag behind in my studies, I would buy lots of handouts to read, and when it was time for exam, I would be there, taking the tests. I never missed a test or an exam. I would always show up, when it was time to take tests. I knew my father would not tolerate truancy. So to please him, I would always make sure I did well in school. Believe it or not, I was always in the top ten in my class," he said, as a flicker of a smile came to the corner of his wounded face.

"In Borno State, you said earlier that Boko Haram was mostly in control of a lot of villages and towns in the state, what areas were you referring to?" I asked, trying to get some kind of clarification on some of the things he had touched on earlier.

"Despite the widely publicized crackdown on Boko Haram by the Nigerian military, with the state of emergency in the state of Borno, we were able to firmly control areas like Marte, Magumeri, Mobbar, Gubio, Guzamala, Abadamin, Kukawa, Kaga, Nganzai, and Monguno. We were the administrative authority in these places, just like the Taliban controlled the border towns and villages in Pakistan and Afghanistan. We even had a training camp called Sambisa, on the outskirt of Maiduguri, the state capital, where I had first received my initial training, after the breakout from the makeshift prison, and the riot afterward. We operated freely in the state, and the police could not stop us. I think the police officers were afraid of us.

Most of the time, we would march across Maiduguri, unchallenged, by the police. The idea of the march was to let the indigenes know that there will be consequences if they were to cooperate with local law enforcement agents, and soldiers. Not that the police bothered us, they did not. The few times they tried to bother us we retaliated by burning down their stations and vehicles. To keep the peace, the police would stay out of our way, and we would leave them alone.

A lot of times, our Fulani brethren would come from Mali and Togo at nighttime to kill those suspected of giving information to the police. I remember a village near Maiduguri, whose residents were slaughtered at night because they had given information to soldiers about Boko Haram. There must have been about 200 Fulani militants, who participated in that slaughter, on behalf of Boko Haram. They beheaded the heads of the men, women and children, and set the thatched houses on fire. A whole village was burnt down, and destroyed by the Fulani herdsmen, who were also members of Boko Haram," he said, without any emotion.

As he talked, I started wondering if the state of emergency imposed by the Jonathan administration was having any effect in the state. So I asked him the next question that I thought would clarify that point. "While Boko Haram and the Fulani Herdsmen were creating these mayhems, where were the soldiers?' I asked, not expecting the answer that I received from him, minutes later.

"The soldiers were even worse. When they were not telling lies about the number of Boko Haram members they killed, they would be killing innocent villagers and burning villages that they felt were harboring Islamic militants. Even if the soldiers were capable of doing anything, there was no way to contact them by phone, where phones exist. There was no communication in the state as the government of Jonathan had blocked out any form of communication, to destabilize Boko Haram and Ansaru. Not that law enforcement agents or soldiers would come to the rescue of anyone that was being killed by militants. If they did come, it would be hours after the mayhem had taken place. You might as well say the soldiers were there to create their own atrocities," he said, shaking his head, sadly, as if in self-pity.

I understood what he meant about law enforcement agents and soldiers showing up hours after a crime had been committed and the culprits had left. It was typical of law enforcement agents in Nigeria to hide while armed robbers or militants were committing a crime. There was a story I had read in one of the newspapers in Nigeria about a man who had received a letter from armed robbers that they were coming to his house on a certain date to rob him. The man had taken the letter to the police. The police had promised to come to his house to protect him, and to apprehend the armed robbers.

The man got home, boastfully informed his wife that his house was being protected by police that she should not have anything to worry about. On the appointed day, the couple ate dinner, and got ready for bed. At the exact time the armed robbers promised to come, they arrived, unchallenged by the police, at the couple's house and started robbing them. The couple waited in vain for the police to come as they were being robbed, but none came, and the armed robbers operated freely for hours on end, without any apprehension. Before leaving the couple's home, the armed robbers showed the couple the letter they had given to the police!

It was eight hours after the armed robbers had robbed the couple's, and neighbors' houses, that police officers arrived, with guns drawn, pretending to be battle-ready to fight the armed robbers. Later on, there were rumors that the police had been hiding in the area, while the armed robbers were robbing the couple and their neighbors. The police had only come out of their hiding places when they knew the armed robbers had left. In that incident alone, several lives, monies and jewelries, were taken by the armed robbers, who operated in the area, unabated for hours on end, while the police were hiding and scared to come out to confront the armed robbers. The couple believed the police colluded with the armed robbers!

A few days later when the police commissioner of police in the area was told about the action of the police, all he said was that his officers were probably overpowered by the superior firepower of the armed robbers; who were probably armed with better sophisticated weapons and hand grenades. After that, no mention was ever made about the incident.

I remember talking to my good friend who was still working

with the Nigerian Television Authority (NTA) about it, and how he had shrugged and said "that is Nigeria for you," saying that in Nigeria, armed robbers often write letters to potential victims that they were coming to rob them, in order for such potential victims to have enough money ready for them. If the potential victims did not have enough money when the armed robbers arrived, it would be a bloodbath for the families, who would suffer death, he had said. The idea of writing potential victims in advance was to allow the victims to borrow the money, or get it by any means possible, my friend had added. It had baffled me that armed robbers could be so brazen and bold to operate in any society with such audacity, without interference or apprehension by the police.

As a journalist, you hear things from citizens, in the grapevine or rumor mills. I was once told by a fellow journalist who was a reporter with one of the newspapers that some police officers often work in collusion with armed robbers. In some cases, corrupt police officers would loan weapons to armed robbers, to commit armed robberies. There were also reports that some of the armed robberies were actually masterminded and organized by police officers, in Nigeria.

I remember talking to a retired journalist with the Daily Times, who had covered the activities of a notorious armed Robber called Anini, a native of Bini, Benin City, in Edo State, who, during his interrogation and capture, confessed to working with a police inspector, called Iyamu. Iyamu was a feared police inspector at the time, who was supposedly in charge of an anti robbery squad, fighting armed robberies! It was the same Iyamu, who was reportedly supplying information and weapons to Anini and his gang, my colleague had said.

Following the confession of Anini, at the time, the police inspector and several other police officers who had illegally enriched themselves, through complicities and collusions with armed robbers, were executed at the firing squad, along with Anini. It was a sad case, according to my colleague, who said the police inspector was a huge disappointment to the residents who had also paid him for protection against Anini, whom the inspector was also sponsoring!

My mind was still in a reverie, that I did not hear the jihadist talking to me at first. I only became aware that he was talking to me when he nudged me with his hand. I looked at him and nodded, as if I knew what it was that he was talking about. He smiled knowingly, and continued with his confession.

"I was going to tell you about the Boko Haram initiation process, which included several rites and ceremonies," he said, waiting for me to give him the signal to proceed. I nodded again, as if in a trance, wondering what sort of rites he was referring to. With the jihadist, I had prepared myself for anything, but the idea of initiation took me by surprise. I had heard about initiations among cultists and secret society members, never among militants.

Journalists, as you may already know, talk with each other more often than the public knows. I don't think there is any group of professionals that work in better and greater unity and camaraderie than journalists. I stand to be corrected if you knew of one. Having said that, because we talk to each other and compare stories, we often hear things that we may or may not print.

A Nigerian journalist I once worked with, while I was covering insurgency in the Niger Delta, in Nigeria, had once told me that within college or university campuses in Nigeria, major crimes like forced initiation, rape of female students, and murder were taking place on a daily basis than are reported by the media. He said the frequencies of the crimes on university and college campuses were so much that such stories were no longer newsworthy. I had asked the Nigerian journalist why he thought such crimes were not newsworthy.

He had said crimes like rituals, rapes, kidnappings, and armed robberies were very common among university and college students in Nigeria. So common, he said, that it was no longer newsworthy. Nigerian politicians, he said, often recruit their political thugs and hired killers from amongst the cultists in university and college campuses. My journalist friend had also informed me that once armed with weapons supplied by politicians, the students often go on crime sprees once elections and political thuggery ended. That thought and mindset led me to my next question for the jihadist. But before doing that, I wanted to hear about the initiation process he was referring to, so I listened to him.

"Are you okay?" the jihadist asked me, as he looked at me intently. "I am okay," I told him, wondering if he was reading my mind again. "If the story I am telling you is disturbing and affecting you, I can stop, he said," and I immediately shook my head, saying it was not affecting me. It was affecting me, but it was affecting me differently than he knew or understood.

"Okay, the initiation process that I went through included having sex with a virgin and bringing the head of an infidel to the ceremony. To do this, my Muslim friend and I, went looking around for a virgin, which as you know, was a hard thing to find, unless you were looking for a young girl who was just entering puberty. After racking my brain for a long time about finding a virgin for the ritual, my friend, Usman Dangari, came up with the solution. He said we could go and raid the homes of Christians in the area, that we could kill two birds with one stone, meaning to kill an infidel and have sex with a virgin, at the same time.

To do this, we were given two weeks to find, and have sex with a virgin, and to kill an infidel. To make it easy, Boko Haram, under Yusuf, gave us fifteen foot soldiers to accompany me and my friend. We were to bring the head of the infidel, and to also bring a white loincloth stained with the virgin's virginal blood, to the ritual.

Since I did not have any household in particular in mind, the only household that came to my mind was my childhood Christian friend, whom I had severed my relationship with, since becoming an active member of the militant sect, Boko Haram. I was an active member before I was initiated into the sect. I guess my activism before initiation was to prove my loyalty.

I went with my other active members, with masks, to the home of my Christian childhood friend, at night, killing, and beheading him, and raping his younger sister, whom I knew was a virgin. I knew the girl was a virgin because the family members were devout Christians who did not believe in premarital sex or any sort of fornication. I chose the family because I knew in my heart of hearts that the girl was a virgin. And she was.

With the rest of the family members hacked to death with axes and machetes, the girl did not offer any resistance as I raped her. At the time of the rape, I had only a loincloth on, as I had been instructed to do. I had also washed my genitals with 'holy' water that I was given. We put the severed head of my former Christian friend, in a plastic bag, and then carefully put the white loincloth in a separate nylon bag, and left the rest of the carnage behind. We celebrated afterward, before taking the severed head and the bloodstained loincloth to the cleric who performed the rituals and ceremony, in front of over 200 jihadists and activists," he said.

If I said I almost threw up, it will be an understatement. I didn't want to give the jihadist the impression that I was affected by the confession, so I held my own, roiling inside. I quickly asked the next question, to conceal my discomfort.

"What was the purpose of the virgin blood and severed head?" I asked, wondering, and thinking, as he answered.

"The virgin blood meant purity. The cleric had instructed that having the blood of an unmarried girl or woman who has not copulated or had any form of sexual intercourse, was a clean beginning for a new recruit, into the sect. The severed head was proof of one's readiness to make the ultimate sacrifice on behalf of Allah. The blood of a virgin also meant that a person's life has been purified, sort of like being reborn as a Christian. Once a proven activist had provided the required ingredients and materials for the sacrifice, he becomes ready for the initiation, which often lasts a whole night.

Part of the initiation process was to also sleep with a virgin Muslim girl, during the celebration. The difference between the Muslim virgin girl and the Christian virgin girl was that the Muslim girl signifies the beginning of a selfless sacrifice for Allah, while the blood of the Christian virgin girl signifies, as I said earlier, purification. The severed head also means severing ties with the past, and any form of western influence or sins," he said. I was feeling repulsive and had to control my bowels with every effort I had left, in me.

I asked the next question for the sake of digression as I needed time to recover from the gory details he had just painted. So, I asked the next question, which was totally incongruous to the earlier discussion.

"I have heard that lots of northern Nigerian politicians are in collusion with Boko Haram and Ansaru, how truthful is that?" He looked at me thoughtfully, and then started to weigh the question before answering.

"If it hadn't been for the support of northern Nigerian politicians, Boko Haram would not have the funds to operate and to recruit foot soldiers and suicide bombers. Most of our supporters are disgruntled northern politicians who felt deprived of their Allah-given rights to rule Nigeria. I remember attending a meeting with a prominent Nigerian politician who gave us a bagful of millions of Naira, with instructions. The instructions were verbal and we had to write them down. Part of our instructions was to create a state of anarchy in the north, and some parts of the south, so that the country would be ungovernable for President Goodluck Jonathan.

The idea was that a state of anarchy would bring down the administration of Jonathan and force the military to take over the government, in a coup d'etat that would lead to an interim government or a military government. The prominent northern politician told us that if the military were in charge, that the Head of State would be a chosen northerner, who will rule for a few years and hand-over power to a new civilian administration that would comprise of northerners. We were told that a military administration, headed by a northerner, will be more sympathetic to our cause than a southern civilian administration that was more sympathetic to insurgents in the Niger Delta than a group of Muslim militants fighting to establish Sharia law in the north.

To buttress his point, the prominent northern Nigerian politician pointed out how President Goodluck Jonathan had bankrolled the insurgents in the Niger Delta with free monthly salaries and wages. The politician said the rise of Jonathan was a conspiracy with insurgents in the Niger Delta. Part of that conspiracy included pressuring former President Umaru Musa Yar'Adua, through Obasanjo, to choose Jonathan as his vice president, who hailed from the Niger Delta, in order to pave Jonathan's way to the presidency.

The prominent politician said the insurgents in the Niger Delta knew of President Yar'Adua's medical background, that the administration of the now deceased president would be short lived, which would then give room for Jonathan to ascend the presidency. And, according to him, it worked, as Yar'Adua, as predicted by them, did not make it through his first term in office.

The zoning system adopted by People's Democratic Party (PDP) that allowed former President Olusegun Obasanjo to rule for eight years, was to pave the way for a northerner to ascend the presidency. Rather than Obasanjo allowing his then embattled vice president, Atiku Abubakar, who was a northerner, to take over as prearranged, Obasanjo handpicked his own successor, in the person of Yar'Adua, a sicklier, who was already looking at death in the face; much to the chagrin of the northern politicians who had handpicked and bankrolled a financially strapped Olusegun Obasanjo into the presidency in the first place. It was a slap in the face for the northern politicians who felt betrayed by Olusegun Obasanjo.

As if the betrayal wasn't enough, when Goodluck Jonathan had finished serving the term of the deceased President Musa Yar'Adua, Jonathan refused to step down for a northern politician to run under the PDP platform. Rather than give in to the party's prearranged zoning system, Jonathan ran for, and won the presidency, under the PDP platform. Recall that PDP was founded by northern politicians that included Atiku. Since the party was then basically controlled by former President Olusegun Obasanjo who served as the chairman of the Board of Trustees (BOT), who had himself wanted to run for a third term in office, by unsuccessfully trying to change the constitution, the northern politicians felt they had lost control of the party they had founded, the prominent politician told us in the meeting.

The prominent northern politician told us that Boko Haram could do what the insurgents in the Niger Delta did, but this time, in a bigger scale than what Movement for the Emancipation of the Niger Delta (MEND), and other insurgents in the area did for Jonathan. He also told us that Boko Haram would be rewarded as the insurgents in the Niger Delta were rewarded by Jonathan. He told us that money and weapons will not be an issue, that we should continue as we had always done, but this time, we should be attacking and targeting government infrastructures and Christians in the area. The idea of attacking Christians was to send a message to Jonathan, who is a Christian. The message was that ruling Nigeria was the birthright given to the Muslim-north by Allah, the prominent politician told us in the meeting," the Jihadist had confessed.

Though I had heard that some northern Nigerian politicians had said Nigeria would be ungovernable if PDP did not keep to its zoning policy by allowing northern politicians their turn, I did not know it was as deep as the jihadist had said. I remember reading in the PM Newspaper that a high profile member of the Boko Haram sect, Commander Shuaibu Mohammed Bama, who was in the list of wanted terrorists by Nigerian authorities, was arrested in the home of a Nigerian senator in Maiduguri, in November, 2011. I also read in a Nigerian newspaper that a Nigerian secret police had arrested a Boko Haram spokesman with ties to Senator Aliyu Ndome.

Listening to the jihadist as he confesses, I began to understand that he was not just a foot soldier. He was also in the top hierarchy of Boko Haram, especially if he was able to attend important meetings as he alleged to have attended. I did not have any reason to doubt him, since he was confessing on his own volition without being asked or forced to do so. He was a dying man who knew he was at the twilight of his life. He did not have any reason to exaggerate or to lie about his position in the Boko Haram sect. What bothered me and continues to gnaw inside me, was the implication that the Islamic militant sect was closely linked with al Qaeda, which has been confirmed by credible sources. If the sect was linked to al-Qaeda, and northern Nigerian politicians, then Nigeria may already be another Yemen, where al-Qaeda in the Arabian Peninsula was said to have infiltrated the government of that country.

So, I asked the next question in line with my thoughts. I looked at the jihadist who was now almost not doing badly for a dying man, in his gurney, with a new meaning. So far, the confession he had given had indicated that he rose as high as a top commander in the sect, than I had previously guessed. That realization made me feel more compelled to ask questions that I figured he would know.

"If it is true northern Nigerian politicians were using Boko Haram to destabilize the government of Jonathan and the country, how come Jonathan doesn't realize this and crack down on the northern politicians," I asked, waiting for him to answer. I wanted a cigarette so bad, but I kept to my promise to stop smoking. But the situation made my resolution to stop smoking difficult to keep. But I knew if I go back that it would be difficult for me to eventually stop, so I held on to my guns of resolution, and did not yield to the temptation that was now very strong. I took my mind off the craving for a cigarette, and waited for the jihadist to answer.

"To answer your question," the jihadist went on, after taking a deep breath, "you need to realize that it can sometimes be difficult to deal with unknown enemies. Though there were rumors that northern Nigerian politicians were bankrolling the sect, there were no credible proofs, other than the implication of Senator Aliyu Ndome who was reportedly harboring the sect's spokesman and wanted terrorist in his house. Though the senator was questioned, he was quickly released for reasons best known to the Jonathan administration.

Another reason I think the Jonathan administration did not want to stir an already troubled pot, in the north, was that he had been personally confronted by a northern politician who accused him of rigging the election that swept him into power for a full term, after the president had finished serving Yar'Adua's uncompleted term. Jonathan knew there were lots of northern politicians who were against him, and for fear of making them angrier, I am sure he stayed with the known facts that Boko Haram was linked to al-Qaeda in the Arabian Peninsula, and in Afghanistan, and left it at that.

Since terrorism had become a global phenomenon, with terrorist cells destabilizing Somalia, Central African Republic, Mali, Libya, Thailand, India, Pakistan and several other countries, the president, I am sure, preferred to let sleeping dogs lie by concentrating on his one-sided belief that he was fighting terrorism like the rest of the world. Another reason, I am sure, was that Boko Haram was founded in 2001, long before Jonathan ascended the presidency, and became a major player in Nigerian politics. With that mindset, Jonathan did not see Boko Haram as the seed of the hatred sowed by his enemies, but of a larger phenomenon sweeping the world," the jihadist said, and it did make sense, if I was to believe what he said, and like I said earlier, I had no reason not to.

So, I asked another question that had formed in my mind about the politicians using Boko Haram to destabilize Nigeria. "In your opinion, would you say northern Nigerian politicians were trying to use Boko Haram to force the military to intervene, as happened in Egypt when anarchy led to the fall of the government of the Muslim Brotherhood?" As I asked the question, I could see he did not think there was any comparison with what happened in Egypt.

Even with that, I waited for him to answer. I knew for some weird reasons that his answer would throw some light in the matter. I was not disappointed when he went straight to the matter. "The Egyptian situation was a total chaos that had no comparison. What you saw in Egypt was a Muslim brotherhood with a political clout that Boko Haram, in Nigeria, could never have. The Muslim Brotherhood was an entity of its own, with no known affiliation to al-Qaeda or large scale terrorism. They achieved their current status by peaceful protests, albeit using violent protests to fight the military for forcing out the government of Mohamed Morsi," he said, and stopped, to think. At that point, I felt the need to move on to a more relevant point.

Although I knew he had answered a couple of troubling questions, in my mind, I still felt the need to get to the crucial part of the matter about terrorism and what training he had received in foreign countries, besides the one he purportedly received in Mali.

"I know you said you received Boko Haram sponsored training in Timbuktu; was there any other training you received through al-Qaeda?" He looked at me with some kind of sadness. I don't know if he was sad about the fact that his life had turned out the way it did or he was sad for me. He started to answer my question by first giving me a background of the link between Boko Haram and al-Qaeda.

"I want you to understand this, my friend, that Boko Haram was founded after the original founder of the sect, Mohammed Yusuf, had received instruction in Salafism or Salafi methodology, which was really a hardcore Islamic training. A lot of people would say there was a link between Salafism and Wahhabism. A lot of Sunni Muslims do not like the link to Wahhabism for obvious reasons. The Salafist movement is a Sunni Muslims movement, that itself was started by earlier Muslims who considered Salafism the best example of an Islamic practice for every Muslim. In case you are wondering what Salafism entirely entails, I will tell you," he said as he looked at me, waiting. Seeing that he was waiting, I nodded my head.

"Salafism can be said to be a literalist, strict, and puritanical way of practicing Islam. There is something about Salafism that you should know. Those who founded the Salafi movement were the earliest Muslim fanatics and extremists who believed that Islam should be wholly puritanical, with rigid morality. Salafi Jihadists believed in using violent jihad against infidels and nonbelievers as an Allah-approved, legitimate way of expressing their beliefs in Islam.

Those adherents of the earlier Salafi movement and methodology, from which Mohammed Yusuf received his training and instructions, followed every literal tenet of the sacred texts, as preached by Ibn Taymiyyah, an Islamic theologian and scholar of the era of Mongol invasions, who himself had received his instructions from extremist, literalist, and puritanical school founded by Ahmad ibn Hanbal, who also introduced his own brand of Jihad, that he later called Hanbalism.

Now, with this background, you can see that Boko Haram was founded on the philosophy of Salafism and Hanbalism, which were based on extremist and literalist puritanical ideologies that were strictly based on rigid morality. That rigid morality explains the meaning of Boko Haram, which in the Hausa language means *western education is sinful*. That puritanical approach is the Islamic philosophy upon which Boko Haram operates its own brand of Jihad," he said, as he rested for a while before continuing. I could tell by his demeanor and body language that he may not have much to live. His breathing was getting irregular and difficult, even with the oxygen on his nose that was helping him to breathe better.

Though I had appreciated the historical and scholarly background of Boko Haram, which in a way threw a light on the historical connection between al-Qaeda and Boko Haram, I still wanted to know more about his trainings and instructions, and if there was a training that was peculiar to the top hierarchy and recruits of Boko Haram.

"I can tell by the confusion on your face that you did not get the answers you sought. But before I answer you, there is something more that I want to clarify," he said, as if he had regained his normal breathing. I waited, as I had gotten used to doing with him. I knew it would be totally useless for me to rush him. Even if I could, the jihadist didn't seem to be the type that could be rushed. So I waited. He didn't wait too long before he gave me my answer. But before he did so, he gave me more unsolicited information concerning Boko Haram and al-Qaeda, as if he wasn't satisfied with his own explanation.

"Hanbalism and Hanbali methodology has a strong following in Saudi Arabia, Qatar, Iran, Iraq, Syria, and several Muslim countries in the Middle East, Asia and in the Arab world. Lots of the adherents of Salafism are also, adherents of Hanbalism. Osama Bin Laden also believed in Salafism and Hanbalism. Now, my friend, you can see the link between Boko Haram and al Qaeda. Osama Bin Laden believed in the same puritanical and literalist philosophy that adherents of Salafism and Hanbalism believed in. \

Bin Laden was once quoted saying that Sharia law was the only hope the Muslim world had, to 'set things right.' That same mindset is what drives Boko Haram, al-Qaeda and Al Shabab. Like Boko Haram, under Mohammed Yusuf, Bin Laden once called on the west to: 'reject the immoral acts of fornication, homosexuality, intoxicants, gambling, and usury,' which had earlier been preached by Ibn Taymiyyah and Ahmad ibn Hanbal," the jihadist said, as he made a weak effort to smile.

I appreciated the explanation but I was eager to listen to his other trainings. As if reading my mind again, for the umpteenth time, he continued. "I was in my final year in the university, preparing for my finals, when I was chosen to be a part of a group of young Muslims to train with Al Shabab. At first I was reluctant but since my final exam was still weeks away and the training would only take a week, I went, taking all my books and handouts with me.

I traveled with the other new recruits of Boko Haram to Somalia, and arrived there in the middle of the night through Djibouti and Kenya, avoiding Ethiopia in the west, because of that country's war against Al Shabab. We knew Ethiopian soldiers were on the alert for any Al Shabab's foot soldiers and activities. We traveled using donkeys, cars, and sometimes ferries. It was the most difficult travels I had ever traveled. We were told that traveling through the most difficult terrains and longest routes and making it to the headquarters of Al Shabab, in Somalia, was part of the training, because of the difficult terrain, in the war-torn area.

When we arrived in Somalia, we were met and received by the leader of the Mujahideen Youth Movement, or what we fondly called the Movement of Striving Youth. At that time, Al Shabab already had its own brand of Sharia Law in the southern part of Somalia, and we were told to study how the Sharia Law was working in the south controlled by Al Shabaab, and to train with *The Boys*, the name given to the most extremist and violent youth division of Al Shabab, the group responsible for enforcing the strict rules of the Sharia Law.

While in Somalia, we did not know we would be helping to fight against the Transitional Federal Government (TGF) of Somalia and the Ethiopian soldiers, who were fighting alongside TGF to run off Al Shabab from the area. Fighting with Al Shabab, we learned, was part of our training. We were given Ak47s, sophisticated riffles, hunting knives, and hand grenades. It was the first time in my life that I saw so many weapons in one place. I saw more Russian made weapons than I did U.S. made weapons. Most of the Russian made weapons, I learned, were supplied by the brethrens in Chechen, who were fighting their own war against Russia.

At nights, we would ambush TGF and its allies, killing lots of the troops who were mostly inexperienced in guerilla warfare. We would take them by surprise, taking their less sophisticated weapons and ammunitions, and sometimes, their military vehicles. It was fun fighting TGF and its allies. There were lots of women who practically threw themselves at us. Having lots of women was permissible in Islam, even though harlotry was forbidden.

The training was so adventurous that at the end of the training and joint military exercises, some of us stayed behind to help fight the war. But because I had a text to take, I had to return after the second week.

Our training was in a camp in the jungle, where we would jump, do pushups, run, and practice martial arts. We also learned to use several weapons. But the greatest training I received in that camp was the act of making bombs. Those who were educated or half-educated were taught how to make different types of weapons, using everyday ingredients and materials. I was surprised that it was that easy to make deadly explosives. At the time I left the southern part of Somalia to go back to Borno State, in northern Nigeria, I was already very good in making explosives," he said.

I wanted to know the types of bombs he was talking about. I

knew I had to wait to ask the questions as I did not want to push him. But he continued before I knew he was ready.

"We were trained to make and use gunpowder because they burn quickly and can produce a high pressure-gas. High pressure-gas often helps to make the bullet to accelerate and fire quickly. Gunpowder was also good for our type of activities because it was used as a propellant in ammunitions. In some cases when we needed to scare the enemy, we would mix gunpowder with other explosive materials to create blasts, and to create fireworks," the jihadist said, as he paused to think.

I already knew a lot about gunpowder and how it is used. I knew about the black powder, which is sometimes used in making muskets, canons, and Dane guns. With my limited knowledge of gunpowder, I knew it is 75% potassium nitrate, 15% charcoal, and 10% sulfur. I remember from high school days in the chemistry lab that you could grind and mix these substances together, to make them lethal. The process was very simple, if I am to remember correctly. It often includes dampening the substances with water and then mixing it into a solid substance, like a cake, with a hydraulic press. The hydraulic process creates a resistance of some sort which creates pressure that is transmitted when a quantity of liquid such as water or oil, is applied.

The solid substance or cake-like matter is usually broken up and cut into different sifted sizes, with added graphite. I tried to remember other useful ingredients or application but my memory did not go that far back. It has been thirty years since high school, even though I had taken a few science courses in college before making up my mind to go into political science and, later, journalism. But I had kept up my interest in applied science, which included a subscription to journals dealing with science subjects such as chemistry, physics, and biology. In high school, chemistry and physics were my favorite subjects, but with my rusty recollection, it was hard to tell, you would say.

The jihadist was looking at me, as if he thought I had lost my mind. I would have thought so too. I had a faraway look on my face that people who were mentally disturbed usually had on their faces. But I was far from being mentally disturbed. I was trying to remember a subject that conjured a fond memory of the past. The jihadist must have been anxious to continue, sensing that he was running out of time, as he asked if he could continue.

"We can change the subject if it is disturbing you," the jihadist said, thinking the discussion about gunpowder and bomb making was affecting me. I quickly reassured him that the subject was a comfortable one for me. I even informed him that chemistry was one of my favorite subjects in high school. He asked why I didn't choose to become a scientist instead of a journalist. I laughed, and told him that journalism was my dream career, that I couldn't resist being one when the opportunity came.

He nodded as if he understood. "Can I then go ahead with answering your question about the different bombs we were trained to make?" I nodded, wondering if the subject was really relevant. For sake of argument, and clarification about the jihadist's involvement in Islamic militancy and terrorism, I felt it was necessary, and did not object to him continuing with his discussion of the subject matter.

"I want to clear a point that you made about gunpowder. Not all gunpowder is powerful. For instance, black powder with reduced sulfur contains 70% saltpeter (potassium nitrate or sodium nitrate), and 30% charcoal. The only advantage that the reduced sulfur in the black powder has is that it is less corrosive on the gun barrel, unlike black powders with full capacity sulfur," he said, as if the clarification was really necessary. I didn't voice out my opinion for fear of interrupting the confession.

He continued after a lasting pause and a spasm of coughing intervals. "My favorite was nitroglycerin, which is an oily explosive liquid that can also be used as a poison. Nitroglycerin is often used in making dynamites, even though most pharmaceutical companies also use it for making medicine. As a doctor, I know this. Nitroglycerin can have a destructive and lasting effect when detonated or used as an explosive. When detonated, the liquid ingredient changes into gas which can create an expansive destruction. The impact of nitroglycerin is several times more effective and powerful than gunpowder, and several times faster.

Even though it is powerful and can have a more expansive destructive effect, nitroglycerin is very easy to make. To make nitroglycerin, all that is required is to carefully and slowly add glycerin to a concentrated nitric and sulfuric acids. As the glycerin is slowly added, a layer is gradually formed on top of both the nitric and sulfuric acids. The layer can be removed with water and sodium carbonate," he said, as if recalling a crammed instruction from memory.

I was impressed by his knowledge and recollection. But then again, I realized he was a doctor that such issues as compounds, matter, liquids, and acids, come easily to him. So, I urged him to continue with the confession, realizing that time was no longer on his side, by the look on his face. I could tell by the look of resignation on his face that he was ready to give up the ghost. But I also knew that the confession was important to him. He wanted to make sure his afterlife was a smooth transition. I don't know when he finally realized that he needed to confess, in order to have a peaceful hereafter, and I wasn't going to ask him. I figured I will probably ask him later, if time permitted.

"Nitroglycerin is often a choice ingredient by most chemists when creating smokeless powders such as cordite," he said. I got curious and wanted to know about cordite. So, I asked what cordite meant or entailed. He came out with the answer, as if he expected me to ask the question. "Cordite is a smokeless powder that is comprised of nitroglycerin, and guncotton," he said as he went into a short spasm of racking coughs. I waited for him to regain himself, before asking the next questions.

"So far, the bomb making ingredients and substances you have mentioned, are not as dangerous as the ones used in making magnetic bombs and car bombs?" I asked. He shook his head as if agreeing with me but I could tell he was thinking as he started looking at the ceiling again, as if asking for a divine help with his recollection.

"There is saltpeter which is really a potassium nitrate, used for making explosives, matches, gunpowder, and fertilizer bombs. Saltpeter is unique in that it is in its own class as far as explosives are concerned. In chemistry, saltpeter is used as a reagent. Reagent is itself a substance used in detecting and measuring tangible things because of its biological components. Saltpeter can be a very dangerous substance because it contains an oxidizer which can be found in liquid rocket fuel propellants," he said.

At this point, my mind was overwhelmed with information, and I was beginning to feel that I was digressing from my intended story. But then again, it occurred to me, for the umpteenth time that the information might be of interest to my editor, and my readers. So I kept listening to him, without bothering to lead him to a different topic.

He continued, as if he couldn't wait to get a signal from me. "The substance, saltpeter is really a crystalline powder with white colorless crystals. What makes it so special is that it can dissolve very quickly, mostly at 337 degrees Celsius. A very important fact you should know is that saltpeter is often created through a chemical reaction between potassium chloride and sodium nitrate or nitric acid," he said. I was a little tired and thought of a ten minute break. I was afraid to take a break because I didn't know if he would die during the break. I felt it was important to keep him talking, to keep him alive.

I looked around me, and I could see that the CIA commander and the Nigerian secret service agents were not happy with my decision to give the jihadist an opportunity to confess. They wanted the dying jihadist to go to hell and rot, but they also wanted to hear what he had to say. The CIA commander was listening attentively to see if the jihadist might say something useful that could help in apprehending other wanted terrorists in the region. None of their reasons mattered to me. I wanted to listen to the confession for the sake of publishing it. Terrorism had become a major news scoop, and I knew it would increase my station's ratings, once the story hits the airwave.

"I want to elaborate on the subject of guncotton," he said weakly. I nodded my head for him to go ahead. "Guncotton has simple components that you see and use every day. To obtain guncotton, cotton or purified wool cellulose, we would soak the purified wool cellulose in a mixture of sulfuric acid and nitric acid. For better effect, we would drain the soaked cotton from the acid mixtures, and then boil it to remove the impurities. Once boiled, we would ground and pulverize it to a pulp and then drain it out. The final stage would be to press it into slabs or solidity while it was still damp. When it is solid enough, it is then dried. Guncotton is a very lethal component as an explosive, and we used it a lot.

The reason I said that is because if it is ignited, dry guncotton can be unpredictable as it can burn very quickly. If not properly handled, it can explode, especially if struck with a heavy object. Guncotton is only dangerous when it is dried. When wet, guncotton will not burn or explode. We would often keep wet guncotton in a freezer until we had the need for it. The beauty of a wet guncotton is that it can be kept refrigerated to keep it wet, or in storage to maintain its wetness. Bear in mind that when wet, guncotton cannot explode on its own," he said, as he took a deep breath. I was wondering when he would talk about something else. I regretted asking him to describe the training he received about making bombs and explosives. It seems he enjoyed describing the processes, and I figured I wouldn't do myself any good to ask a new question, since it didn't appear he was done with the subject.

"Another explosive you should know about that we were trained to use is TNT. TNT is a dangerous solid explosive," he said, as he scratches his head. I wanted to know about TNT and asked him to explain what the acronyms stood for. He surprised me again, reading my mind and answered. I felt the man must have studied psychology or had psychic abilities. "TNT means trinitrotoluene. Trinitrotoluene is comprised of nitrogen, hydrogen, carbon and oxygen," he said, as if reading a script from memory, once again impressing me with his knowledge of chemistry.

He continued, as if suddenly in a hurry to finish the discussion. "TNT is usually through the process of adding a nitro group to an organic compound, what we called nitrating. We would nitrate the chemical compound toluene to make TNT. TNT often appears pale yellow crystals, at first, and often darkens to brown. The beauty of TNT is that it is less dangerous. A novice can handle it without worries that it would blow up on him. TNT can be melted in a low temperature heat without the danger of it going off on its own. TNT is a charge-component for shell bombs. It can be very dangerous and effective when used in conjunction with PETN, RDX and ammonium nitrate," he said.

He was going deeper into the processes of making explosives, and I was wondering if the end of the discussion on the topic was in sight. I was tired and even bored with the topic. But at the mention of PETN, RDX and ammonium nitrate, my interest suddenly came alive, as if the fatigue had been removed from my system. Not surprising, considering his ability to psych me up, he continued.

"For the uninformed, not referring to you," he smiled, "PETN means pentaerythritol and is considered more powerful than TNT.

It can explode smaller devices. PETN can sometimes be used as a core for detonating caps and fuses. For greater chemical reactions, TNT and PETN can be mixed together for greater effect. When TNT and PETN are mixed together, the final outcome is called pentolite," he said. I felt as if I was back in my chemistry lab, in high school, the way I was learning about these explosives, chemical reactions and compounds.

He continued, as if tired of psyching me up. "There is a dangerous bomb component or explosive you should know about. It is called picric acid. The chemical name for picric acid is trinitrophenol. Trinitrophenol is mostly used as an explosive. Its popularity has gone down among bomb makers because it often corrodes metal casings. It can be very effective when combined with metals to form salts known as picrates. Picrates are unpredictable and can be used as an apparatus to set off predictable explosives," he said. I could no longer hide my boredom as I yawned. I was tired of suppressing my yawns. I didn't think he paid me any attention, as he continued.

"The most common explosives are plastic explosives which are substances that can be molded into any shape or size. Plastic explosives usually result from a mixture of RDX and PETN. Plastic explosives are commonly used in crowded places. They are mostly used in Iraq, Yemen, Afghanistan and Pakistan, by the Taliban. Boko Haram often uses plastic explosives because it can be kept hidden for days or years. It is safe to hide in a building or a highly populated place, as only a powerful detonator can set it off. I have used several plastic explosives in my jihad, and it is very lethal," he said.

It was at this juncture that I felt it was time to ask him more questions. I knew in my heart of hearts that my readers will be bored to death if I put this on paper the way he had narrated it. I figured I may have to seriously edit out the irrelevant parts in the story. Though I liked the full explanation of the processes involved in making explosives and bombs, I knew that not everyone will be into it. I knew I got bored somewhere in the middle of the discussion. Since I was obligated, somewhat, to listen to him, I had hidden my boredom, until towards the end.

To renew my interest, and hopefully the interests of my readers who would read this, I asked him more relevant and interesting questions.

"Earlier in your explanation and discussion," (he smiled with understanding as I was trying to use the right word), you mentioned that you had helped Al Shabab to fight government and allied forces in Somalia. Did you do any fighting with any militant group, elsewhere?"

"I am glad that you asked that question. Yes, we had often joined forces with our brethrens in other countries to fight the enemies of Islam. I was part of a group of Boko Haram soldiers sent to Mali, Central African Republic, and Algeria to fight French soldiers and African Union peacekeepers. We fought French and Malian soldiers with guns supplied to us from Chechen and Russia. For a while Islamist fighters, including Boko Haram, al Qaeda and the local Islamic group in Mali, fought the French and Malian soldiers as they came into the towns of Diabaly and Douentza, in central Mali. We fired rocked propelled grenades and retreated into the bush, when the French airstrikes became too much for us. Though they did not really inflict any casualty on our members, we wanted to remain safe to fight them from the bushes and desert.

And we succeeded as we burnt their armored vehicles with bombs and rockets. To teach the French a lesson, we bombed and sabotaged the gas plant in Algeria because of the French interests in the plant. At the plant, we took several hostages and created fears among the indigenes. The whole idea was to frighten them not to cooperate with French and Malian forces, and we succeeded.

Even though we had lost a couple of towns to French and Malian forces, we were able to hold on to towns like Mopti and Sevare, where we mostly operated freely. We made the indigenes pay us taxes, while running a makeshift government, and imposing Sharia Law.

I want to point out that we did lose a few vehicles but no casualties. We had used most of the residents as human shields against French airstrikes, and it worked. The French were mostly concerned with not taking innocent lives, we did not care. The burden was on them, not on us. After a couple of weeks of fighting, I had to go back to school, as the last of my final exams was approaching. For me, at that time, it was very important that I finished my school," he said.

At this point, I figured it was time to get him to talk about his activities in Nigeria and how Boko Haram became such an internationally known terrorist organization within a very short time. He gave me the look that I had come to recognize as the *duh* look.

"When you attack a United Nations office in any country, especially in a nation's capital, you are sending a message; and you immediately get headlines across the world, and that is what we got, in August of 2011, when we crashed a car loaded with explosives into the UN building that killed 21 and wounded 60 people. The point of the bombing of the U.N building was to make sure we were taken seriously by the international community. We did not want to be known or seen as a local group. We felt we had done enough carnage in Nigeria to be heard and recognized like al-Qaeda and Al Shabab," he said, as he closed his eyes.

For a minute I was worried that I had lost him, and then just as suddenly, he opened his eyes and smiled, as if in mockery of my anxiety. I felt an instantaneous relief that he was still alive. I did not want him gone until I was satisfied he had told me everything he wanted to say. I figured he was as eager to tell his story as I was eager to publish it.

I remember the horrendous explosion he was talking about. I was in Abuja, covering a story when the attack had taken place. My friend who was then working for the NTA had called me at my hotel to inform me about the attack. I immediately abandoned everything I was doing, including the Nigerian girl I was with, and had rushed to the site of the explosion.

What I saw took me by surprise. I did not think Boko Haram would target the U.N building, but then again, I could see it as being relevant to the sect, since it was part of the western edifice that the sect abhors.

I remember interviewing a source who had witnessed the attack. He had said the suicide bomber had driven the car, loaded with explosives, crashed it through two security barriers, to the reception area, in the diplomatic zone of the building, and detonated the bomb. The impact of the explosion had immediately devastated the building, destroying it to its lower floor and foundation. The building was said to have had around 400 U.N employees at the time of the attack, which was probably the reason it was targeted. Terrorist groups often preferred to attack huge crowds. The magnitude of the bomb and the timing of the attack indicated the bomb was meant to kill as many of the 400 U.N employees as possible, for greater effect.

By attacking an international organization like the U.N, and provoking condemnation from the U.N Secretary General, Ban Ki-Moon, who described the attack as "assault on those who devote themselves to helping others," the Islamic militants achieved the lofty objective of getting international recognition and attention.

As I recalled the tragic event at the U.N building in Abuja, I looked at the jihadist and wondered about the evil that men were capable of. Taking innocent lives to promote a cause is barbaric and primitive. But then again, I realized that with Boko Haram, they thrive on barbarism. The sect had often preached against civilization as they had come to know it. The objective of the sect was to establish Sharia Law, and to forego anything western and its corruptive influence, or so they proclaimed, in Nigeria.

I had heard how the founder, Mohammed Yusuf, had lived a lavish lifestyle, driving around in expensive luxury vehicles, while preaching to his followers that they should reject western influence and anything western. Cars and expensive homes, decorated with western furniture and ornaments, were western, but the deceased leader preached against the lifestyle he enjoyed, till his untimely death in the hands of the Nigerian soldiers and mobile police.

Most hypocrites, I had come to realize, often preached what they did not practice. Historically, and in the current dispensation of leaders who preach one thing and do something else, it is not surprising that Mohammed Yusuf would live one lifestyle and preach a different lifestyle to his followers. In communism and socialism, the leaders were often known to preach to their followers to live an austere life, while maintaining an expensive and opulent lifestyle in secret themselves.

In George Orwell's *1984*, big brother often was seen rationing food to the citizens while the leaders enjoyed a lavish lifestyle of bountiful foods and drinks, while the commoners suffered and lived on rations. In North Korea, the leader is said to enjoy western lifestyle, while at the same time rebelling against the west. In Iran, and other rogue regimes, leaders preach what they don't practice.

The jihadist was looking at me with a worried look on his face. I caught the look on his face and smiled to let him know I was still with him. He smiled back, as if relieved that I had not lost my sanity.

"Are you okay? For a minute there, I thought my confession had caved-in your sanity," he said. I laughed and said I was okay. He nodded his head and continued to talk again.

"As I was saying, the attack on the U.N building in Abuja in 2011 brought us instant recognition. International media and news organizations started listening to us. Even the U.S. formally recognized us as a terrorist organization, something that was totally nonexistent before the attack on the U.N building. There were bounties on the heads of our leaders. Even the U.S. placed a bounty on the heads of some of our leaders. With that acknowledgment we felt we had arrived.

Like al-Qaeda and Al Shabab, we had a spokesman, whose name was really an alias, who acknowledges attacks carried out by us, to the media. We became important overnight. But that importance had a price. Not that most of our foot soldiers cared about deaths, we never did. Death was part of the inheritance and reward for fighting for Allah. It was the expected end result for a foot soldier, even for the leader," he said.

I begged to differ that the leaders were ready to die the same way the foot soldiers were ready to die, as martyrs. I knew from experience, as a journalist, that terrorist leaders do not make the same sacrifices for the sake of the principle that they preach about. Mohammed Yusuf was in hiding from Nigerian soldiers, until he was discovered, captured and killed. Osama Bin Laden was in hiding in Pakistan, for nine years, living with his wives and children, before he was killed in a CIA led operation that included Navy Seals.

Sensing my silence, he took that as a signal to proceed, and continued with his confession. Rather than being absentminded as I had been in-between the confession, I actually maintained eye contacts as I reflected on the capture of Bin Laden in Pakistan.

Though I disagreed with his comment about the readiness of terrorist leaders to sacrifice their lives, as martyrs as their followers, I did not voice out my opinion. Terrorists revered their leaders as they do their Allah. To say anything derogatory was to invoke their anger, so I maintained my silence and kept my opinion to myself.

"There is something I should tell you. It is something I have never bothered to tell anyone before, not even my parents when they were alive. There was a time when cannibalism was an accepted practice in the sect. Once, in our camp, an infidel who had been giving information to the Nigerian soldier about our activities was captured, and to prove a point, we actually roasted him and served him as meat to all the members in the camp. It was the first time I ever ate a human being. Before then, I had eaten dogs, snakes, snails, but never a human being.

What was so bad about the experience was that I did not feel bad about it. The sect members who were in the camp ate the bones, the flesh and the entire body as if it was a regular bush meat or cow meat. After that particular incident, I did not come across any sort of cannibalism again, except when we were in training in Somalia when I witnessed two 11 years old soldiers eat the thigh of a Somali government soldier," the jihadist said, with a straight face, as if the experience was a normal experience.

I have heard of cannibalism among rebels, terrorists, and insurgents. Not too long ago I saw a Syrian rebel eating the heart of a Syrian government soldier who had been captured and killed, on you-tube. In the years I have been practicing journalism, I have written about cannibalism in North Korea, in Ibo land of Nigeria, during the civil war, when the Ibos were being starved. I have also written about cannibalism in Thailand were primitive natives use humans for rituals and later serve the body as meat.

As far as I know, most governments are against the practice of cannibalism, but there is strong evidence that cannibalism still exists in many parts of the world, especially in very poor countries of the world. As I listened to the jihadist tell of his experience with cannibalism, I began to fully understand why he would want to confess at the twilight of his life. For him, it was time to come clean with his sins, if he calls his actions sins, that is.

After a while I felt it was time to leave the subject of cannibalism and concentrate on a decent topic. The topic was becoming gruesome, repulsive and repugnant to me, and I was no longer comfortable with it. When I had written about the subject several years ago, it had been a very difficult subject for me to tackle, as it is for me now.

I asked a different question, one that I was more comfortable with. "We have talked about your various training; did you at any time join the al Qaeda insurgents in Iraq and Afghanistan?" He shook his head vigorously as if the question was a taboo.

"As much as we hated western influence and corruption, we at Boko Haram, did not believe in fighting sectarian wars in other countries. In Somalia we fought against government forces as part of our training. It would have been against our methodology to go to Iraq or Afghanistan to fight. We did what we did because we believed in it, not because of any other reason," he said, as if confused about what to say next. I kept quiet. I could tell he wasn't comfortable with discussing the topic of fighting with jihadists in Iraq and Afghanistan, so I left the topic alone and thought of a new topic to ask him.

"I know there are different types of Muslims, what type are you?" I asked, not sure if the question was offensive or not. I was trying to see if one particular sect of Muslims were more violent than the others. As usual, he started with a long explanation before answering the question.

"In Islam, there are several types of Muslims. There is the Sunni Muslim, which are the largest group of Muslims in the world. The Sunnis practice orthodox Islam, according to the actions, examples, and words of Prophet Muhammad.

And there is the Shiite Muslim, which is the second largest group of Muslims in the world. The Shiite Muslims believed that Prophet Muhammad's family, Ahl Bayt, and his descendants, such as the imams, had greater spiritual authority over other Muslims, while the Sunnis believed otherwise.

The third largest are the Wahhabi Muslims. These groups of Muslims base their beliefs in the teachings of Muhammad ibn Abd al-Wahhab. Wahhabism is very dominant in Saudi Arabia. Abd al-Wahhab had preached purging out impurities in Islam. That is why the type of Islam practiced in Saudi Arabia today is different from the type of Islam practiced elsewhere in other Muslim countries. Most of the modern day jihadists originated from Saudi Arabia, because of the hardcore belief in Wahhabism.

The last groups of Muslims are Sufi Muslims. Sufi or Dervish Muslims are adherents of the inner, mystical dimension of Islam. Sufi practitioners believe they have divine powers," he said, without elaborating.

"And to answer your question, I am a Sunni Muslim," he said, smiling, as if reading my mind again. I knew what he was doing. He wanted to make sure I understood the different types of Muslims in Islam, before answering the question. In a sense, I appreciated what he was trying to do because I did not know about Wahhabism.

I was feeling giddy, tired and out of ideas. I decided to let him talk rather than direct him. He waited for me to ask him a question and when he saw that I was not going to, he started to talk again.

"After my medical school education, the question became whether I should open a clinic or work for a clinic. My father was ready to support any move I decided to make. All the years I was going to school and getting trained by Boko Haram and al-Qaeda my father was not aware of it. He did not know that I had participated in insurgencies, and militancy in Somalia, Mali and even at home in Nigeria. I think my good grades sort of overshadowed his thoughts of me as an Islamic militant.

I opted for a clinic for obvious reasons. The temptation to have my own clinic, even though I had no experience as a medical doctor, was too much. After all, this was Nigeria, I told myself. No one really cares whether you have experience or not, as long as they have access to a real doctor, which was what I was. Most of them had also known untrained pharmacists who pass themselves as doctors to unsuspecting and naïve customers. Some of them have never known or had the privileged of having a real doctor.

I opened my clinic in the heart of Maiduguri, completed with everything a clinic should have. Since nurses were practically cheap, especially those trained by the ministry of health, I hired eleven of them. The place was always swarming with nurses in white uniforms. It had the look of a medical facility – Nigerian style!

As expected, the villagers brought their sick, wounded and dying to the clinic. I did as much as I could with the cases, within my power to handle. Cases that were too serious were immediately referred to the teaching hospital where there were surgeons and different doctors who specialized in different types of medicines.

Believe it or not, I never rejected any patient on the basis of religion. As a doctor, I did the job of saving lives. In a sense, I led a double life, sort of like Dr. Jekyll and Mr. Hyde. As a doctor, I was the best you could find, and as an Islamic militant, I was also the best in the sect. I killed without conscience as a jihadist. I saved lives with compassion as a doctor. Now you can begin to understand why I said I was like a Dr. Jekyll and Mr. Hyde. I committed a lot of atrocities when I was not working as a doctor.

At first my fellow jihadists did not even know I was a medical doctor, that I had a clinic. It was one summer, after Ramadan, when a serious religious violence had broken out, that it became known to my brethrens in the sect that I was a medical doctor," he said. At the mention of himself as Dr. Jekyll and Mr. Hyde, my vigor had returned as if I had had an infusion of energy or mood enhancer.

"Can you tell me exactly what triggered the violence, and if the violence was started by your sect?" I asked, trying to understand since he was playing Dr. Jekyll at his clinic when the violence had broken out. He saw my point and shook his head.

"Boko Haram and its members had nothing to do with the religious riot. Let me mention that northern Nigeria has been having its fair share of religious uprisings and violence before Boko Haram came into existence in 2001. Don't forget that Boko Haram was only interested in establishing Sharia Law, in order to remove the impurities that had become the lots of Muslims in northern Nigeria," he said, as he waited for my reaction to his comment.

I responded by asking if Ansaru was formed at that time. The question was really unnecessary because I knew Ansaru was founded in January of 2012, and was not even in existence then. But the jihadist answered the question I was hoping he would touch on when he provided a detailed explanation on the subject.

"For a long time, majority of the members of Boko Haram had the erroneous belief that the sect was not radical enough, and that there was too much political influence. I think the part concerning political influence concerned the sponsorship of violence and targets by several prominent politicians who were using the sect to disrupt the government of Jonathan, following the presidential election of 2011, which most of the northern politicians felt was rigged.

Ansaru was formed in 2012 by members of Boko Haram who did not like the direction of Boko Haram. The disgruntled members who left to form Ansaru were upset with the group leadership for allowing northern politicians to dictate its actions. You have to understand that most of these disgruntled members hated northern politicians whom they knew as corrupt and greedy, with western lifestyles.

After unsuccessfully trying to persuade the leadership of Boko Haram to refocus the objective of the sect, some members left to form Ansaru, which was known as the Vanguard for the Protection of Muslims in Black Lands. Ansaru was created with the intention of creating awareness about the rise of terrorism in Nigeria and in black lands. Ansaru wanted to take the sect international, and make it an international terrorist entity, different from the misguided focus of Boko Haram, which Ansaru saw as being controlled by northern Nigerian politicians to carry out their agendas against the Nigerian government.

What was very ironic about Ansaru was the comment of the founding leader, Abu Usmatul al-Ansari, who described Boko Haram's actions as 'inhuman to the Muslim Ummah.' But the violence perpetrated by Ansaru appears to contradict that comment, as the group continues the same domestic jihad that was also the trademark of Boko Haram. The group claimed not to be associated with politics, but there was a rumor that a few prominent northern politicians had bankrolled the sect."

I nodded when he had said that. I had also heard the same rumor. As a journalist, the rumor mill can be very useful. Sometimes the rumor mill triggers interest to investigate the rumor, which often leads to bigger stories and news. The rumor mill, or grapevine, as most people call it, can sometimes be the bread and butter of a journalist.

Sometimes, some unscrupulous journalists will publish a rumor, garnered from the grapevine without any further investigation. We called that sort of journalism: *yellow journalism*, the practice of publishing stories without first verifying the facts. In journalism, if one wants to be taken seriously, it was always necessary to verify a story before rushing to put it out.

"I see you are back to your usual daydreaming or absentmindedness," the jihadist said, trying to get my attention. I quickly brought my mind to the present and started to pay attention to him. I realized that the jihadist, like most people, hated talking in vain or to the air, without anyone listening. Since the objective of the jihadist was to confess and clean his mind of past sins, he wanted to make sure that I put everything he was saying down as accurately as possible.

To let him know I was not daydreaming, I asked a question that had been bothering me, for some time. I wanted to know about the Christmas day bomber, and if Boko Haram was involved in his training. So I asked him about Umar Farouk Abdulmutallab, the Nigerian underwear bomber who attempted to detonate a plastic explosives hidden in his underwear while aboard Northwest flight 253, en route from Amsterdam to Detroit, Michigan, on December 25, 2009.

He cleared his throat as if that was a difficult question before answering the question. "I knew you were going to ask me this question sooner or later. First let me clear the misunderstanding that Abdulmutallab was trained by al-Qaeda. Boko Haram recruited and trained Abdulmutallab, not al-Qaeda, as was erroneously reported in the media. The only accurate statement in the media report was the fact that Abdulmutallab had traveled to Yemen. He traveled to Yemen because we sent him, along with six other Boko Haram jihadists to learn the procedures of the al-Qaeda operatives in the Arabian Peninsula.

Abdulmutallab became influenced and inspired by the teachings of Anwar al-Awlaki when he had attended several of the cleric's lectures. Abdulmutallab met Ibrahim Hassan al-Asiri, during a lecture organized by al-Awlaki. Abdulmutallab had returned to Nigeria, to Maiduguri and consulted with the leadership of Boko Haram, which included me, at the time, and said he was ready for the journey of martyrdom. We started to prepare him but because we were not ready for what he suggested he wanted to do, we loaned him to our brethrens in al-Qaeda in the Arabian Peninsula, for the jihad, which had failed.

I want you to know that we not only trained him but paid for his travels to Yemen, Dubai, Kuwait, Saudi Arabia, and Qatar, where he was tremendously influenced. We believed in him, and trusted his sincerity when he said he was ready for jihad. The only problem was that we were not ready for the international jihad, which involved the United States that he had proposed. We thought he would be better suited for the al-Qaeda in the Arabian

Peninsula, which was then managed by Anwar al-Awlaki," he said, as if angry by the media report that the al-Qaeda in the Arabian Peninsula had trained Abdulmutallab.

I didn't quite agree with him on everything he said about Boko Haram's influence. I did hear a rumor then that Boko Haram had initially trained Abdulmutallab, before the young man traveled to Yemen to meet with Anwar al-Awlaki and Ibrahim Hassan al-Asiri. Since there was a strong connection and link between Boko Haram and al-Qaeda in the Arabian Peninsula, I did not particularly dispute his claim that the Nigerian underwear bomber was recruited by Boko Haram.

I wasn't particularly interested in the underwear bomber discussion because it had been widely reported in the media. Any discussion on the subject might not be of interest to my readers. I wanted to hear something that hadn't been reported or made public, so I asked him about the method the sect uses for recruiting and brainwashing suicide bombers. He didn't particularly like the word *brainwashing*, but it was my preferred word, and after a few minutes, he gave up and answered the question. I felt he was the one who requested to have a confession, not me. I didn't feel I was under any obligation to lean towards his commands and wishes.

"Let me start by saying that the method of recruiting volunteers to make a sacrifice on behalf of Allah is not suicide. Islam forbids suicide. Any adherent that takes the route of martyrdom on account of a religious belief by suffering death on account of adherence to a cause is not a suicide, as is mostly reported in the media.

I have been personally involved in recruiting martyrs in several countries, and it has always been voluntary and optional, not by coercing or cajoling, as most unbelievers think. As the head of the martyrdom division, I would sometimes get letters from men, women and children, who wanted to make a sacrifice on behalf of Allah.

My policy was to always interview them as to why they were interested in martyrdom. The majority of them had often said they lost a family member, a child, a father, a mother, or an entire family, and had nothing to live for. For some, it was just a personal disgust with the way Muslims were being persecuted, harassed, profiled, and abused across the world.

I remember an invitation I had received from a young Muslim woman whose children and husband had been slain by Buddhists in western Burma. She had written me that she would like to join the holy war, so as to get killed and join her slain family. In her letter, she said her family had become victims of Buddhist mob attack, and that she had escaped because she had been at work when the attack had taken place. I went to meet her in Rakhine State, in western Burma, where I personally talked to her, to make her think seriously about her option.

I made it clear to her that jihad was not an act of revenge but a holy war waged on behalf of Islam as a religious duty. She then broke down and told me how she had always wanted to make a sacrifice on behalf of Islam but hadn't had the opportunity until her entire family members were wiped out. I offered to take her with me to Yemen, where I was temporarily residing at the time, working with al-Qaeda in the Arabian Peninsula.

During her visit, I had introduced her to Ibrahim al-Asiri, who had further given her more instructions on the duty of a jihadist. After the instructions and readiness, she had returned to Burma, and made the ultimate sacrifice, that resulted in the death of several Buddhists. For her, it was not a vengeance but a holy war against those who were killing and persecuting Muslims in western Burma," he said, looking at me for understanding.

I remember covering a Buddhists' riot in western Burma, where hundreds of Muslims had been killed by Buddhists, a few years ago. I knew he was telling the truth about Muslims being killed by Buddhists in Burma. I remember interviewing one of the most vocal Buddhists then, who had expressed his desire to wipe out the Muslim population in his country because of their increasing population. The warmongering Buddhist had said in that interview that he hated seeing Muslims in his country.

I had accompanied the mobs, who were wielding machetes and deadly weapons, rampaging through Muslim neighborhoods. I witnessed several Muslims getting killed and beheaded by a mob of Buddhists. I had felt weakened by my powerlessness to stop the carnage. I had returned to my post, sickened by the experience, for several weeks. Years later, the experience still haunts me, in my sleep.

I had seen people getting killed in warfronts but never the sort that I had experienced in Burma. When my editor had asked me to return to cover another Buddhists' rampage, I had refused. It was not always that 1 refused an assignment but I had to refuse that assignment. I know as a journalist I should separate my personal feelings, but that is often hard to do when you are witnessing murders that you feel powerless to stop.

I was in deep thought when I noticed that the jihadist was becoming restless. I knew immediately that I had to limit my thoughts in order to concentrate on the matters at hand. I knew it was hard not to reflect on some of the issues that came up in the jihadist's confession. But as time continues to be of essence, fearing that the jihadist could die at any time, I started to think hard about any loopholes I may have neglected to cover.

I thought of the next possible question to ask him, as his head slumped to the left, making me think that he was no longer with us, that he was dead. Just as I thought he was gone, he straightened his head and smiled. I could see he was trying to be funny, despite his dying mien. "I gotcha, now I got your attention!" he said, still smiling. I didn't find it amusing, as the joke impacted me a great deal. When he saw that I was not smiling, he nodded his head as if he understood my shock and relief.

"Okay, let's get serious," I said, looking at him. He nodded his head without saying anything, and I continued with the question I was going to ask him before the practical joke he pulled on me. "You were talking about suicide bombers, and how it was against the tenets of Islam to commit suicide. I know you said it was martyrdom and not suicide, but when one takes his own life, don't you think it is suicide?" I asked.

He shook his head vigorously again, and for the umpteenth time I worried that his head would fall off. "Like I told you earlier, martyrdom is not suicide. When one sacrifices his life for his religious faith, that person is not committing suicide but making a sacrifice," he said, with emphasis on martyrdom. I knew when it comes to martyrdom that the thin line between suicide and sacrifice is debatable. But I didn't say anything, knowing it might offend his belief. My goal was not to be judgmental but to listen, I told myself, as I continued to weigh the next question in my mind.

I was thinking of the Fort Hood Shooter, of Nidal Hasan, a U.S. Army Major and psychiatrist, who fatally shot 13 fellow soldiers and wounded 30 others, at a military base in Fort Hood, near Killeen, Texas, in November of 2009. I remember the reluctance of the authority to call it a terrorist attack at first. I knew it was later determined that the act was a terrorist attack, following an investigation that revealed that Hasan had been influenced by the Yemeni based al-Qaeda leader and cleric, Anwar al-Awlaki, through email communication.

As if reading my mind again, he nodded. I did not exactly know why he nodded his head. I figured it had to do with my thoughts about the Fort Hood Shooter. But I didn't say anything. I didn't want to continue to give him the impression that he was correctly reading my mind. As much as I liked to listen to his confession, I was not trying to be friendly, even though I was polite to him. Any person that killed innocent women and children will never get any form of friendship from me.

I could understand fighting for a cause and belief, but knowingly taking innocent lives of children is no longer fighting to protect a cause or belief, but pure coldblooded murder. To maintain civility and decorum, as it applies to my profession, I kept my opinion and disgust hidden from my facial appearance. I didn't want to give him the impression that I find him repulsive, even though I knew he suspected that I didn't like him or what he represented.

My job was to report stories and news, not to hate or dislike. I felt I had an obligation to inform the public about anything that represents oddity and weirdness, in order to create awareness. The essence of this story was to also fulfill that professional obligation. So, I kept on maintaining my objectivity, albeit with a profound difficulty to do so.

"Major Hasan was not only influenced by the teachings and instructions of cleric al-Awlaki but by his own knowledge of the atrocities that were being committed against Muslims by U.S. soldiers in Iraq and Afghanistan. As a psychiatrist, Hasan was obligated by the duties of his profession, to listen to the atrocities confessed to by soldiers who had returned home from the battlefield. Listening to the returning soldiers who were troubled by the carnage and atrocities they committed while on a tour of military duty in Iraq and Afghanistan had also troubled the psychiatrist.

With each psychiatric session, Hasan learned firsthand that the soldiers who came to see him were troubled by the sins and atrocities they had committed in the war against terrorism. He began to seek counseling himself by sending emails about his thoughts and troubles to cleric al-Awlaki, who dutifully responded, instructing the psychiatrist to do what was right in the eye of Allah.

Major Hasan continued to communicate his thoughts to the cleric, and with each response from the cleric, he gradually became radicalized. With the burden of vengeance on him, the psychiatrist was no longer thinking of himself as a counselor but as a man on a mission. He began to walk around the military base, weighing his obligation to fellow soldiers and to Islam, to see if there was a way out without taking the lives of those who had made it their obligation to kill Muslims in the guise of fighting terrorism.

The psychiatrist could not see a way out. He felt he had to stop the next batch of soldiers going to Iraq and Afghanistan by any means possible. After weighing the many possibilities, he finally decided to communicate with the cleric one more time to make sure Allah would approve of his action. The cleric's response to his email finally convinced him he was on the right course of action. He saw it as his duty to derail the U.S. soldiers from committing further carnage against Muslim in the name of terrorism.

For years, Muslims across the world had been victimized. It continues to this day, in countries like Thailand, Burma, and places where Muslims are in the minority. Buddhists have been waging wars against Muslims for years, butchering them with machetes and deadly weapons. Unlike the Jews who faced similar atrocities during the first and second world wars, we did not have a big superpower country like the U.S. to protect us. Instead the superpowers were trying to deface us from the face of the earth," the jihadist said, as if the matter had been another source of extra burden on him. He had a look of defiance on his face.

I listened attentively, not bothering to interrupt him. I had learned it was better to listen than to talk. As a journalist, listening comes natural to me. There was a lot to be learned and garnered from the confessions of the jihadist without imposing the burden of interruption. But as I remained quiet without saying anything, the jihadist stopped, and was looking at me, obviously wondering at my silence. I wasn't about to give him the privilege of second guessing me or reading my mind.

"As a Muslim, did you feel that you were being discriminated against by the west?" I asked him, and to my surprise he just stared at me without saying anything. Just as I was thinking I had said something outlandish, he suddenly spurted with a sudden but brief burst of effort to answer the question without looking at me as he had often done when answering an offhanded question.

"As a Muslim, it was an obligation to feel like an underdog of the west, one whose lot was of utmost disregard and disrepute. After September 11, 2001, Muslims across the world became a target by virtue of their religious faith. At airports, shopping malls, and in the streets, Muslims would be physiologically and psychologically abused, sometimes with bodily harms. In the Middle East, Israel, and in the streets of western countries, Muslims became targets of religious and racial profiling. For a Muslim, radicalism and martyrdom comes natural due to the perception of others towards him. To answer your question, yes, I felt discriminated against. In my case, reading stories of other Muslims who were facing persecution and abuse, affected me indirectly," he said, looking at me as he finishes his comment, as if waiting for my approval.

I mentioned earlier that I had reported stories where Muslims had been victims of persecution, especially in countries where Muslims were in the minority. I had also reported and written about cases where Muslims had victimized people of other religions, especially Christians. In northern Nigeria, and elsewhere in the Muslim world, Muslims often wage the holy war of jihad against those who did not believe in, or practice their religion of Islam.

Christians in northern Nigeria are frequently harassed and killed because of the simple fact that they are Christians. Recently, I read in a Nigerian newspaper about the story of Christian children who were slain as they flee from Muslims who were chasing them with machetes, and guns, in Kaduna as they attended a funeral. The victims were a six month old baby and a 13 year old girl who was murdered as their parents ran from the rampaging jihadists in northern Nigeria.

Apart from the carnage often committed by Boko Haram, Fulani Muslims were often encouraged and incited by Islamic extremists to kill Christians. As I mentioned earlier, Fulani Muslims would come at nights, dressed in blacks, to attack unsuspecting villagers who felt safe from Boko Haram. It was the same normally safe and quiet villages that several underage children were shot and killed with machetes by Islamic extremists, in Kaduna recently.

The villagers were reportedly under attack for several hours without any intervention by security agents, and even the soldiers who were supposedly deployed to the area to stop such carnages. According to the newspaper account, those who survived the carnage likened it to Armageddon, sort of like a battle between the forces of good and evil. In this case, the forces of evil appeared to have prevailed over the forces of good. The Fulani Muslim attack was also reminiscent of another similar attack in a village near Jos, where 10 Christians were killed by Muslims who had attacked them as they worshipped in the wee hours of the morning in a church.

As my mind went through the various attacks that Christians have suffered in the hands of Muslims, in countries where Muslims were in the majority, I found it hard to sympathize with the jihadist. There was no justification for killing others because of religion. It was primitive, barbaric and a throwback to the forgotten days of Muhammad's early crusade of jihad.

But as I said, earlier, the call of my profession precludes me from prejudgment and presupposition. I had to maintain objectivity in order to be fair in my profession. And I have always been, even though in my heart of hearts I sometimes feel the pain of victims who faced religious persecutions across the world, whether Muslims or Christians.

Chapter 4

The tropical weather was as predictable as the tropics. But surprisingly it had not rained as the weatherman had predicted. The sun was sitting in its usual spot on the equator and shinning overhead, directly into this part of the world, as if the inhabitants were doomed with the curse of constant heat. Though the heat was overbearing and almost unbearable to a visitor to this scorched part of the earth, the inhabitants didn't seem to mind. To them, it had become the norm in this part of God's earth.

The evidence of an unforgiving mother nature was profound, as I inwardly wished that the confessing jihadist lived long enough to give me the scoop I was hoping for. So far the story he had given me in the way of a confession did not seem strong enough to persuade my editor to give it an airtime. Most of what he had told me was nothing new. As a reporter, you were bound to know these things, things that create sensation and make a page-turner.

I was still waiting for the page-turner in his confession when he delivered what I thought was close enough to be called a page-turner. I was absorbed in my usual reverie, when he surprised me by asking a question. "Have you ever seen or witnessed the anger of a jihadist?" He asked, with a deep thought on his face. At first I couldn't understand the question. It was after a few minutes that the reality of what he meant dawned on me.

"No, I have never experienced the anger of a jihadist," I responded. He looked at me as if he couldn't believe that I hadn't experienced the anger of a jihadist. After a while, he started to explain. "The anger of a jihadist is mayhem and death. When a jihadist is angry, death occurs," he said. I was more confused than ever as I could not figure out the path his explanation was headed. I had realized that anger and death were synonymous in Islam. The wrath of a jihadist was equals to death, meaning that death was the ultimate outcome of the wrath of a jihadist.

It follows that when a jihadist is angry he expresses his anger by killing those with opposite views and faiths. I wanted to know what causes the wraths of a jihadist and why such wraths often resulted in murder and mayhem.

"The jihadist is a Muslim who feels he has been called to be a soldier in Islam, in order to protect the core values of Islamism, as preached by Prophet Mohammad. As you know, Prophet

Mohammad was the messenger of Allah, who delivered messages directly from Allah to Muslims. The idea of jihad, as you may have already known, came from the prophet himself, who first used it to wade off, and convert or kill unbelievers who were either against Islam or did not believe in the message of Allah," he said, as he took a deep breath.

I still did not understand the path his explanation was headed. I wanted to see how I could get him to really talk about jihad as profound as I would appreciate it. It was not that I was fishing for anything sensational and bloodcurdling. I was not. But when you really think about it, everything about jihad is sensational. Jihadists arouse lurid and intense details about their activities. And I was no exception as I knew my readers or listeners would be. In journalism, you have to envision what you think will interest your listeners or readers, and then try to provide such interests. A lurid story that causes horror, revulsion or gruesomeness, is one such story. So, I probed for details, hoping that the gist would finally begin to flow from his lips.

I was aware that time was no longer on his side, that death was already at his doorstep. The realization presented an urgent desire to hurry, so as not to miss the once-in-a-lifetime golden opportunity to let the world hear his confession. It was not every day that a journalist gets to sit down with, and to hear the confession of a remorseful jihadist, if one could call his confession remorseful.

As I dwelled on his confession and jihad, I started to wonder about the influence jihad has had on Muslims across the world. Islam, as the world knows it, is the religious faith of Muslims who are faithful to Allah and Prophet Muhammad. As the sole deity, Allah is seen as the revered Supreme-Being, whose only Prophet is Muhammad.

Jihad's origin can be traced to Mecca, going back to 620 CE. Mecca was said to be the birthplace of Prophet Muhammad and the place where Muhammad was first given the revelation about the Koran. The place or site, according to legend, was in a cave, several kilometers outside of Mecca, the holist city in Islam. As the home of Kaaba or sacred house, where Muslims of all nation and creed pray, Mecca is said to be the ultimate journey, for every devout Muslim.

During prayers, Muslims must face the direction of Kaaba, called Qibla (the name of the direction faced during prayer), wherever their stations or place in the world, for such prayers to be meaningful and impactful. The significance of Kaaba is emphasized by the sacred mosque, Al-Masjid Al-Haram that was built around Kaaba.

For Muslims to be confirmed as true believers, they must perform the holy pilgrimage to Mecca, and adhere to the five pillars of Islam. The five pillars are essentially basic tenets that Muslims must abide by, in order to be true Muslims. The five pillars are considered the foundation of a true Muslim believer. Contained in the Hadith of Gabriel (which contained the reports and actions of Muhammad), the five pillars of Islam are:

1. Shahadah: that there is no other god except Allah, and Muhammad His messenger and prophet;
2. Salah: Obligatory prayers, five times a day;
3. Sawm: Maintaining a fasting period and self-control during the holy month of Ramadan;
4. Zakat: giving a portion of one's earning to the poor and needy, preferably a 2.5% portion;
5. Hajj: performing a holy pilgrimage to Mecca in one's lifetime, if able to do so.

The five pillars of Islam are sort of like the Ten Commandments in the bible, which has the same connotation or meaning as the five pillars of Islam. I rummaged through my duffel bag for a bible, and quickly read through the Ten Commandments. I flipped through the pages until I got to exodus, where I looked for the Ten Commandments. I found it on chapter 20, verse 2-17:

1. I am the Lord your God, who brought you out of the land of Egypt, out of the house of bondage. You shall have no other gods before me.
2. You shall not make for yourself a carved image, or any likeness of anything that is in heaven above, or that is in the earth beneath, or that is in the water under the earth; you shall not make for yourself a carved image, or any likeness of anything that is in heaven above, or that is in the earth beneath, or that is in the water under the earth; you shall not bow down to them nor serve them. For, I, the Lord your God, am a jealous God, visiting the iniquity of the fathers

on the children to the third and fourth generations of those who hate Me, but showing mercy to thousands, to those who love Me and keep My Commandments.

3. You shall not take the name of the Lord your God in vain, for the Lord will not hold him guiltless who takes His name in vain.

4. Remember the Sabbath day, to keep it holy. Six days you shall labor and do all your work, but the seventh day is the Sabbath of the Lord your God. In it you shall do no work: you, nor your son, nor your daughter, nor your male servant, nor your female servant, nor your cattle, nor your stranger who is within your gates. For in six days the Lord made the heavens and the earth, the sea, and all that is in them, and rested the seventh day. Therefore the Lord blessed the Sabbath day and hallowed it.

5. Honor your father and your mother, that your days may be long upon the land which the Lord your God is giving you.

6. You shall not murder.

7. You shall not commit adultery.

8. You shall not steal.

9. You shall not bear false witness against your neighbor

10. You shall not covet your neighbor's house; you shall not covet your neighbor's wife, nor his male servant, nor his female servant, nor his ox, nor his donkey, nor anything that is your neighbor's.

The jihadist was looking at me, wondering what I was doing as I compared the Ten Commandment to the five pillars of Islam. I could see a slight similarity. The jihadist looked at me, and shook his head. I could almost tell what he was going to say.

"The bible and the Koran are almost the same. You cannot compare the five pillars of Islam with the Ten Commandments. They are very different in connotation and meaning," he said, as he waited for my response. I was not a religious expert and didn't claim to be one, and because of that, I remained silent.

I didn't want to make the subject of jihad the main topic of the discussion. I was more interested in his confession than the understanding of Islam, which I knew enough to get me around. As a reporter, I knew the basics, and was not interested in going further, since it was not my religion. As I thought about it, I realized that I did not particularly pay allegiance to any deity or religion, even though I claimed to be a catholic.

I looked around me and saw that the CIA agent and the Nigerian secret service agent were no longer interested in me and the jihadist. I could be wrong to say they were not *interested*. I think the right word was *bored*. They were in the other part of the house, still investigating the kidnapping, and identifying the dead bodies. I had already taken pictures and gotten enough information on the dead and maimed in the bungalow, and I did not see any reason for me to show further interest in the aftermath of the kidnapping.

Since I met the jihadist, who had approached me, albeit in an odd way, to hear his confession, I had somehow lost interest in everything else; hoping that the confession from the jihadist would suffice to keep my readers engrossed. But as a precaution, I had taken pictures of the scenes and videoed the relevant newsworthy actions.

One thing I had learned as a journalist was to never underestimate the value of a confession or an informant. As repulsive as the jihadist was, I found his confession overwhelming and engaging, even though some of what he said was not news to me.

As I mentioned earlier, the task of a journalist goes beyond the mere act of trying to report a story. A journalist may sometimes become an investigator, or what is often called an investigative journalist, in order to make sure a story is valid or factual. Believe it or not, every journalist always tries to verify a story before rushing to beat a deadline. I also mentioned earlier that lazy journalists practice yellow journalism, especially those that are too lazy to verify a story before publication.

A good journalist must verify a story before publication or airing it. A proper investigation is needed to make sure a story has validity. Failing to do so may result in libel, if the story had no merit, or is without a just cause. If such a story exposes others to public contempt and ridicule, it can also result in a defamation of character. Oftentimes, a story can become blasphemous, treasonable and seditious.

To avoid tort, sedition, or the crime of publishing a libelous story, a journalist may become an investigative journalist.

Investigative journalism is an act of investigating hearsays for validation. Another aspect of investigative journalism is when a journalist takes it upon himself to find out about an issue that is pressing and taking a center stage. For example, if I felt a story needs further investigation, I would go after sources to reconfirm or validate the story.

Sometimes, investigative journalism can go as far as ascertaining the essence and validity of a crime or corruption in order to expose the perpetrators. If a public official awards a contract to a contractor and asks for a kickback, an investigative journalist could try to get a comment from the contractor, and those who may have witnessed the kickbacks and the discussions leading to it, to establish a prima facie evidence.

The job of an investigative journalist can be dangerous as the parties involved may want to silence the investigative journalist, if the matters being investigated implicate highly placed individuals who may not want such matters exposed. In such cases, the perpetrators will employ any means to silence the investigative journalist.

I once experienced such an issue in Nigeria when I was investigating illegal oil bunkering by some powerful businessmen and businesswomen in the country. I had unearthed evidence that politicians and some prominent businessmen and businesswomen were responsible for the hacking of oil pipelines to steal crude oil in order to refine and resell it to consumers. During the investigation of the story, I found out that there was an international conspiracy involving the exchange of arms and ammunition for illegally bunkered oil by some prominent politicians who were also exporting the oil to some unscrupulous third party countries.

My well investigated story revealed that the Nigerian oil sector was losing over $5billion in revenue to illegal oil bunkering. The same government officials who were in charge of protecting the oil from being illegally bunkered were also the ones who were privately profiting from the illegal activities.

When the story came out, several attempts were made on my life by assassins who were employed by those affected by my story, to eliminate me. When it became clear my story was putting my life in danger, I went underground and dug up some more dirt on those who tried to kill me.

And the more dirt I dug up, the more I discovered that the illegally bunkered oil that were being illegally refined and sold to consumers. The money was also being used to sponsor terrorism in Nigeria, Mali, Tunisia, Sudan and Somalia. The international ring of the crime brought me face to face with wanted criminal elements that were bent on establishing Sharia law in several parts of African countries, including Nigeria.

The perpetrators of the illegal oil bunkering, I discovered, went as far as the presidency, and those in the inner circles of the presidency. The trail went cold at the most inner circle of the presidency. Though the president himself was not implicated in the conspiracy of illegally bunkering oil for private profits and enrichment, some members of the president's inner cabinet were involved.

I also discovered that some Indian, Lebanese, Chechen and Ukrainian nationals were involved. Those who were helping to illegally refine the bunkered oil were some Chinese and Indian nationals in the country, and believe it or not, it was being done in the open, with total impunity, and under the watchful eyes of soldiers and military police that were supposedly posted in the area to prevent such acts.

The fact that local law enforcement agents and soldiers were allowing the acts was the first indication that the theft was deeper than I had first thought. Everyone, from those who had the obligation to protect the oil, to the local extractors, was in the take. And because of the deepness of the corruption and theft, I found myself constantly on the run.

Being a white man investigating a crime and conspiracy in a country of over 160 million black people can be a daunting and dangerous effort. It was more so when the people you would expect to protect the national asset were involved.

My investigation did not only reveal that Nigeria was losing over $5billion annually due to illegal oil bunkering but also that an estimated 150,000 barrels of oil were being stolen on a daily basis, through a very complicated process of tapping oil pipelines. The process, I found, involved tapping pipelines, and siphoning the oil, then pumping it to offshore barges, where it was sold to third party foreign countries or oil firms.

In some cases, as I mentioned earlier, illegal oil bunkering can also be crudely refined for local consumption, and was often sold on the roadsides by local merchants for quick profits. This particular business is very profitable because of the perennial shortages of fuel in Nigeria, even though Nigeria is one of the top oil producing countries in the world.

The fact was that Nigeria produces oil that is refined abroad and then imported back to Nigeria for consumption. Several factors are responsible for this. The first is that Nigeria's very few refineries had become too old to refine oil for local consumptions, plus the fact that lots of businessmen, businesswomen and politicians benefit tremendously from the import of oil to Nigeria. Importing oil to Nigeria has made so many Nigerians very wealthy, to where some are now the world's wealthiest.

On the issue of illegal oil bunkering and how oil was often siphoned by highly placed crooks in Nigerian society, the method even gets more complicated and daunting. To steal oil in Nigeria, the method involves installing a valve into a live, pressurized pipeline, to siphon the oil. Once the oil is tapped or siphoned, it is then loaded into waiting crafts, for transport to barges or rudimentary or makeshift refineries in the jungle, to be refined for local consumption.

Makeshift refineries are often used to refine stolen oil that is also sold to third party countries and international oil thieves. The extent of the criminality, as I mentioned earlier, goes deep, and involves oil firms, Nigerian officials, law enforcement agents and some members of the president's cabinet.

As you read this, you begin to wonder how a few local indigenous crooks could have access to such capability and financial wherewithal to carry out such a large scale operation. My investigation revealed that illegal oil bunkering was usually sponsored by some prominent businessmen and politicians, and in some cases, by unscrupulous oil companies.

Coming back to the jihadist, since there was no way to verify some of the things confessed to by the jihadist, I made a mental note to verify what was possible to verify. Confessions seldom need verification as they were generally from the horse's mouth, or directly from the sources. It did not occur to me that it was unnecessary to verify everything that was confessed to by the jihadist. For precautions, I had also recorded every word of the confession. But even with that, publishing or airing the story could still be seditious or libelous, and may result in a tort, if the facts were not authenticated.

To avoid tort or libel, an editor would sometimes edit out names of those mentioned in a story, as was the case with this story. Names of those mentioned or implicated in the confession of the jihadist were carefully edited out of the story. The essence of such editing was to leave the investigations to law enforcement agents, and to avoid the act of obstruction of an ongoing investigation.

Terrorism in Nigeria, as in the United States, is a troubling problem that continues to occupy the resources of both state and federal governments. As a journalist, my job was to rouse an issue, by stirring up an action.

Looking at the jihadist as he took a quick break while my mind did its own foraging into the past and the future, in search of moments in time when my profession had taken me into the realms of dangerous spots in the world of journalism, I suddenly became cognizant of the fact that I may have lost the confessor.

Just as I was getting worried, the jihadist stirred from his break, as if becoming conscious of my probing eyes. He smiled when he saw the anxious look on my face. My journalistic instinct told me that he may have been playing possum to get my attention. I smiled inwardly, not wanting to give him the satisfaction that he succeeded, even though it was apparent that he did succeed in getting my attention.

"Welcome back from the land of the sojourner," he said, still smiling. I could not fathom his use of the word *sojourner*, but I pretended to ignore him, while thinking of a storyline that would take him back to his confession. As I looked harder at him, it occurred to me that the jihadist was somehow recovering, or was trying to remain alive for the story. There was no doubt that his injuries were severe and that he could die any moment. But his demeanor and body language, albeit in a gurney, bespoke good health, even though I knew he was dying.

"Recently, a navy reservist walked into a navy shipyard where he worked as a navy contractor, and opened fire on several civilians and contractors working in the shipyard, killing 12 people. Would you say, in your opinion, the act was terrorism or the act of a crazed man who probably had a private grievance against his employer?" I asked, using a current act of violence to get him back into his confessional mode.

The jihadist looked at me as if saying *duh*, which almost infuriated me to a certain degree. He started without any form of preamble as he had often done. "What happened at your navy shipyard was definitely a domestic act of terrorism, caused by the insensitivity of the government to the plight of an aggrieved black disadvantaged population whose lot is still very pitiable and insignificant even though a black man is the president of the United States.

I can almost tell you that the action of the naval reservist had nothing to do with jihad of any sort. Now, he may have been a copycat of the carnage and jihad committed by the former army psychiatrist, Major Nidal Malik Hassan, who shot and killed 13 fellow soldiers in a military base, in Fort Hood, Texas, in 2009," he said, as if reading a script or a news report from memory. I waited for him to continue, as I reflected on what I knew about the story myself.

"What you have to understand is that the plight of Muslims in the hands of those who chose to persecute them, often attract sympathizers who are not necessarily Muslims. You westerners often called these types of people *copycats* but they are actually sympathizers. Timothy McVeigh, who detonated a truckload of explosives and bomb, in front of the Alfred Murrah federal building in Oklahoma City on April 19, 1995, that killed 168 people and injured over 600 people, was a domestic terrorist who had Muslim sympathies.

Recall that Timothy McVeigh's bombing of Oklahoma federal building was before the 9/11 attack. The bombing of the federal building in Oklahoma was what gave the idea to those who carried out the jihad of 9/11. The tremendous success of the Oklahoma federal building bombing was so well publicized due to the humongous number of those killed in the blast that Osama Bin Laden gave the orders that buildings with economic importance be monitored and studied to see how attacking such buildings could shake the economy of the United States.

Bin Laden's idea was to destroy the economic structure of the

United States and to reduce the country's economic importance in the world, and as a result reduce its superpower influence among nations. As far as the parochial minds of Osama Bin Laden and his lieutenants were concerned, the destruction of the economic source of the U.S. would precipitate the destruction of the country. But they were wrong as they underestimated the resiliency of Americans who would do anything to uphold the strength of the country's economy and psyche.

As far as we were concerned, and that includes Bin Laden, if a large number of casualties were recorded, it would expose the United States as a country with weak national security, where terrorists could unleash terror when and where they choose to carry out terrorism.

If you think back to the terrorist attacks on U.S. infrastructures before 9/11, you will see that al-Qaeda had experimented with small scale attacks, before embarking on the attacks of 9/11, which took several years to plan.

Remember the USS Cole bombing that occurred in the Yemeni port of Aden that killed 17 and injured 39 American sailors, in October of 2000? That attack on U.S. Navy guided missile destroyer was to test the power of the U.S. military, to see if there was a weakness in it, by the then growing al-Qaeda in the Arabian Peninsula. To a large degree, the suicide bombers succeeded in creating enough damage to impact the foundation of the U.S. stronghold. Recall that the attack on USS Cole happened five years after the Timothy McVeigh's bomb attack of the federal building in Oklahoma.

Though the U.S. government held the country of Sudan liable for the attack, it was actually the work of al-Qaeda in the Arabian Peninsula, not a poor country like Sudan that did not have the resources and sophistication of the attack on USS Cole. At the time of the attack on USS Cole, the CIA did not have enough details on al-Qaeda to go after its members, and decided on a scapegoat, which was conveniently Sudan, at the time. The freezing of Sudan's assets of $13 million was responsible in part, for the rise of Al-Shabab in Somalia and Sudan," he said, taking a break.

I could not agree on a lot of the claims he made that Sudan was chosen as a scapegoat for the attack on the USS Cole. I did not agree that blaming Sudan gave rise to the emergence of al-Shabab.

I did know that al-Shabab was already in existence when the USS Cole was attacked.

I recall writing a story on Al-Shabab and its rising influence in East Africa, soon after U.S. embassies' attacks in August of 1998. The well coordinated simultaneous attacks on U.S. embassies in Dares Salaam, Tanzania, and Nairobi, Kenya, was said to have been carried out in protest against American forces in Saudi Arabia. But the motives were far deeper than that.

In my story then, I wrote that the Egyptian Muslim Brotherhood or Egyptian Islamic Jihad, under the auspices of al-Qaeda, that first made Osama Bin Laden and Ayman al-Zawahiri, household names in the U.S., were responsible for the attack. The attacks on U.S. embassies in East Africa made Bin Laden one of the top ten most wanted fugitives in the world.

I also wrote then that the FBI had linked the attacks on U.S. embassies in East Africa to Azerbaijan because of the calls that were made by Bin Laden to his associates in Baku about the attacks. Even though Bin Laden was linked to the attacks, Fazul Abdullah Mohammed was said to have masterminded the coordinated bombings. Law enforcement agents scrambled to find the reasons for the attacks on the U.S. East African Embassies. The clandestine report that the attacks on the embassies were the direct revenge for the U.S. involvement in the extradition and torture of four members of the Egyptian Islamic Jihad, who had been arrested in Albania, months before the attack, was laughable.

I did not believe that the arrest of four suspected members of the Egyptian Islamic Jihad who were named as Ahmad Isma'il 'Uthman Salem, Ahmad Ibrahim al-Sayyida al-Naggar, Shawqi Salama Mustafa Atiya and Mohamed Hassan Tita, who were said to have participated in the assassination of Rifaat el-Mahgoub, and in the attempted attack on the Khan el-Khalili market in Cairo, in Egypt, was the motive for the East African embassies' attacks. I remember writing then that it didn't seem plausible that the accused assassins were important enough in the terrorist network to lead to the coordinated bombings of U.S. embassies in East Africa.

When my version of the reason why al-Qaeda attacked U.S. embassies in East Africa hit the airwave, several other motives began to surface. The first was that Osama bin Laden was angry with the U.S. for double crossing him in Afghanistan. The second was that Bin Laden was angry with the west for its ongoing support of Israel. The third was that Bin Laden was angry that the CIA did not pay him for his work in Afghanistan, when he worked with the U.S. against the then Soviet Union, during the cold war.

I was amused by the different versions that were presented. It was amusing because a significant part of the reason for the attacks was deliberately left out of the motives and reasons for the attack. The fact that Bin Laden saw himself as the new prophet of Islam, with the duty to spread jihad, was also deliberately ignored.

After my report hit the airwave about the activities of the al-Qaeda in the Arabian Peninsula, and the reemergence of the Muslim Brotherhood in Egypt, including the growing terrorist cells in Africa, the word AQAP began to be used ubiquitously, even in the media.

My story also exonerated Sudan as the main culprit for the attacks on U.S. embassies in East Africa. Since I specifically linked al-Qaeda to the attacks as part of the assertions being used by Bin Laden, to create awareness about his holy jihad, Sudan gradually began to be taken out of the conspiracy theory and equation.

Sudan was by no means a country devoid of terrorism or carnage. But the country's brand of terrorism was localized, and mainly a civil war type, such as is happening in Syria today, where rebels are fighting to oust Bashar al-Assad, the Syrian President. The theory that the U.S. embassies were attacked because the U.S. had hatched the plans to divide Sudan into two countries was also debunked by my story at the time.

Another absurd conspiracy theory was that the attack on the U.S. embassy in Nairobi had relevance to the Holy Kaaba in Mecca. There was also mention that the Dares Salaam attack had relevance to the Al Aqsa mosque, which is said to be the third holiest site in Islam. The al-Aqsa mosque is located in the old city of Jerusalem. The absurdity of these conspiracy theories was laughable, especially because of the huge publicity the theories received in the media.

My coverage of the attacks on U.S. embassies in East Africa was based on a six month investigation into how the plan was hatched and the parties involved in the attack. A memo that was said to have been written by Mohammed Atef in 1988, that was intercepted and seized by the FBI, which was leaked to me by a reliable source, indicated that al-Qaeda was deeply active in Afghanistan, and that Bin Laden was concerned about a possible U.S. intentions in that country; a country he had chosen as his home and stronghold. There was also a mention in the memo about an ongoing negotiation between the Taliban and a U.S. based gas pipeline consortium.

Though the memo was authored and intercepted at the time of the attack on the U.S. embassies in East Africa, there was hardly any relevance between the memo and the attacks, and I remember emphasizing this point in my media report at that time.

My coverage did however reveal the plot and the preparation that occurred months and weeks leading to the attacks. At the time, an unnamed source who had witnessed the preparations, told me, exclusively, after a couple of hundred dollar bills had exchanged hands, that he witnessed the purchase of a flat in Nairobi by one of the perpetrators for the purpose of housing the bomb paraphernalia and materials. The same source also told me that Sheikh Ahmed Salim had purchased a gold colored Toyota Dyna in Nairobi, including a 1987 Nissan refrigeration truck, for the attack. My source told me that metal bars were used to create a box on the back of the Nissan to store the bomb.

From the same anonymous source, I also gathered that in June of 1998, a house was rented in the Ilala district of Dares Salaam, a few miles from the U.S. embassy. A Suzuki Samurai was also purchased and used, to transport bomb materials in disguised food sacks from the house on llala district of Dares Salaam.

In both attacks, another terrorist, Mohammed Odeh, helped in creating massive 900kg explosive devices that were used in the attack in both Nairobi and Dares Salaam. In the Nairobi attack, 500 cylinders of TNT, with aluminum nitrate, deadly aluminum powder and detonating cords, were used to construct the devices.

The elaborate planning included constructing wooden crates where the explosives were housed. With the explosives in the bed of the truck, the terrorists ran wires from the bomb to the batteries in the cab of the truck, with a detonator switch on the dashboard, where it was accessible to the terrorist, in the driver's seat. In both the Nairobi and Dares Salaam attacks, different sizes and types of explosives were used, for impact. For the Dares Salaam explosives, TNT was fixed to oxygen tanks and gas canisters, with four bags of ammonium nitrate fertilizer and sandbags, for maximum effect of the blast.

Immediately my story hit the airwave, several media houses published the story, and soon, the explosives became very popular among terrorist wannabes in the west. There were reported cases of copycats who had tried to use similar bombs, but were immediately apprehended by law enforcement agents who had been alerted by the stores where the explosive materials had been purchased by the terrorist wannabes.

The jihadist made a startling and deliberate coughing noise to get my attention, and I immediately looked down to see him smiling. "Is it my confession that is affecting you; or something else is bothering you?" he asked, when he finally got my attention. I knew what he meant and pretended I didn't understand.

"I want to ask you about fatwa and the significance of it, in Islam," I asked him, to get him talking again. Although I had a faint idea of what fatwa symbolizes, I wanted him to explain it in his own way. With jihadists, things are usually implied differently than they seemed.

"In Islam, fatwa is a form of judgment or interpretation by an Islamic scholar, cleric, authoritative figure or an appointed person or persons. In Sunni, fatwa may not be as encompassing as other Muslim faiths such as Shiite Islam where fatwa has a different meaning. A fatwa can be a ruling or an opinion, depending on the reasons for its ruling. In Sharia Law, fatwa can be an opinion or an interpretation of how Muslims should behave and live their lives.

In some cases, a fatwa can only be binding on, and to, the followers of the cleric or mufti who issues it. If a cleric ruled that a certain offense is punishable according to Islamic law, that ruling or opinion can also apply to those who believe in the cleric or mufti. In the same token, if an imam gives a fatwa regarding an issue, only the followers of the imam may be affected by the imam's opinion or ruling," the jihadist said, leaving me as confused as when I first asked the question.

I have always had the impression that a fatwa was an order by a cleric that certain Muslims adhere to. When the Koran was set on fire by an American pastor, Terry Jones, on Saturday April 28th,

2012, a fatwa was issued that the pastor be killed for desecrating the Koran, and for burning images of Prophet Muhammad, by a few clerics in both Sunni and Shiite Muslim faiths.

My understanding was that a fatwa was only an order that applies to the followers of the jurist, cleric or mufti issuing the ruling. Several years ago, Ayatollah Khomeini, issued a fatwa that Salman Rushdie be put to death for writing a book, *Satanic Verses*, which the Ayatollah said desecrated Islam and Prophet Muhammad.

It spooked me when the jihadist spoke up as if reading my mind. "Contrary to popular beliefs, fatwa is not necessarily a death sentence. In the case of the Ayatollah versus Rushdie, the bounty placed on the writer's head can be interpreted in different ways. As I said earlier, a fatwa is a ruling or an opinion. To some people or followers of the person issuing the fatwa, it can be taken as an order.

If a cleric like the Ayatollah ruled that Rushdie be put to death for desecrating Islam, and Prophet Muhammad, then that ruling itself is a fatwa; as had been the case at the time. The interpretation of a ruling can also be termed, in Arabic, to mean a fatwa. Remember that a fatwa is a form of ruling or an opinion that applies to a certain issue that affects Islam. Depending on whose opinion you seek, a fatwa may sound like a clarion call to take up arms or simply an opinion or an interpretation," he said, sounding like a scholar himself, despite the aroma of death surrounding his persona.

I once wrote an article in a popular newspaper, *Integrated Herald*, in which I explained that different opinions existed in Islam, but that the most meaningful and widely misinterpreted form of opinion or ruling was the *fatwa*. It is noteworthy that the word fatwa connotes a profound ambiguity that different Muslims of numerous leanings interpret in their own different ways. A call by a supreme leader about an issue may be interpreted as a call to arms.

Depending on who was asking, the order given by the Ayatollah regarding the writing of *Satanic Verses* was a *fatwa* because it was a ruling that the followers or the adherents of the Ayatollah took to be a death sentence against Rushdie, which consequently drove the writer into hiding.

Another interpretation of fatwa is when a Muslim asks his imam a question for clarity regarding an issue. The opinion given by the imam regarding the question asked by the Muslim is in itself a fatwa. On the other hand, if the cleric gives a ruling to a certain breach of the Islamic faith, that ruling can also be a fatwa, because a ruling is considered a judgment.

The reason while an opinion or a ruling can be misinterpreted is because qualified opinions are often supposedly based on knowledgeable evidence, not on an uninformed opinion. Here a different type of ambiguity arises because fatwa is generally an opinion by a qualified jurist or a learned Muslim scholar, but for that opinion to be a meaningful fatwa, it must be deemed evidential. If an opinion in Islam is not backed by evidence, that fatwa becomes a ruling. Here again, another form of ambiguity exists.

I was getting confused by my own interpretation of fatwa and decided to look at the person whose understanding of the word has a deeper implication. Again, the jihadist surprised me by beating me to the punch again.

"The Islamic understanding that Muslims should pray five times a day at specific times, as contained in the five pillars of Islam, is a different type of fatwa that all Muslims must abide by. The act and understanding of praying five times a day at specific times, means that Muslims of all calling, should pray five times a day when it is time for prayer, regardless of where they may be. When it is time for a prayer, a Muslim must quickly abandon whatever he or she was doing to carry out his or her religious obligation. That obligation is in itself a fatwa that exists in the five pillars of Islam.

Just like the law of a land that is based on a written constitution, fatwa is usually based on several sources such as the Holy Koran, whose tenets are said to have been inspired by Allah as revealed to Prophet Muhammad. The other source is the Sunnah which chronicles the words and actions approved by Prophet Muhammad. The other source is often based an opinion pool or consensus knowledge of clerics, or scholars. A consensus agreement reached by Muslim scholars can be considered binding as a fatwa.

If a fatwa is not backed by evidence or a passage in the Koran, or the consensus opinion of Muslim scholars, then a stalemate called ijtihad is reached. Ijtihad means an uninformed opinion which may not qualify as a fatwa, regarding an issue. Consequently, a fatwa must be backed by the Koran or informed sources to be valid," the jihadist said, clearing his throat and burping at the same time.

His explanation of fatwa did not especially surprise me as I had already known that fatwa was some sort of a decree handed down by an Islamic leader such as a Supreme Leader, or as the jihadist said, a cleric or a jurist, or even a mufti. I did not want to pursue anymore discussion about fatwa and quickly thought of a different diversion. At this time, I knew the jihadist's confession was taking a new meaning as digressions upon digressions had mired the so-called confession.

Don't get me wrong, I had often, from time to time, steered the jihadist back to course, to make sure the confession did not become a message of some sort, being discreetly delivered via my medium. I knew how jihadists and martyrs operate. They are usually after publicity, lots of it. Anything that would generate an enormous publicity is what they seek, to promote their cause.

As the confession was taking place, several terrorist attacks were also taking place that linked al-Qaeda, al-Shabab, and Boko Haram, which almost made me to abandon the confession, to go after those breaking stories. My editor had called me to travel to Nairobi, Kenya, where gunmen suspected to be members of al-Shabab had stormed an upscale mall in Nairobi, on a day marking children's day, and killed over 100 shoppers, including children in the mall.

Reading about the story in a Nigerian daily newspaper that one of the soldiers had brought into the building, as I was taking a break from the jihadist's confession, I gathered from the paper that 20 gunmen had been identified as the culprits of the terrorist attack. The paper said over 30 hostages were held, and later rescued, by the Kenyan military.

Pictures of bullet ridden mall were shown in the paper, as I continued to read about the carnage. There were also pictures of several Kenyan soldiers who appeared battle-ready to combat the terrorists who were using the hostages as human shield. My experience with covering situations like the hostage issue, in

Nairobi, tells me that more carnage would likely occur, as the 20 gunmen did not seem to have come to make any demands. And more casualties did occur. The gunmen had seemed like the type of jihadists that would fight to death. And they did.

As I had read more about the deadly attack, it had suddenly occurred to me that the gunmen did not intend to release the hostages; that more carnage would occur. The feeling was sickening as the situation was beginning to look more like another carnage that had occurred several years ago at the U.S. embassies in Nairobi and Dares-salaam that killed 200 people.

As I read more stories about the carnage, I could see from the corner of my eyes that the jihadist was looking at me very curiously. For some weird reasons, something told me that the jihadist knew about the attack at the mall, since it was the work of an affiliated terrorist brotherhood. Recall that I mentioned earlier that al-Shabab and Boko Haram operatives and recruits had trained and fought together in Sudan and Somalia.

I picked up another Nigerian daily, and read more in-depth stories. The paper said the attack was well planned to coincide with a popular weekend meeting spot, where Kenyans and expatriates often gathered at the luxurious Westgate mall, for lattes and fun, and to shop in the over 80 stores in the mall. I also read in a renowned U.S. daily that only five gunmen were actually involved in the attack, not 20 gunmen as reported in the papers.

Something caught my attention in the paper that said Muslims were first escorted out of the mall, before the planned attack took place. As I read this, I began to wonder if there were any security personnel in the mall. Kenya was a known terrorist hotbed, and it would seemed incongruous to me that a potential target for a terrorist attack like the Westgate mall where expatriates often gather to drink lattes and shop would be left unprotected without soldiers and police.

Kenya had supported the fight against al-Shabab and had often fought its own war against the terrorist group. To expose the lives of expatriates, who were often targeted by terrorists, in a potentially terrorist dreamed place, was a failure of the local and central government.

Another Nigerian newspaper quoted a statement made by al-Shabab, which was actually called an Al-Qaeda's proxy in

Somalia, saying that "when justice is denied, it must be enforced," in its twitter account. While claiming responsibility, al-Shabab had said it was not ready to back down from the carnage until justice prevailed. Another paper quoted al-Shabab vowing not to negotiate with Kenyan authorities. It was obvious that the group was looking beyond Kenya, and were hoping for, and getting the international attention and media coverage it craved, to promote its dastardly cause and business.

A foreign newspaper quoted another twitter comment by al-Shabab, saying that "the Mujahideen are still strong inside the Westgate Mall and still holding their ground," as the gunmen held their ground and fought on. It appeared the terrorists were sending pictures and messages to their leaders about their activities and efforts.

The incident reminded me of another terrorist attack by members of Lashkar-e-Taiba, the Pakistan -based militant organization in 2008, in Mumbai, when gunmen stormed the Oberoi and other luxurious hotels, often frequented by foreigners, in coordinated attacks that resulted in the death of hundreds of people. The attackers in Mumbai were said to have received some sort of reconnaissance assistance before the attack. Like the Westgate mall attack, the gunmen had also been sending messages, and talking on the phone with their leaders who were also making demands that all Mujahideens be released.

I almost lost my cool as I looked at the smiling face of the jihadist who seemed to be enjoying the fact that another terrorist attack had taken place. I could be wrong but I could have sworn I saw a smile on the face of the jihadist. But then again it may very well have been my imagination. I didn't think a man who was seeking redemption by confession would enjoy hearing that his brethrens had killed and maimed several innocent people, including children.

It could also be that the jihadist was luring me into telling his story to the world in a form of testament, telling the world that he had succeeded in carrying out his jihadist assignment. I don't know. But the jihadist looked like a man who wanted to clean his soul and transition peacefully to the world beyond. Though unclear about the jihadist's motive, I did not feel I should be judgmental or presumptive about his objective. As I said at the beginning of the story, I am a journalist, whose primary objective was to be objective and not presumptive.

Chapter 5

A nurse was brought in to check the pulse of the jihadist, and to check his wounds. I felt he should have been taken to the hospital because of the enormity of his injuries, but that opinion had been overruled by the commander who had told me in private that it wouldn't serve any purpose to let the jihadist live. "Look at what is happening in Guatanamo Bay detention camp where those captured terrorists are being detained and released. As soon as the injured and captured terrorists are released, they become terrorists again, creating the same havoc they had been arrested for earlier," the CIA commander said, with a hint of anger in his eyes.

I understood his frustration very well. Personally, I don't think captured terrorists should be allowed to live, let alone be detained and released. If a terrorist is responsible for the death of an innocent person, that terrorist should pay with his or her life. Returning captured terrorists to their countries' governments is a bad idea. Most of those countries are reportedly in collusion with the terrorists. They believed what the terrorists believed. Having been reporting on terrorism for a long time, I had come to realize that a lot of Muslims believed they are being unjustly persecuted by the west.

I will however point out that not all Muslims are extremists or jihadists, but a good number of them nurture the tendencies to commit jihad. I have spoken with lots of Muslims who told me that they believe in jihad against unbelievers. I have also met Muslims who condemned terrorism in public and sympathized with terrorists' causes in private. Some Muslims even donate to terrorist organizations in private. There was a case of an imam I met in Jordan who would often work with the CIA and American embassy in Amman. The imam told me that he understands the reasons a Muslim would take up jihad against the west.

I was careful not to question what such reasons might be, as the imam was said to be an influential figure in Jordanian politics and in the King's palace, and of course, the American embassy. Years later, I would occasionally reflect on the words of the imam and wondered about his double standards. The imam was often on television condemning Muslim extremists, while in private condoning Muslim extremism and jihad.

I heard the imam was involved in brokering a peace agreement between Jordan and Israel once, and I had also heard rumors that the imam's eldest son was part of a jihadist movement that continues to harass and persecute non-Muslims in Jordan and across the Middle East.

After a few minutes of personal reflection, I decided to wait for the nurse to finish examining the jihadist. The CIA commander and three senior Nigerian secret service agents were fanning around the gurney the jihadist lay in, as if fearing that something was about to go wrong. I did not at first understand the reason for the sudden tight security. More armed Nigerian soldiers, fully dressed in battle-ready uniforms, complete with green military helmets arrived. Looking at the soldiers' red eyes, I could see they were ready to kill.

Something had gone wrong that I was not privy to, or was yet to be privy to, I told myself as I watched more and more soldiers arrived. It was almost ten minutes later that the CIA commander told me that the security was tighter in the bungalow because Boko Haram had twitted that it was sending a reinforcement to take its dead members who had been killed, in the bungalow.

I knew from experience that Boko Haram's so-called spokesperson often put out comments that were not even the intentions of Boko Haram. The self-appointed spokesperson would sometimes say something that would contradict the actions of Boko Haram. There was once a talk of amnesty and peace with the government, that was later debunked as untrue by captured Boko Haram members who had said the group had no intention of negotiating any peace agreement with the government. This was after the so-called spokesperson for Boko Haram had written to the media that the group was ready to negotiate with the government.

I don't even know that Boko Haram had a spokesperson or if the so-called spokesperson actually represented the group. Everything he puts out was often contradicted by the sect. Now, it maybe that there was actually a spokesperson and the group was using a distractive technique to lure the government into its traps.

When one understands that the group is striving to establish a Sharia Law in Nigeria and do away with western interests and influence, it begins to make sense that there is an ulterior motive for the misinformation that is often deliberately put out through the spokesperson. Miscommunication is a healthy technique in a war.

Whether the government wishes to acknowledge it or not, the group believes it is in a war with the government and Christians in Nigeria.

And as I mentioned earlier, there are also those northern Nigerian politicians who are known to fund and sponsor Boko Haram. My sources informed me that the government was aware of such criminal acts, and refuses to acknowledge the conspiracy for fear of stirring a full-fledged civil war, even though there was already a tactical civil war in the country.

The number of people that Boko Haram and government troops kill and maim on a daily basis was the same equivalent, if not more, that dies in Syria's ongoing civil war with rebels and al-Qaeda linked rebels. Like Syria, Nigeria is fighting several rebellious interest groups, which includes Boko Haram, Ansaru, militants in the Niger Delta, and organized kidnappers and armed robbers. Whereas Boko Haram and Ansaru, operate in the north, the militants in the Niger Delta operate in the south, while organized kidnappers and armed robbers operate in both north and south.

When the number of daily deaths caused by Boko Haram, Ansaru, militants in the Niger Delta, and organized kidnappers and armed robbers, are tallied, the same casualties and death caused by openly declared civil war is reached. In Syria, the number of deaths caused by the civil war in that country, since the war started in 2011, had reached over 100,000 deaths and counting. In Nigeria, the number of deaths acknowledged by, or known to the Nigeria government, far surpasses 100,000, within the same period.

And if truth be told, the Syrian casualties or deaths may be far less than those of Nigeria. The reason I said that is because during declared wars, the number of deaths are often deliberately inflated in order to lure in other countries for support by either parties in the civil war. This happened in the Biafran war against Nigeria, when people of eastern part of Nigeria decided to secede from Nigeria. Or better still, when greedy politicians and soldiers felt the need to secede from Nigeria in order to have access to the newly discovered oil in eastern Nigeria.

The Biafran war, can easily be tagged a war of attrition, an act used by the Ojukwu-led dissidents to weaken or attack the infrastructures and federation of Nigeria as it was known at the time, following the discovery of oil that the east did not feel was being evenly distributed since the oil was discovered in the then eastern region.

The Nigerian civil war that lasted from 1967 to 1970 was perceived as a political conflict rather than a war of attrition. The attempted secession of the southeastern provinces of Nigeria by the Ojukwu-led dissidents, who had proclaimed themselves as a separate country that they had aptly named the Republic of Biafra, in order to have, as I mentioned earlier, access to the oil in the Niger Delta, which was in the southeastern province.

Like the Syrian war, or as the war against terrorism in the current day Nigeria, as it was in the declared civil war in Nigeria between 1967 and 1970, there was a profound economic, cultural, political and religious interests involved. The Niger Deltans felt exploited by the oil companies, controlled by the Nigerian government. Though there was evidential justification for the grievances of those who lived in, and made a living from the Niger Delta's fishery, because of the havoc created by the oil companies on the land, fishery and water supply in the Niger Delta, there was no justification for the act of violence.

There is always room for a diplomatic solution if applied tactfully. A diplomatic solution is usually tenable if the interests of the aggrieved parties are genuine. In the case of the Niger Delta, though there was evidence that the livelihood and economic mainstay of those who live in the Niger Delta had been noticeably destroyed by greedy oil companies, any diplomatic solution that could have been worked out, had been deliberately derailed by those who benefit directly from the conflict and militancy, such as the politicians from the area, and of course, the militants and their leaders. The people really suffering from the total depletion of their economic mainstay and livelihood still continues to suffer, while a few unscrupulous wannabe freedom fighters have become unprecedentedly wealthy from the chaos.

The resolution of the Bakassi conflict between Nigeria and Cameroun by the United Nations is a true testament to a conflict resolution of an economic conflict, which resulted in Nigeria abiding by the resolution brokered by the United Nations to handover the land to Cameroun and to withdraw all its troops at a certain date. Though the agreement left so many Nigerians in the area disadvantaged and confused as to what country to settle in, after years of being called Nigerians, it was still an agreement that settled a protracted territorial conflict. The Green-Tree agreement stipulated that Nigeria must withdraw from the oil-rich Bakassi Peninsula by August 14, of 2008, and it was an agreement that Nigeria abided by.

Whether such an agreement could apply to the aggrieved people of Niger Delta who purport to be fighting a freedom fight is arguable. First the fighters of Niger Delta would have to be internationally recognized as freedom fighters, and then the concerns of the parties involved would have to be genuine. And on top of that, since conflicts are usually resolved between countries at the United Nations, Niger Delta would have to be a country for the international body to intervene or for the case to be heard by the International Court of Justice, in Hague. That of course will be impossible as long as the militants in the Niger Delta remain insurgents and militants.

While I had been doing my personal reflection, it suddenly dawned on me that the jihadist was no longer surrounded by soldiers. I began to wonder what had happened. I beckoned to the CIA commander and asked about the situation. "Oh, it was a propaganda rumor by Boko Haram to create a sense of reinforcement. Our sources have confirmed that Boko Haram is so broken right now, that it will take a while for them to regroup to attack again.

I doubted that, but I could see that the Nigerian soldiers were not taking any chances. There was a heavy presence of soldiers around the bungalow. I looked at the jihadist who seemed amused by it all.

"Why do you think Boko Haram would use a tactical subterfuge in a situation like this?" I asked the jihadist who appeared to be doing better than he was, before the break. His smile was more direct and less forceful. The tiny smile that often played around the corner of his mouth when something amuses him was back. I could tell that he knew what the tactical subterfuge was intended to achieve.

"A tactic like creating a ruse would be the kind of scheme that Boko Haram would use to create a pandemonium. The subterfuge had the trademark of Boko Haram, but I doubt that such a fruitless exercise would be of any interest to Boko Haram. The activity at the bungalow, and the death that occurred with our men, would only signify that Boko Haram wouldn't have the time or the inclination to carry out such a ruse," he said, talking as if he was not one of the leaders of Boko Haram.

A stranger listening to him would think he wasn't part of the group. But he was part of the group, and very proud of the fact that he had participated in the deaths of several innocent men, women and children. Like I said at the beginning of this story, the jihadist did not have the persona and demeanor of a jihadist. Appearances can be very deceptive and *there is no art to tell the mind's construction in the face,* Shakespeare once wrote in Macbeth: Act 1, scene 4. With the jihadist, it was very easy to build a trust if one was gullible enough to fall for the charade.

I have seen people like the jihadist throughout my career as a journalist. Sometimes, you would think they are your friends, but if you turn your back they will stick a knife in you. Such is the extent of human deception.

"As a jihadist, did you ever think of the ultimate sacrifice like wearing a suicide vest or belt, to please Allah with your sacrifice?" He shook his head so hard that I almost feared that he was going to hurt himself. Whatever was left of his eyeglasses almost fell off.

"To be a suicide bomber, you have to be chosen or called, like being called to serve as an imam, a pastor or a minister of a church. A person does not just become a suicide bomber as you westerners choose to call it. The act had to have the blessings of Allah or it will not be the will of Allah. Suicide is forbidden in Islam. When a Muslim brother or sister chooses to make the ultimate sacrifice, we do not call it suicide. We call it martyrdom, meaning a sacrifice on behalf of Prophet Muhammad and Allah.

If I had been chosen to serve in that capacity, I would have gladly accepted the role of a martyr," the jihadist said, wiping the sweat from his eyebrow as if the thought had made him sweat. I could almost understand why a thought like that would create cold sweats. Or maybe the jihadist was really sweating. I could not see how it was possible for him to sweat when the air condition was in full blast, African style blast.

The thought of suicide bombers made me think of a story I had written in the, Integrated Tribune, several years ago about a

Tibetan monk who had set himself on fire in Nepal, to protest Chinese rule over his country. For that story, I had traveled to the Boudhanath shrine in the northeastern edge of Katmandu, to investigate the story. The monk was severely burnt and was in a critical condition, and was taken to the Tribhuwan University hospital for treatment.

Self immolation is very common among monks and Tibetans who see personal sacrifice as not only a way to draw attention to their plights but as a statement that they would rather die than allowed themselves to be ruled by China.

Like suicide bombers, monks who use self immolation know that death will occur and still chooses to go through the process. There was a rumor that self immolation was also a calling, that a monk or a Tibetan must be called to make the ultimate sacrifice of self immolation. Though the monk involved in the self immolation survived, albeit critically burnt, most immolations often end up in deaths.

During my research for that story, I had found that thousands of Tibetan refugees who lived in Nepal, around Boudhanath, within the Buddhist monasteries, crave immolation, and fervently line up to be called to make the ultimate sacrifice. Self immolation, I found out, was a privilege for a chosen few.

In the researched story about immolation among Tibetans, I wrote that over 100 Tibetans had been involved in, or participated in self immolation, in the last three years, in their ancestral homeland in Chinese regions. Those Tibetans who had self immolated are said to have adhered to the clarion call from their spiritual leader, the Dalai Lama, to return to Tibet. The call for Tibetans to return to Tibet had often been interpreted as an incitement to chosen monks and Tibetans to participate in self immolations. Though the Dalai Lama had denied ever inciting self immolation among Tibetans and monks, it is no secret that as the spiritual leader of Tibetans, that every call from the Dalai Lama is closely listened to and interpreted as a call to action.

Muslims, suicide bombers, based on my investigations, are recruited rather than called by divinity as some clerics would want people to believe. The brainwashing technique of recruiting suicide bombers or what some Muslims would prefer to call martyrs, is making potential suicide bombers believe that they will be

inheriting paradise if they were to die on behalf of Allah and
Prophet Muhammad.

I looked at the jihadist, and noticed a changed demeanor, than
he had been for the most part, during his confession. I could see
that his demeanor had visibly changed. I wanted to call the nurse
back to see if he was alright, but the jihadist's eyes were fluttering
as if trying to tell me something. I immediately changed my mind
about the nurse, and when I looked back at the jihadist, I saw a
visible relief on his face, which tells me the nurse had something to
do with his changed demeanor.

"Okay, what's going on?" I asked the jihadist, when I was sure
no one was within earshot of the conversation. He looked around,
before answering. "I think the nurse gave me something that is
hastening my death. Since she examined me and gave me some
weird looking medication, I have noticed something totally
different inside me. It is as if I am drowning or something, into
some kind of abyss. I can't explain it, but I am sure she put
something in my medicine. You know I am a medical doctor and
can tell when something is not right, medically speaking," he said.

I couldn't argue with the man on that point. He had been
practicing medicine for a long time, and had had his own clinic
that was always packed with Muslims, in Maiduguri. At one time,
he was rumored to be the point-medical man for injured foot
soldiers of Boko Haram, al-Shabab, and al-Qaeda. I also heard
there were several occasions when an al-Qaeda fighter would be
flown from Yemen and Pakistan to Maiduguri, to be treated. There
were unconfirmed rumors of Taliban sending its wounded soldiers
to the jihadist for treatment.

There was a time I had wanted to do a story on the subject but
had to kill the story because the trail had died in Kabul,
Afghanistan. When it became known that I was investigating a
story about wounded terrorists that were being sent to Maiduguri,
the capital of Borno State, for treatment, no Muslim would talk to
me about the topic. My sources went dried and cold. There was
even a rumor, though unconfirmed, that a fatwa had been issued on
my life.

Like I explained earlier, a fatwa can be a ruling by a cleric, a
mufti or jurist. When a fatwa was said to have been issued against
me, I knew what it meant without trying to get anyone to interpret

what it meant. Contrary to what most Muslim scholars would say, an issued fatwa can be a death sentence or a ruling. If it involves an individual, it means the individual it is issued against should be put to death. That is my opinion on the subject of fatwa.

I looked at the jihadist again, still in a deep thought and asked. "Do you think she was ordered to kill you by putting something in your medicine?" He nodded in the affirmative. "The nurse may have been just doing her job, and not involved in the conspiracy to finish me off, but I can assure you that the plan was concocted and hatched by the Nigerian secret service agents who do not want me to live. I am not worried about death. As I am lying on this gurney, I know I am dying, that my last breath is within minutes or at best, days away. I am ready for the moment of truth. I have paid my dues.

My only wish now is to make sure my soul will rest in peace once my body gives up on me. The only thing that concerns me is that I have not fully finished my confession to you. My soul will not rest if I die now. My soul will be restless and be wandering around this place and my clinic, in torment. I know as a Muslim I am not supposed to think like this, but I am smart enough to know that hell will open its door quickly for me if I do not repent before my time expires here on earth.

Looking at me now, you can see that I am half dead. My vital organs are damaged. I believe it is by the special grace of Allah that I am still alive. The injuries that I sustained during the confrontation with rescuers from the CIA, M15, and Nigerian soldiers, is life-endangering. I didn't expect to live this long. I think the reason I am still alive was due to my urgent desire to finish my confession and for that I thank you, for giving me the opportunity to do so.

I know that you are supposed to confess to a priest or a clergy in your last moments, but I am not a Christian and do not believe in that. The only way my soul can repose is if my confession is made known to the world through the media," he said, as he shook his head sadly.

I was not stupid. I knew a desire to be heard when I saw one. Once a Muslim, always a Muslim. I knew what he was trying to do. He was trying to make his last mark, or a testament of some sort, if you will. The testament I am referring to in this respect concerns a method of illuminating the effectiveness of a mission that had been completed. It was common among Muslims to create a legacy of their jihad, for others to abide by, before passing on.

Though I suspected he was trying to use me to create his twisted legacy, I wasn't going to give him the opportunity to achieve his goal. I knew better than to allow him to use me to further and pass his jihad to the next generation.

I had known instances where Muslims used the media to promote their propaganda. But that was not the objective of the jihadist. His objective was more purposively sinister, even though he claimed to want to clean his soul and repent. Recalling that he had told me, minutes before, that he was a Muslim and not a Christian, and does not believe in Christianity, I knew he was not being remorseful and trying to repent. Only someone who had sinned and knew that he had sinned will want to repent.

In truth, my initial perception was that the jihadist was trying to repent and show remorse for the atrocities he had committed during his holy war as a jihadist. Though I had subconsciously questioned the honesty of the confession, I was not there to judge him. My job as a journalist was to report what I was told as accurately as I could.

As a rule, I take pride in being an honest, truthful and objective journalist, who often keeps his personal suppositions and prejudgment from his report. Though I often analyzed and edited what I am told by my sources, I always reported every news report, verbatim, so as not to misquote the source. Now, I do use paraphrases in my analysis; that was as far as I usually go.

Once again, I looked down at the jihadist, wondering how I should respond to his assumptions that the nurse who treated him was trying to kill him. I was anxious to return to the confession as much as he was. I wanted to hear more of how he practiced his jihad. I felt there was more that he hadn't told me.

I didn't want to be insensitive even though I didn't really care about his feelings. I felt it was necessary to show a little concern even if it was a pretense, so I made a face as if I was empathizing with him. "Maybe she didn't put anything in your medicine, because if she did, you would be dead by now," I said. He thought about that possibility for a few minutes and suddenly smiled as if an epiphany had suddenly given him an edge in understanding.

"I think you are probably right. If she had put something in my medicine to kill me, I would be dead by now, wouldn't I?" He asked, acting dorky, and making a face to seem as if he was actually thinking about the possibility that he could be paranoid. "It could be that whatever she put in my medicine will probably kill me gradually, until it finally kills me," he said, almost sheepishly.

I thought of what he said and instantly knew he was right. Though I was not a medical doctor, I knew there were some poisons that take its time to kill its victims. Such poisons would remain in your blood until your life was sapped and then taken. A friend once told me that they often used such a 'medication' at hospice to kill or finish off dying patients. I didn't think that any hospital would kill its patients, even if such patients were in the throes of death. And because I didn't believe the friend, I didn't pursue the story. Hospice was supposed to be a facility created to provide care and hospitable environment that meets the physical and emotional needs of the terminally ill.

Once, though, there was that doctor of death who used to assist his patients to die, or even kill them. Jacob or Jack Kevorkian was a pathologist, euthanasia activist who specialized in assisting the hopelessly sick to die in a painless way as a form of mercy killing. Aptly named Dr. Death, Kevorkian was known for championing the cause of the terminally ill patient's right to die through doctor-assisted suicide. Kevorkian confessed to assisting over 130 patients to die in a physician-assisted suicide, throughout his career as the doctor of death. He was quoted saying "dying is not a crime," when he was asked if he thought his actions were murder.

Dr. Kevorkian was arrested and tried for his role in a case of voluntary euthanasia, and was convicted of a second degree murder by a jury that did not believe his actions were mercy deaths at the behest of the terminally ill patients. Dr. Kevorkian served eight years of a 25 year prison sentence and was released on parole in 2007, with a court order that he should not participate or offer suicide advice to terminally ill patients.

Other than Dr. Death, no other known cases have been reported, other than husbands or wives assisting their terminally ill loved ones to die painlessly. Hospice on the other hand, prepares terminally ill patients for the inevitable. Several relatives of patients who had been taken to hospice had complained that their terminally ill loved ones had died faster, and too soon, soon after they were placed in the care of hospice.

I think the notion that hospice is a death support facility was succinctly made clear in their website. The Hospice Advantage, as advertised in their website, offers a safe environment for comfortable death support. Translated, it means that Hospice makes death an easy journey for the terminally ill, so that the patient doesn't have to wait until the hospice death occurs. The website also said patients "can reach out to us ahead of time." To "reach out to us ahead of time," means you can die before your appointed time with death, through hospice.

When one reads the advertisement or contents on the hospice website, it wouldn't be difficult to reach the assumption that hospice is a facility that often helps terminally ill patients to die quicker. If a patient is medically considered to be beyond the help of doctors, and taken to hospice for final preparation for appointment with death, that *preparation* could mean anything. In a nutshell, hospice is a facility that offers death support. Death support is an ambiguous phrase that denotes a lot of subtleties. Hospice offers *resources available* to families of loved ones in terms of death support. The question remains what those *resources* are.

Thinking about all these possibilities, it occurred to me that the doctor-jihadist may not be totally wrong. The jihadist knew about the possibility of death support, since he was in the throes of death. Though the jihadist was not fussy about being gradually killed with medication, he felt he might not be able to complete his confession before dying.

I did not agree with him that he was being gradually killed with medication. Or it could be I refused to agree with him out of repulsion. Either way, I was not prepared to go along with him. My mind was more on how to get as much confession from him as possible. As a journalist, getting the story was my primary objective. Empathy and shared-sympathy were not part of the equation.

"I am aware that most terrorist networks are intertwined in some way or another, but is Boko Haram associated with the

Islamic jihadists in the Philippines?" I asked, trying to lure him into confirming something that had been tugging me at the back of my mind. He gave me that hideous look that had become a part of his demeanor, before answering.

"Don't confuse Bangsamoro Islamic Freedom Fighters (BIFF) with Boko Haram, Al-Shabab, Al-Qaeda, Ansaru. Bangsamoro is fighting for political gains, not for Allah or Prophet Muhammad. Though he often claimed to be associated with al-Qaeda, he does not share the same beliefs, and ideologies as al-Qaeda or Boko Haram."

I wanted to press him for clarification but instead reflected on what I had read in a British newspaper about the attacks, and guerilla tactics used by BIFF. Not too long ago I had read that BIFF, armed with chainsaws and guns, had launched coordinated attacks across 11 towns in southern Philippines, leading to clashes with government troops. In what the paper had called an attack by Muslim rebels, an army detachment was attacked by rebels, with the Muslim rebels touching off gunships, and military infrastructure, in the southern province of Maguindanao.

During the mayhem, the Muslim rebels vandalized and cut down electrical poles, cutting off power supply to several towns, before attacking the towns. I also remember reading in the said paper that there was a strong al-Qaeda affiliation with the jihadists in the Philippines. For a starter, the head of BIFF was Ameril Umbrakato, who was influenced by his education in Saudi Arabia. The British newspaper had traced the background of Ameril Umbrakato to his days in the 12,000 strong Moro Islamic Liberation Front (MILF), to the time he had splintered from MILF to form his own terrorist cell.

The major contention Umbrakato had for splinting from MILF, according to the paper, was because MILF chose to reach a peace agreement with the government, which the rebel leader did not agree with. Later on, the splintered group led by Umbrakato became a sworn enemy of MILF when the latter had agreed to help the government stop or derail Umbrakato, which itself resulted in more clashes and deaths of innocent civilians. The choice of weapon often used by terrorists loyal to Umbrakato was chainsaws and machetes.

A famous British newspaper had also mentioned that the

government of Philippines had somewhat agreed to share territories with the jihadi rebels, in order to allow peace to rein. Though the government had denied having a secret agreement with the rebels, with the enticement of shared wealth, the immunity that the rebels enjoyed in the areas they control, gave credence to the rumor that the government had a secret agreement with the rebels.

Unlike most countries where Muslims were in the majority, like Nigeria, Yemen, Saudi Arabia, Somalia, Senegal, Algeria, Mali, Pakistan and Afghanistan, the Philippines was 95% Christians or catholic. The former American protectorate, according to the paper's opinion should not have any problem quashing the Muslim insurgents, especially due to the small numbers of Muslims in the country.

The paper had also traced the history of insurgency to the 1970s, in Philippines, which had killed over 165,000 Filipinos since its inception. Quoting the Mindanao Examiner, the British newspaper reported that rebels had occupied several towns in the southern region of Mindanao.

Despite the peace agreement reached with the government, rebels still continued to fight amongst themselves, and government troops, which had led to insecurity in several small towns like Shariff Aguak, Datu Saudi Ampatuan, Talayan and Datu Unsay, and in Midsayap, in North Cotabato province, according to the British paper.

With the rebels controlling towns and highways in several towns, in rural Philippines, it was easy to compare their tactics to that of Boko Haram and the Taliban in Pakistan and Afghanistan. The problem with the insurgency in the Philippines was that the Muslim rebels in that country, as in Nigeria and Yemen, were not as organized as their counterparts in countries where Muslim extremism was rampant. The Muslim rebels existed in splinter groups and dissents in Nigeria and Yemen.

Like Boko Haram whose main goal was to topple the Nigerian government and establish Sharia law, the Muslim rebels in the Philippines want an unstated and undefined freedom from the central government. A statement made by Abu Misry, a rebel spokesman for one of the splinter groups, accused the government of attacking them and igniting the conflict, which had led to their rampage in retaliation to government attacks in the Basilan province. But that was just one of the many instances where government and Muslim rebels had accused each other of inciting violence and revenge.

With al-Shabab, al-Qaeda, Boko Haram and Ansaru, their methods and agendas were different and more defined. With al-Shabab, the goal was to establish Sharia law in Somalia, and if possible, in neighboring countries of Sudan, Kenya, etcetera. With al-Qaeda, the goal was to spread holy jihad in every corner of the world. With Boko Haram and Ansaru, the goal was to eradicate western influence in Nigeria, and to establish Sharia Law, which already existed in some parts of northern Nigeria, where citizens are often forced to abide by the age-old primitive Sharia law of keeping women as slaves to the whims and caprices of their male partners, who were free to marry as many women as possible.

Sharia Law, in Islam, allows men to marry as many women as they can afford. Polygamy is one of the perks that Muslim men enjoy in exchange for giving up alcohol of any kind, even though lots of Muslims are known to be drunks. Another hypocritical part of Sharia Law was that women were regarded as sacred beings whose bodies should not be exposed to the lustful stares of other men. Adherence to the archaic policy of stoning women who fornicate to death is very common in lots of Muslim countries. In Saudi Arabia for instance, women are not allowed to drive, participate in sports, and in government. Though few changes are being made in the Saudi kingdom, women are still seen as second class citizens, while at the same time holding them in high esteem. A great deal of inconsistencies in policies regarding women, one would say.

I looked down again to see how the jihadist was faring since my mental sojourn, only to see him looking at me meaningfully. Another thing that I didn't like about the jihadist was my inability to read his stoic expression. He had a way of presenting an inscrutable face that made it hard for a person to read into the ambiguities presented by his facial expressions.

He spoke up as if he had been waiting for me to give him an attention. "Were you satisfied with my answer to your question about the Muslim rebels in the Philippines?" He asked, with a small wry smile playing at the corner of his mouth. For the umpteenth time, I had the feeling that the jihadist was playing me, or using me for a task I could hardly decipher. The only thing I knew was that he was using me to clear his conscience by way of confession. But something else also bothered me, that he had some kind of sinister motive behind his confession.

The feeling that the jihadist had a sinister motive started to grow as I gave myself room to think about jihad and the methodology of jihadists. As the jihadist talks and reacts to my sundry questions, my journalistic instinct began to suspect that there was a different motive to the confession.

First, the jihadist had been on a mission, which was the unsuccessful kidnapping of foreigners who had been unsuccessfully rescued by the combined team of the CIA, M15, and the Nigerian secret service, and had been severely injured in the process. Though the kidnapping had been somewhat successful and unsuccessful, judging by the casualties that resulted from the rescue effort, it would seem that Boko Haram had achieved its objective of getting both local and international media to cover its nefarious activities, to promote its jihad.

What bothered me was how the jihadist had suddenly reached a state of epiphany that he wanted to confess to his sins in order to have an easy transition to the world beyond. It didn't make sense as I had never heard of a jihadist wanting to show remorse through confession at the twilight of his life, when he was in the throes of death. Again, as a journalist, it was my job to reserve my prejudice and judgment in order to present a fair and balanced report to the public. But I couldn't help thinking I was being played.

Chapter 6

In Baghdad, Iraq, a teenager quietly walked into a meat market, passing a police officer who was stationed at the market, and approached the busiest part of the market, and detonated the bomb strapped to his vest, killing thirty bystanders, in a suicide attack. In another busy part of Baghdad, a day after the Ramadan, a beautiful young girl in her early 20s, walked into a mosque where several Muslims were praying on a busy Friday prayer session, and detonated the bomb planted in her body, killing more than 60 worshippers, in another suicide attack.

In Sanaa, Yemen, a Saudi born suicide bomber dressed in a Yemeni army uniform with a captain stripes, walked into a sporting event, passing several soldiers who were stationed at the stadium to prevent violence, and to protect the fans watching a soccer game on a Friday afternoon, a day after the Ramadan, and detonated the bomb laden vest he was wearing, killing himself and 100 other spectators at the game.

On the same day and on the same hour, another coordinated attack was taking place somewhere in Sanaa, as a Saudi born suicide bomber detonated a bomb in his vest, killing 200 bystanders. In another venue, a group of al-Qaida militants, numbering six, also disguised in Yemeni army uniforms, detonated multiple car bombs in a military posts, in southern Yemeni province, killing 50 soldiers and wounding several others, during a heavy fog.

Yemen, considered the poorest among other wealthy Arab neighbors, continues to unsuccessfully fight its own endless war with al-Qaeda in the Arabian Peninsula. For years now, Yemen has become the hotbed of al-Qaeda operatives. AQAP continues to wage its own holy jihad against the Yemeni military, which has resulted in several assassinations of top military officers, and top government officials in suicide attacks and motorcycle shootings.

Since 2001, the al-Qaeda in the Arabian Peninsula has become stronger as the al-Qaeda operatives in Pakistan and Afghanistan became weaker. As the al-Qaeda in Yemen renewed its jihad with vigor, the branch became known as the most dangerous al-Qaeda cell in the world. The success of the AQAP has been evident in its effectiveness in recruiting young Americans and Europeans to commit suicide attacks in the west. The success of AQAP has also been evident in the attempted attacks on British and U.S. soils.

With the daily attacks on both Yemeni government infrastructures and western interests, it became necessary for the west to mount its own campaign of terror against AQAP. The U.S. established an enduring drone attacks, targeting AQAP leaders. Considered the most successful campaign against al-Qaeda in the 21st century, the drones have killed several visible leaders of AQAP, destabilizing the group, which still remains strong in Yemen.

In Maiduguri, Borno State, Nigeria, three Boko Haram operatives, wearing suicide vests, entered a packed Catholic Church on a Sunday mass, detonated the suicide vests they were wearing, killing more than 500 worshippers, while injuring several others. The attack was considered the most vicious in the history of the terror group's activities.

In Abuja, the capital of Nigeria, two nicely dressed young female members of Boko Haram, adorned with hidden suicide vests, entered a popular Baptist church, close to Aso Rock, the seat of the legislative body of the Nigerian government, where known top politicians often worship with their families, and detonated the bombs strapped to the vests they were wearing, killing over 200 worshippers who were praying and dancing to the music provided by the choir.

The coordinated attacks in Nigeria, and Yemen, attested to the already known fact about the affiliation that exists between al-Qaeda and Boko Haram. The arrest of a Nigerian citizen, said to be a member of AQAP, charged with aiding and abetting a foreign terrorist organization, was also another proof of the link between Boko Haram and al-Qaeda.

Lawal Olaniyi Babafemi, was arraigned in a federal court in New York City, after being extradited from Nigeria, for terrorist activities, and for aiding and abetting AQAP. Though charged with supplying guns and ammunitions to the terrorist group, his main crime was in helping to promote terrorist attacks against the U.S. and its allies. Babafemi was said to have received over $10,000 in cash from AQAP, to recruit young Nigerians to join the group, and for the supply of weapons. The Nigerian was also said to have met and trained with leaders of AQAP.

Babafemi was also known to be an AQAP propagandist who

had helped in promoting the terrorist group's agenda in Nigeria through a jihadist magazine called, *Inspire*. The Nigerian was said to have been recruited and personally trained by Anwar al-Awlaki, the American born jihadist who was killed in a CIA-operated drone attack, in 2011.

Chapter 7

It was approaching sunset, and I could tell that the local law enforcement agents and their British and U.S. counterparts were willing and ready to close the case and move on, to another case. With forensic evidence collected, and all necessary precautions taken, it seems to me that everyone was ready to close shop, except of course me. I knew instinctively that if I were to let the law enforcement agents have their way that I would never be able to get the confession out of the jihadist.

I was told that the jihadist would be taken to a military hospital and from there to a military detention camp, where he would continue to receive treatment for his wounds. I knew the CIA would like to get hold of him to get as much information as possible out of him. Though they liked the confession that the jihadist was willingly giving, they did not believe the jihadist was revealing everything he knew. In their textbook minds, they thought the jihadist was using me to promote his jihad, and to leave a legacy.

None of those reasons or motives appealed to me or agreed with my sense of obligation as a journalist. I was not interested in reasons or motives. I had one interest in mind, and that was to get the gist of the confession on paper. From the way things had been going, it seemed as if I might get my wish, with the story.

Reading my mind again, or appearing to do so, the jihadist crackled to life, making those small repeated noises that I had come to recognized as a way of requesting my attention. "There is something that I should tell you that I have never told anyone, living or dead," he said. I wondered about the *living or dead* inference, but I didn't say anything.

"Earlier, I told you about the blood swapping oath taking, right? And I also told you that to be considered a member of Boko Haram that a new recruit had to kill an unbeliever, and that the new recruit must sleep with a virgin, as a way of being reborn. What I did not tell you was that, once a recruit had performed all the rites of initiation, a select number of those new recruits would be castrated to make sure there was no room for any form of temptation. The belief was that once a selected new recruit was rendered impotent, he would be deprived of any vitality that would cause him to fornicate," the jihadist said, stroking his moustache.

I have heard stories about religious entities castrating their inner circle adherents to make sure they remained loyal to the Order. The chosen ones who were often castrated were often required to take solemn vows to ensure they did not stray from their calling.

Castration in the Catholic Church dates back to the 16th century when male children were chosen to be castrated before they reached puberty. The rationale behind the castration was to prevent the vocal cords of the chosen, from lengthening, and the voice, from deepening.

Earlier version of the reason for castration of male children was that some male children were born with defects like the medical condition called endoctrinological that prevents such male children from sexual maturity. Once castrated, the castratos were able to preserve the soprano or contralto range of their voices.

Once chosen, the candidates for castration were often sedated with opium before the operation. The operation often included being soaked in hot water, while sedated with opium, until the chosen candidates become unconscious, for the operation. Though not all the castratos became professional soprano singers because of insufficiency in the quality of the voice, those that did not, were said to have died prematurely. For a boy to be chosen for castration, he had to be between the ages of 7 and 9, and after castration, must undergo a voice training procedure. Though lots of the castratos became big-time international opera singers, such as Farinelli, with three octaves, castration would gradually become unpopular toward the end of the 18th century.

In the Vatican, the seat of the Catholic Church, the castrati continued to perform in the Sistine Chapel as recently as the beginning of the 20th century. The last known castrati was said to be Alessandro Moreschi, who passed on in 1922. Moreschi was said to be the only castrato who actually made sound recordings.

The early life of Moreschi attests to the fallacies that some churches, especially the Catholic Church, used to encourage the castration of children under the age of 10 years. For Moreschi, he was born into a Roman Catholic family in the Italian town of Monte Compatri, near Frascati. Legend had it that he was born with a defect called inguinal hernia, in the region of his groin, and in the lowest lateral region of his abdomen. At that time, it was thought that castration was the only cure for such a defect.

Another legend was that Moreschi was castrated before he reached puberty around 1865, because he was vocally talented. Moreschi's talent was said to have been noticed by a member of the Sistine Chapel choir, who was scouting for new talents at the time. The scout, Nazareno Rosati, took Moreschi to Rome around 1870, where he became a pupil and was taught by Gaetano Capocci, a maestro di cappella of the Papal basilica of St. John Lateran, around 1873.

As I reflected on my knowledge of the castration in the Vatican and Italy, between the 16th and late 18th century, it began to make sense to me why jihadists would want to castrate those they admitted into their inner circles. With jihadists, trust and loyalty were big stuff. With the leaders of Boko Haram, al-Qaeda, al-Shabab, Ansaru, and other terrorist organizations, trust was an integral part of membership. I had heard that those who were found to be untrustworthy were sometimes beheaded and their families wiped out, to serve as a lesson to those who may nurture the intention to betray the group.

The issue of castration as a way of preventing temptation among those chosen to be castrated was mostly confined to soprano and opera singers until after the ritual became very unpopular towards the end of the 18th century. Secret societies and religious extremists adopted the procedure to create loyalty and also to prevent temptation. The temptation in this respect pertains to worldly temptations and the lusts associated with the opposite sex. With impotency used as a method of creating loyalty, it soon became a pattern amongst sects that the way to gain and create loyalty was through the castration of the chosen.

The castrated inner circle members of the Muslim sects were also the ones chosen for dangerous missions like suicide bombings, assassinations, and daredevil tasks. Since the castrated members were considered elite members of the inner circle, they were also called the chosen ones by Allah. For a while it was considered a privilege to be castrated and chosen as a member of the inner circle, amongst extremists.

Having reflected on the little I could recall about what I knew of castration among Muslim inner circle jihadists, I started to wonder if the confessing jihadist was also castrated. I had to ask the question because I couldn't resist the urge. So I asked. "Were you also one of those chosen or privileged to be castrated?" I asked, knowing it was an absurd question since he was once married with children.

"No. To be chosen for castration means to be chosen for the tasks of martyrdom. With divine help from Allah, those entrusted with the tasks of picking the inner circle members were often assisted by Allah with divine guidance. Purity was one of the most essential keywords in the divine selection process. In times past, only male virgins were selected to be members of the inner circles. But as those types of male virgins became scarce and hard to find, Allah gave a new divine guidance for picking those who may have eaten the forbidden fruit and exposed to the knowledge of sins and life.

Even amongst those who had eaten the forbidden fruits of sins and knowledge, only males were at first considered bold enough for the sacrifice of martyrdom. Later on, clerics and imams blessed with visions to see purity among those made impure by the forbidden fruits of sins and knowledge, began to recruit females for the inner circle. The females were at first considered easy prey for the infidels in the west who may use the females to infiltrate the inner circle. After repeated tests, and deliberately created mousetraps, it became clear that the females were as determined and impenetrable as their male counterparts.

Another reason that led to the recruitment of females for the inner circle tasks was that females were, for a while, less suspicious than males. Soon, female members of the inner circle were given more tasks than the male members, until security agents in the west and in Israel began to screen suspected Muslim women. Women had become very successful as martyrs before it dawned on security agents in the west that some female Muslims were now involved in martyrdom.

The clerics and imams had to seek divine guidance for help in finding new recruits when the male inner members increasingly became objects of profiling before their missions could be accomplished. It was not long after, that another cleric had a vision that children could also be chosen to be members of the inner circle. With children ranging between five and ten being recruited, success came again as children were known to be less objects of suspicion than adults.

The success of children as martyrs led to a new recruitment drive for young adults who still possessed innocence for the service of Allah. Those targeted were first orphans and children who had lost their parents in wars with the infidels in the west. Those children were easily recruited because of their bitterness toward those they accused of murdering their parents and siblings.

The idea of recruiting children for suicide attacks, as the west liked to call it, first started in Afghanistan, where Taliban were using teenagers and children to wage suicide attacks against Soviet forces, and later on, U.S. forces. I was one of those privileged to go on a recruitment mission to find children who had been orphaned by wars. I would visit orphanages, and shelters, with gifts, money and toys, praying for those children while also recruiting them.

As a cleric, those children would lean on my every word, believing that I was there to help them, which in a sense, I was. I would advise them that the best way to fight back against those who had murdered their parents was to work for Allah. Majority of them were always very eager and happy to be called to work for Allah. A few though, would ask deep and troubling questions, regarding the nature of work that was required. With those, trickery was often used to get them to go on missions. But generally, bitterness and revenge were always the best ingredients of recruitment," the jihadist said, as I nodded my head.

The mention of the Taliban, by the jihadist, triggered my memory of a story I had covered in Kabul and Kandahar, years ago. My editor had sent me to Afghanistan to investigate the surge in the recruitment of minor children by the Taliban for suicide bombings against foreign troops and government forces in that country.

I had interviewed several children who had been intercepted by security forces before they could carry out their suicide bombing missions. A ten year old girl who had been rescued told me, after I had persuaded her parents to let me talk to her, that she had been approached by an imam, a cleric, who had told her to do him a favor, for money. She said she had been scared when the man had approached her, but because the man was an imam, she wasn't worried, because she knew that imams were religious clerics.

She said the imam gave her a heavy duffel bag tied with wires connected to a small cellular phone that had a big red button in the middle. The imam had tricked her that she was doing something very important for Allah and Prophet Muhammad. She was told by the imam that she should press the red button on the cellular phone when she gets to a police station where several Afghan police officers were gathered, for an early morning instructions.

When the little girl had reached the police station, she had forgotten the instructions and had asked a U.S. soldier loading military equipment in an army jeep to assist her. The soldier had quickly noticed the different wires and had realized that the duffel bag contained bombs. He had quickly called for a backup, while immediately taking the duffel bag from the little girl. It was not long after, that U.S. bomb experts had arrived and tested the items in the duffel bag, that it was later confirmed to be bomb.

The little girl had been rescued and handed over to her parents. There was also the case of a12 years old boy who was given a backpack loaded with bomb strewn with wires, connected to a remote control; and was told by a man who gave him a handful of Afghani to go near security forces and press the button on the remote control, in Kandahar. The boy had been arrested before he could press the button on the remote control. The boy later confessed to having been misled by the Taliban, saying he did not know the backpack was loaded with bomb.

When told about the bomb in the backpack and how he could have blown himself and others to pieces, the boy was shocked and said he did not know that the backpack contained a bomb, saying he was not trying to kill himself and others. Another case that I investigated was that of a14 years old boy whose father had sent to a religious school in the Helmand province to learn about Islam. Rather than teach the boy what he had come to school to learn, the teachers had sent him to Pakistan for further studies. While supposedly going for further studies in a seminary, in the Quetta city of Pakistan, the mullahs started to brainwash him with lies that Afghanistan was being forcibly occupied by U.S. forces in other to turn Afghans into slaves.

Convinced he was fighting a holy war to free his country from invading U.S. forces, the boy was brainwashed that he could help free his country if he played his part. He was also told by the

Taliban that his holy war was approved by Allah, that in a vision received at night by a Taliban, he was instructed to carry out the mission. Given a suicide jacket to go back to Kandahar, with the instructions on how to carry out a suicide attack, the suicide bomber had left Pakistan and arrived in Kandahar for his deadly mission.

Before he could carry out the suicide attack, the boy was captured by security forces who had immediately noticed that the boy was acting suspiciously. The boy was arrested and the suicide jacket tested for explosives. The boy was asked how he came about the suicide jacket. He confessed to being a student who had been sent on a mission to free his country by the mullahs in his school.

Since the U.S. led invasion of Afghanistan in 2001, hundreds of innocent children and women have been killed in suicide attacks and missions, by Taliban forces. Children and women continue to be used for suicide attacks in Kabul and Kandahar for suicide missions against Afghan and NATO forces.

My mind came back to the present, as I continued to watch and observe the jihadist, who by now, appears to be sleeping. He opened his eyes slightly, and saw my renewed interest in him, and suddenly opened his eyes fully and smiled. "Welcome back, my good sojourner. How was your mind-travel?" he asked, obviously mocking me for having a momentary retrospective recall. Rather than ignored him as I had done before, I smiled back, without saying anything.

"As a master strategist for Boko Haram, did you ever work with al-Qaeda in the Maghreb and in Iraq?" I asked, as he looked at me with that stern look that seemed half gloomy and half austere. "First let me explain that the word *Maghreb* commands a far deeper meaning than non-Muslims understand it to be. Maghreb is a word often used to describe Muslims who fight for Allah or struggle in the path of Allah in Africa. In a nutshell, Maghreb means people involved in a jihad or fighting the holy war in the northwest of Africa, west of Egypt, as outlined by the holy prophet Muhammad. In a sense, Maghreb is in a way synonymous with Mujahideen.

In Arabic, Mujahideen also means jihad and a struggle. After 9/11, Mujahideen became associated with radicalism and extremism in Islam, which in a sense is not so far from the meaning of the traditional definition of Maghreb in the region including the Atlas Mountains, and the coasts of Morocco, Algeria, Tunisia and Libya, at the outset of the formation of the Arab Maghreb Union in 1989. So when you say al-Qaeda in the Maghreb, what you are essentially saying is al-Qaeda that is involved in holy jihad or struggle in the path of Allah, in the northwest of Africa

Every Islamic militant in Africa, Asia, Middle East, and everywhere, is involved in the struggle to free Muslims from persecution and injustice of the west. I guess you could call that al-Qaeda in the Maghreb. But there is hardly any al-Qaeda operative who is not involved in Mujahideen, and who is not in the Maghreb," he said as his eyes focused on something in a distance.

I turned to look at what he was looking at and did not see anything in particular. He smiled without turning, obviously enjoying the curiosity of my eyes' odyssey. Reading my mind again or attempting to do so, he said, "I am wondering about hereafter, my friend, how it is going to be like. I sometimes ask myself if the good book actually meant well, when it stated that paradise awaits men like me, who had fought the good fight for Allah," he said, this time totally ignoring me and staring back into space.

I was confused. I recall the jihadist telling me earlier that he did not believe that he will go to paradise, that he had been misled by the preaching of paradise for jihadists. Saying now that he wondered if he would go to paradise seemed like a double standard or something of that nature, to me. Since it was somewhat difficult for me to really understand what he meant or inferred in his confessions, because of his double talk, I chose not to confront him about the inconsistencies in his confession.

After a few minutes, the confusion must have still been evident in my eyes because of what he said immediately afterward. "You are probably thinking about what I said earlier about paradise. Yes, I have changed from my earlier position about paradise, if it truly exists. I was raised, and nurtured with the belief and understanding that paradise awaits the soldiers of Allah, meaning men who fought the holy war, on behalf of prophet Muhammad and Allah," he said, this time with his eyes downcast and dejected.

"Are you saying you backslid in your belief in Islam or in the promise of a paradise in the hereafter?" I asked him, trying to get a clarification. "What I am saying is that I have often been confused by shaken belief in paradise and hereafter. My actions as I understand them are in line with the dictates of Prophet Muhammad about fighting the holy war. I have often wondered if killing innocent people or anyone at that is actually something that Allah would approve of. We were told by our clerics and imams that waging a war against those who are against Muslims and Islam is fighting the good fight," he said, still leaving me in confusion.

"An imam is a Muslim leader who is divinely appointed and a sinless, infallible successor of Prophet Muhammad. As a religious leader who exercises spiritual and temporal leadership in his religious belief, why would your belief in his instructions be shaken?" I asked.

"My belief in the instructions of the imam as a spiritual leader, or in Allah, has never been shaken by any distraction whatsoever. What had bothered me, and in a sense, continues to bother me is whether the killing of innocent people who did not offend me, in anyway whatsoever, is right and justified. I have struggled with this in my conscience for years, and as I neared my end, that struggle has become stronger and overwhelming, hence the need to confess my sins in order for me to set my soul free," he said, with a shaky voice that almost invoked my sympathy for him.

But there was nothing to feel sorry about for a man who had lived his life killing innocent people. It would be a travesty of justice for those who had been unjustly murdered to spare any kind of sympathy for a sworn enemy of humanity. I knew I was not judging the jihadist by having these feelings as my feelings remained neutral in the process. I said earlier that my profession as a journalist forbids me from exercising any presuppositions or prejudgment about anyone or sources, during the process of gathering reports or investigation.

I never wavered or attempted to play double standard in my beliefs. That has never been part of my belief or what I believe in. I am a patriot of the word, and will always remain dedicated to the calling that I have sacrificed my young adult life to fulfill. It did not bother me, feelings-wise, that I was helping a jihadist to promote his jihad, or establishing his legacy as an accomplished jihadist, because I knew in my heart of hearts, that this was a confession, nothing more or less.

If his motive was to use me to send a message to his fellow jihadists or to publish his jihad as part of the process of fulfilling his paradise-lost or paradise-won intentions, then that understanding was not part of the reason I chose to listen to, and write the story about his jihad. For me, writing about the atrocities the jihadist had committed is part of fulfilling my professional calling as a journalist.

I am saying this as a form of justification for choosing to write this story, which I believe is about crimes against humanity, even though he said his actions were dictated by the instructions of his spiritual leader. I am not a Muslim or believer in Islam. Like I said earlier, I am a Christian of the catholic faith, even though I do not attend church on a regular basis. I do not even claim to be a devout Christian. Saying I am a Christian may be stretching it. It will be probably right to say I believe in God, which I do, with all my heart. If believing in God makes me a Christian, then you could say I am a Christian.

The jihadist must have been feeling guilty or pretending to feel guilty about his actions or motives, if my reading of his facial expression is anything to go by. In the few hours I had known the jihadist, I had somewhat come to see him as an actor of some sort, with regards to his facial expressions or body language, even if his words had not been leaning towards that indication. Having said that, I am not saying the jihadist portrayed the hypocrisy or actions of an actor. Actors are not hypocrites, but by their actions, in acting, they may portray themselves to be someone they are not, but that is purely the calling of their profession. Concerning the jihadist, one could easily read his facial expressions as acting or humorous.

A dying man with a humor, I am sure, is something that you are not buying. I am not buying it either. If his facial expression is not humorous, then it is acting, or an act to give me a false impression about him, even though I already knew all I needed to know about him. Again, this is not a prejudgment. I was going by what he had done as a jihadist. He had confessed to killing and maiming innocent people, which made him a monster of some sort, even though he claimed to be fighting to free his brethrens from persecution.

Chapter 8

Terrorism has always been part of modern civilization from time immemorial. Before the emergence of al-Qaeda, the Irish Republican Army (IRA), a few lesser known jihadists were the only known terrorists that the world worried about. Of course there were terrorisms that were sponsored by rogue regimes like Libya's former dictator, Muammar Gaddafi, which resulted in several innocent deaths. One of such terrorism was the Gaddafi-sponsored bombing of Pan Am Flight 103 transatlantic flight from London Heathrow to J.F. Kennedy Airport, in Queens, New York, which crashed the plane in Lockerbie, Scotland, that resulted in the deaths of 243 passengers and 16 crew members in December of 1988.

The Lockerbie bombing was the first known Gaddafi-sponsored terrorism. Other known terrorism sponsored by Gaddafi includes sending hit men to the United Kingdom to assassinate Libyan dissidents living in Britain. According to British secret service (M15), in the 1980s, Gaddafi used a squad of hit men to kill his opponents abroad in order to dissuade others from becoming dissidents. It was a fear tactics that worked for several years, as Libyans were scared to go against the dictator, fearing that, like the mafia, Gaddafi was capable of getting them anywhere, anytime, in the world.

Gaddafi was also known to frequently use his embassies, which he renamed the Libyan People's Bureau, to gather information about Libyan dissidents living abroad, for Libyan assassins. Libyans living abroad were often careful not to criticize the dictator or openly go against the regime.

Reported cases of Libyan dissidents who were assassinated by the dictator's assassins included the killing of Muhammad Ramadan who was assassinated outside the Regent's Park mosque in 1980. Another known assassination sponsored by Gaddafi included the murder of a Libyan-born lawyer, Mahmoud Abbu Nafa, in his Kensington office, in Britain.

In Africa, Gaddafi's actions made Idi Amin, the third president of Uganda, looked like a novice in the world of terrorism and butchery. On his part, Amin Dada, was known to have sponsored terrorism during his regime, from 1971 to 1979, killing thousands of innocent Ugandans at home and abroad. Though infamously known for his human rights abuse, political repression, ethnic persecution and cleansing, extrajudicial killings, terrorism, and sponsorship of terrorism abroad, his style of terrorism was not as widespread as that of Gaddafi. Amin was said to have killed over 500,000 in both Africa and abroad, mostly Ugandans.

Gaddafi did not only sponsor terrorism in the west, but also in Africa, where he attempted to create a United States of Africa, and become its president for life. To achieve his objective, the former dictator embarked upon sponsoring religious uprisings in countries like Nigeria, Mali, Algeria, Niger, Chad, and Togo.

Secret Agents in Nigeria, United Kingdom, and the United States, were aware that Gaddafi was supplying arms to insurgents, and creating terrorist cells in Africa. It was said that Boko Haram was first indirectly sponsored and bankrolled by Gaddafi with the aim and ambition to create an Islamic State in Africa. The intention was to use Boko Haram to destabilize and disintegrate Nigeria, to make way for a Libyan intervention and eventual takeover.

In Mali, Gaddafi created an army of terrorists who constantly fought the Malian government, in order to topple the regime in that country. Eventually, the rebels and insurgents in Mali would succeed in destabilizing that country. Nemesis would later catch up with the dictator as diehard dissidents, assisted by al-Qaeda operatives and sworn enemies, openly rebelled against his regime. The assistance of western countries like France, Britain and the United States, would eventually topple the Libyan leader, thus ending the most notorious state-sponsored terrorism ever known to mankind, besides Iran's sponsorship of terrorism in Lebanon and Syria.

Another known state-sponsorship of terrorism is Iran. According to the CIA, M15, and Mossad, Iran is now the most visible sponsor of terrorism in the world. Iran is said to be the new sponsor of terrorism in Nigeria and Pakistan, funding Boko Haram and al-Qaeda.

According to the CIA, Iran's terrorist activities are usually carried out through IRGC, Quds Force, Hezbollah, and Hamas, to destabilize countries around the world. New evidence had shown that plots like the attempted assassination of Saudi Arabia's ambassador to Washington, continues to be part of the terrorist strategy Iran uses to assassinate its enemies around the globe; and to enhance and further its foreign policy goals.

Iran is also known to be training members of Boko Haram, Hamas, Taliban militants, by allowing the militants to use its territories to supply arms and ammunitions to terrorist cells around the world. Iran is also said to be a sponsor of al-Qaeda in the Arabian Peninsula, al-Qaeda in the Maghreb, al-Qaeda in Iraq and several Middle Eastern countries and emirates. According to the CIA, Mossad, and the M15, Iran's intention was to create destabilization in western countries like the United States and Britain, in order to continue its enrichment of uranium and plutonium, for nuclear weapons capability.

Al-Qaeda in the Islamic Maghreb is also said to be getting its funds from Iran, as well as through ransoms from kidnappings of high profile targets. The instability in Libya, Mali, Syria, Somalia, Sudan and Yemen, is also known efforts of Iran to spread jihad; with the promotion of Sharia Law in the world.

The strengthened increase of terrorism in Nigeria, after Gaddafi's death, in the northern states and cities of Borno, Yobe, Bauchi, Gombe, Plateau, Kaduna and Abuja, perpetrated by both Boko Haram and Ansaru militants, was also said to have links to Iran, who was said to be the biggest sponsor of terrorism in the world, filling the void left by Gaddafi.

Pakistan remains the central haven for terrorists seeking to unleash terrorism, especially the Haqqani Network and Lashkar-e-Tayyiba terrorist cells. With increased terrorism in the world, and with Iran continuously using terrorism to defy the sanctions imposed by the west, terrorism, according to the CIA and M15, will be the new menace the world will need to find solutions to, besides drug trafficking in Columbia, Mexico and Panama.

Chapter 9

The Nigerian nurse came back again to check on the jihadist. By her demeanor, I could hardly confirm the paranoia of death, exhibited by the jihadist. The dark skinned nurse looked to be in her fifties, with a kind face and bedside manner. She was short, around five feet tall, and chubby, with three visible tribal marks on both sides of her cheeks, which made me believe she was of the Yoruba tribe. The Yoruba natives are the only known people with such long noticeable tribal marks on their cheeks.

I watched the nurse as she went about her business of redressing the wounds on the body of the jihadist. She went about it, in the most efficient manner, as if she had been doing it all her life. I could tell nursing had become a second nature to her. Looking at her, I could tell she enjoyed her job, and took pride in her work.

When she had finished redressing the wounds, she had checked the jihadist's temperature, and given him some liquid medicine, which she almost forcibly made the jihadist drink. I could tell that the jihadist was reluctant to take the medicine, but he had very little choice. On each side of the nurse were three tough looking Nigerian soldiers, strapped with automatic rifles and AK47s. By the look on the soldiers' faces, I could tell they enjoyed killing, and wouldn't hesitate to pull the trigger at the least provocation.

The jihadist also knew that the Nigerian soldiers would kill him if he presented any problem for the nurse. Soldiers, anywhere in the world, were government sanctioned killers, who were licensed to kill at any given time, when there was the smallest perception of threat. I did not envy the jihadist, as he was at death's doorstep, dying, and being carefully watched by the angels of death. Though there was no immediate clear and present danger presented by the jihadist, having been stripped of any clothing, he was still a threat to the world.

Jihadists everywhere carry different forms of danger. There were those suicide bombers, or martyrs, as Muslims would like to call them, who carry visible vests-laden-bombs, to kill others. And there were the unintentional suicide bombers, like the teenagers in Kabul and Kandahar that I described earlier in the story, who were often lied to, to carry bags loaded with bombs to crowded places, and areas crowded with security forces, for detonation. The latter groups of suicide bombers often do not know that their actions involved death to themselves and others. Some though, are told that they are working for Allah, by trusted imams and clerics, like the kid who was sent by his parents to go to school in Kabul but ended up in the hands of mullahs in Pakistan.

I have heard that some suicide bombers were now being implanted with bombs in their bodies. Stories abound about the new tactics being used by Islamic extremists to kill non-Muslims. Using surgery to implant bombs in the belly of the bomb carriers or, if you like, suicide bombers, had gradually replaced the visible suicide vests. The new method of spreading terror and killing innocent people was designed by the so-called chemical jihadist, al-Asiri, to make suicide bombers more invisible.

Ibrahim al-Asiri, the chemical jihadist, was said to be working on a new bomb that would make his underwear bomb a child's play. As the chief bomb maker for al-Qaeda in the Arabian Peninsula, al-Asiri was reportedly well funded for his research on new methods of making undetectable bombs. Having once used his brother, Abdullah al-Asiri, as a guinea-pig for one of his earlier bombs, in a suicide bomb attack, the bomb maker was continually working on new bombs that could stay in the body for weeks, undetected by electronic surveillance and metal detectors at airports and train terminals.

The bomb maker's initial experiment was testing the bomb he had made on his brother, Abdullah, whom he recruited to test the new bomb. Using a mixture of PETN bomb that Ibrahim had ingeniously created, and hidden in his brother's rectum, to use against the Saudis security chief, Mohammed bin Nayef, in Jeddah, the experiment had backfired. Approaching the security chief had been easy for Abdullah who was a master of disguise. Acting as if he was a changed man who was no longer interested in jihad and militancy, Abdullah had succeeded in persuading the security chief to meet with him. It was during the meeting that Ibrahim had detonated the bomb in his rectum, in an attempt to kill the security chief. The security chief, Nayef, had survived but Ibrahim didn't.

The bomb was believed to be improperly detonated as the body mass of the bomber did not effectively direct the explosion. The failure of the suicide bomb attack to get its target, and the unnecessary death of his brother, made Ibrahim al-Asiri, to embark upon a new effective bomb technique, which has proven to be successful.

Ibrahim's known bomb attacks included the 2010 cargo plane bomb plot, in which he had used PETN explosive materials. Another known attempt to create a mass murder was the attempted bombing of a commercial plane by a Nigerian recruit, Umar Farouk Abdulmutallab, in 2009. The device worn by Abdulmutallab was also said to be the work of Ibrahim al-Asiri that went awry.

The new liquid implants which are usually surgically implanted, contained devices that are hard to detect by x-rays. The new device was said to be one of the latest devices being developed and enhanced by Ibrahim, to beat security checks around the world.

My Nigerian friend, whom I said had retired from the local television station, once told me that Nigerian law enforcement agents had found out that Boko Haram operatives were being trained and instructed on how to effectively use surgically implanted bombs. Top members of Boko Haram had been known to attend several lectures organized by Ibrahim al-Asiri, in Mali, and in Yemen. According to my sources, Boko Haram has not only acquired the liquid bomb but has also successfully used it in northern Nigeria, against school children.

I turned to the jihadist to see if he had recovered from the treatment the Yoruba nurse had given him. As our eyes met, he was smiling into my eyes, which made me think he had been waiting for me to say something. It occurred to me that patience comes with his training as a jihadist.

I once wrote an article in a popular global newspaper about the patience of al-Qaeda operatives in planning and executing attacks. Al-Qaeda was known to carefully study a situation, then recruit and train those chosen for an attack. The methods of recruiting potential suicide bombers included first using money to lure them. Once the recruits were lured into the sect with money, the next step often included teaching them the Koran in details. Once deeply taught the Koran, the new recruits were then sent on an *endurance resistant* training in a desert, in Mali, which included physical exercises, martial arts, and weapons training.

After the mental and physical training, the next step, according to my sources, was usually to teach them about the glory that awaits believers and adherents of Islam, for martyrdom. Videos and scriptures from the Koran were some of the methods used in brainwashing new recruits. Paradise and the inheritance of it, in the hereafter, is a significant part of the brainwashing instructions. The brainwashing instructions also included hypnotizing the recruits and nurturing their minds during the process of hypnotism to think with a different mindset, which were usually suicide attacks.

Chapter 10

In the northeast of Nigeria, north of Cameroun and Niger, was the headquarters of Boko Haram, in Maiduguri, capital of Borno State. A nondescript fading sign announced the town, in the southwest suburb of the city, called Goram, to a traveler to the town. The town was said to be the hotbed of Boko Haram activities. The street leading to the town from a potholed road in the southwest of Maiduguri was called Mohammed Yusuf Street, the founder of Boko Haram. Since Boko Haram was founded in 2001, Christians and government employees have all disappeared from the town, called Goram, which was said to have been renamed by Yusuf.

Since declaring a state of emergency by the government of Jonathan, the town of Goram remained the only place where the state of emergency has not been felt. Nigerian soldiers knew it was suicidal to traverse into Goram. They knew that nonmembers of Boko Haram do not enter, or leave the town alive. Rather than extend the state of emergency to Goram, the soldiers had stayed away from the small town of Goram, a town of jihadists.

Muslims who had lived in the town, that were nonmembers of the Islamic establishment, had either been assassinated or bludgeoned to death by Boko Haram. The once estimated 10,000 residents of this small town had dwindled and now given way to Islamic extremists and members of Boko Haram. The town even had its own police force, complete with Sharia Law emblems and insignias. The law in the town of Goram was structured according to the tenets of Sharia Law. Since its foundation, the town had become a symbol of how Boko Haram would govern Nigeria, if they should prevail over Nigerian soldiers.

Boko Haram's efforts to replicate another Goram in the states of Adamawa, Kaduna, Bauchi, Yobe and Kano, where they exerted the most influence in the northeast of Nigeria, had met with tough resistance from the Nigerian army. Though there was no visible structural chain of command in the sect, there was a top-down unwritten administration that members strictly abided by. The sect would seem to an outsider like an ungoverned sect, but in reality, there was a very strict governance of the sect by a few invisible hands that controlled the activities of the sect. Various newspapers and media organizations had dubbed the governance of the sect diffused with a so-called cell-like management, with various factions and splinter groups. There was no doubt that the sect was tightly governed by a select group of leaders.

Though security agents in the western world linked Boko Haram to al-Qaeda in the Islamic Maghreb (AQIM), there was no evidence of such links. Though there were reports of Boko Haram members training with al-Qaeda members in Mali and Yemen, there was no known link that Boko Haram was affiliated with al-Qaeda. The new leader, who took over after the death of Mohammed Yusuf, was Abubakar Shekau, whose method was different from al-Qaeda's methods of jihad. The group's ideology and radicalism was said to have been inspired by the now deceased Islamic preacher, Maitatsine.

I was curious about the recent U.S. Special Forces' capture of a wanted fugitive in Libya, and the attempted capture of an al-Shabab wanted terrorist in Somalia, and asked the jihadist what he knew about the futile attempt to capture the terrorist leader in Somalia. His answer surprised me. I didn't expect him to know as much as he told me.

"First let me tell you that the reason the capture of Anu Anas al-Libi was successful was because the U.S. did not inform the Libyan government in advance about the mission. If the U.S. had informed the Libyan government, someone in the government would have told al-Libi; and the mission would have been unsuccessful," he said, as he once again stared into space as if there was something of interest he was trying to invoke and conjure.

The answer surprised me because the U.S. said the Libyan government was informed prior to the capture of al-Libi. Whether the U.S. took advantage of the anarchy existing in Libya to capture the wanted terrorist was not exactly clear. As a journalist, I do know that the government in Libya was not entirely in control of the country. The militias that helped toppled Muammar Gaddafi were still roaming the country with impunity, which made the country ungovernable. The almost lack of law and order in the country, largely due to the existing factions of militias, made it impossible to tell if there was a central government.

Continuing, as if urged by invisible hands, the jihadist said: "those fighting the holy war of jihad knew that the U.S. armed forces and special agents were constantly on the hunt for our members, especially those of us who had taken part in any mission. What the U.S. government did not know was that, being hunted by the great Satan was a privilege that members of the terrorist community craved. Sometimes, we committed an act of terrorism with the hope that we would get in the U.S. most wanted list. The jihadists who had attained the honor of being wanted by the U.S. were called heroes, and were given red-carpet treatment in the Islamic jihad community.

The reason the U.S. Special Operations forces failed in Somalia was because the Somali government was informed about the raid, prior to it taking place. Someone high in the government had tipped off al-Shabab about the raid. At the time the Special Operations forces landed in the port of Baraawe, south of Mogadishu, al-Shabab had already set up a trap comprising of armed militants, waiting for the arriving navy seal. It was supposed to be a surprised amphibian operation, designed to be quick. But what the commanders of the operation did not know was that there were lots of Somali government officials in the payroll and protection of al-Shabab. Some top government officials had tipped off al-Shabab about the raid.

When al-Shabab had carried out the attack on the Westgate Mall in Nairobi, it was an attempt to provoke the U.S. to react as it did, by sending the Special Forces. The operation was anticipated and closely monitored by al-Shabab. The initial idea was to once again humiliate the U.S., as it once did when a U.S. soldier was dragged in the streets of Mogadishu in the 1990s, when a black Hawk had gone down. Al-Shabab knew the U.S. was going to retaliate. What they did not know was that the U.S. would retaliate soon after the attack. Al-Shabab had thought the government shutdown in the U.S. would derail the country's war against terrorism. They were mistaken.

The U.S. had been looking for the opportunity to go after al-Shabab for a long time; and that opportunity came when Westgate Mall was attacked. The attack on Westgate Mall gave the U.S. the opportunity to go after al-Shabab. We were hoping that the U.S. would do the same with Boko Haram, so that we could attain the prominence we have been fighting for, since 2001.

Sending an elite U.S. Navy Seals and fighters after al-Shabab was a symbol of success on the part of al-Shabab, all terrorist sects strive for. So far, only al-Qaeda enjoys that privilege, and a lot of terrorist organizations were tired of allowing al-Qaeda to take credit for their work, while they remained in perpetual anonymity. To achieve any kind of legitimacy and renown, every terrorist network must link with al-Qaeda. A lot of terrorist networks like Boko Haram and al-Shabab were trying to change that. They would like to gain their own international reputation of being branded a terrorist organization," the jihadist said, with a torrent of coughs that scared me.

In a way I could understand what the jihadist meant. The terrorist attack on the World Trade Center and the Pentagon established al-Qaeda as a legitimate terrorist organization, known worldwide. Being able to bring the great Satan to a standstill and its knees, as occurred following 9/11, made al-Qaeda a bona fide organization that all terrorist organizations, big or small, sought to emulate or surpass.

De facto organizations like al-Shabab remained a regional terrorist organization that had no significant legitimacy outside Somalia, and that continued to irk the leadership of the organization that felt al-Shabab was being overshadowed by al-Qaeda. The struggle to outdo al-Qaeda by hitting the great Satan where it hurts was said to be one of the reasons for the attack on the swanking Westgate Mall in Nairobi, Kenya. The 20 gunmen, including a woman, who attacked the Westgate Mall, were trained to undergo the suicide mission by al-Shabab, with the intent to raise international awareness about the potency of al-Shabab. Much to the chagrin and disquietude of al-Shabab, al-Qaeda was given the credit for the attack.

According to my sources in Kenya and Somalia, an American who was a naturalized citizen of Somali descent was used as part of the contingent that carried out the attack. Khattab al-Kene, an American Somali, was said to have been recruited for the Westgate Mall because of his American citizenship, as part of a plan to humiliate the U.S. To make sure the attack had an international scope, Abu Baara al-Sudani, from Sudan; and Omar Nabhan, from Kenya, were also chosen as part of the contingent to attack the Westgate Mall.

The Westgate Mall was chosen because of the perpetual

presence of a huge number of westerners, especially Americans, at the mall. Another reason the mall was chosen was because the president of the United States, Barack Obama, had a root in Kenya, because of his father who was born in Kenya. Though al-Shabab claimed the reason for the attack was because Kenya had sent troops to Somalia to fight against it, the main reason was to gain some kind of international reputation. Kenya became a very important country following the election of President Barack Obama as the 44th president of the United States. Prior to that, Kenya was just another east African country, whose embassy was bomb-attacked by al-Shabab, in 1998.

My reflection of the deadly attack on the Westgate Mall in Kenya was still heavy on my mind when I noticed a commotion behind me. I saw the nurse again, followed by a light-skinned African who could have passed for a Middle Easterner, approached the jihadist. It seemed as if something was wrong, judging by the quick strides of the light-skinned African, who had the demeanor of an important man of some sort. I didn't dwell much on the importance of the man as most Africans with any form of authority always carried themselves with pomposity to show authority.

The nurse and the light-skinned African came over to the jihadist who cowered at the sight of the man. It seemed as if the jihadist knew who the man was, judging by the fear that jumped into his eyes at the sight of the man. I waited patiently. I had an arrangement with the CIA commander to let the jihadist remain alive until the man finishes his confession. Since the commander was nowhere in sight, I began to worry. I knew the Nigerian soldiers did not want the jihadist to live. I had at least sensed that by their action. They wanted the man dead.

The Nigerian government did not want to waste money to try the jihadist in a court of law. They wanted to exert their own form of jungle justice on the man. To them, it was cheaper to kill captured terrorists than to try them in a court of law. They did not understand the rationale behind allowing a mass murderer to live, under the pretext of interrogating him or giving him a fair trial. The U.S. was good at capturing terrorists and interrogating them later, and in some cases releasing them to their host countries. But in Nigeria, it was eye for an eye and tit for tat.

I had heard some Islamic extremists say that being captured

alive by U.S. soldiers was often sought by terrorists as it gives them the opportunity to gather information from other terrorists.

I once interviewed an inmate in Guantanamo Bay detention camp in Cuba, who confided in me that some terrorists would like to be captured by U.S. forces for several reasons. The reasons were that being captured by U.S. agents would allow them the opportunity to know and understand the enemy, the great Satan. Another reason was that they would get to eat good food and get a first class medical treatment, especially if captured injured.

While it was true that most Islamic extremists sought martyrdom, if injured, they often want to remain alive to carry out more suicide attacks. My source once told me that the more attacks a jihadist carries out, the greater the glories he would enjoy when he made it to paradise, in the hereafter.

From the corner of my eyes, I saw that the jihadist was no longer scared. He seemed relax. I looked around to see the reason for his ease of fear. The light-skinned African only looked at him, while the nurse made notes and took dictation from the man. After that, he left, without doing anything.

"Who was that man?" I asked the jihadist, because I was sure he knew who the man was, because of the way he had flinched at the sight of the man. "That man is a killer. He is a trained killer," the jihadist said. "But he looks like a doctor," I said, trying to get him to give me details. "Yes, he is a doctor, but a doctor of death. He specializes in killing jihadists, with potassium nitrite, to induce heart attack in them. The Nigerian secret service uses him to get rid of jihadists like me that they do not want to shoot outright, to avoid international scrutiny and condemnation. By using potassium nitrate, that was largely untraceable in the blood, the government makes such deaths natural deaths," the jihadist said, with disgust on his face.

I was not quite sure if he was telling the truth or simply exaggerating. But the look on his face when he saw the so-called doctor of death convinced me he was not exactly exaggerating. People like the jihadist were not easily scared. Jihadists expected death as the ultimate consequence of their actions. Death, to jihadists, was a welcome reward. Death was not supposed to scare or make them cower as happened with the jihadist. Something else was amiss. I wanted to know why the mere sight of the man he referred to as doctor of death scared him.

"I needed some clarifications on some things," I told the jihadist, trying to get his attention. He immediately looked up at me. I could see doubts in his eyes. I did not understand the nature of the doubts in his eyes. I left that part of my curiosity alone. I had other things in mind, so I asked. "Why did the thought of death bother you? You are already dying anyway, so it shouldn't bother you. Another thing I need clarification on is the matter of the potassium nitrate you mentioned earlier. How can it be used as a poison when it is known to be a sort of fertilizer? I know it can also be used in medicine, but I didn't know it can be used as an undetectable poison," I told him.

"To answer the first question, let me say that death is a necessary end that we, will all suffer at the end of our journey on earth. As a soldier of Allah, I understand death to mean a privilege earned at the end of my mission on earth. That mission was fighting the holy war, as instructed by Allah, through Prophet Muhammad. When my day is done, and my mission completed, then death will become a welcomed relief. Until that mission was completed, any form of induced death by anyone other than the natural consequence of fighting the holy war of jihad, would make my transition to the hereafter impossible.

It is hard for a non-Muslim to understand because it is sort of complicated. The doctor of death himself is a Muslim. But he is a different type of Muslim. His belief as a Muslim is very different from my belief as a jihadist fighting the holy war. By him being a Muslim, and on the other side, with the enemy, his job as an assassin of jihadists is against the tenets of Islam. I am not afraid of him. I am only afraid of the bad omen he carries with him. That bad omen, my friend, could hamper my transition to paradise, the same way non-repentance would.

On the other question you asked, regarding potassium nitrate, I will give you my most candid expert medical explanation. There are so many types of potassium. Potassium chloride is often used as a fertilizer because of the crystalline salt, KCI, as a mineral, which you often see in natural water. That occurring mineral in it makes it useful as a fertilizer. There is potassium bromide that also contains a crystalline salt, KBr, with a saline taste, which can be used as a sedative.

There is another type of potassium, called potassium carbonate, which is a form of a strong alkaline solution. The alkaline solution in the substance makes it useful for making soaps. The other type of potassium is called potassium chlorate, which is used as an oxidizing agent in matches, fireworks, and explosives. Potassium chlorate is a deadly substance.

Potassium dichromate is another oxidizing agent with a soluble salt, used in making dye. Another form of potassium is potassium hydroxide which is a white deliquescent solid, KOH that easily dissolves in water when heated to the right temperature. A strong alkaline and caustic liquid can also become the outcome of the heat. Potassium hydroxide can be used for making soap.

Now, potassium nitrate is different but not as deadly as you described. I will tell you about deadly potassium shortly. Potassium nitrate contains crystalline salt that is sort of a product of nitrification in soils. It is a strong oxidizer which can be used as a fertilizer, and in medicine, but never as a poison.

Potassium permanganate is another form of potassium which is a dark purple salt. Potassium permanganate is an oxidizer which can be used as a disinfectant. This contains a small amount of poison because of the disinfecting agent in it, but not enough to kill a human being.

Potassium sorbate contains sorbic acid which can be used for preserving food, as a preservative. It is a good acid because it is used as a food preservative. Yes, there is such a thing as a good acid, if you ask me.

There is another form of potassium called potassium sulfate, which contains a white crystalline compound, which is also used as a fertilizer. You see, potassium is generally a compound that is used as a fertilizer," he repeated unnecessarily. He continues as if he was reading a script from memory.

"The most deadly of all the potassium family is the potassium cyanide, which is what I think you were referring to. Potassium cyanide is a very poisonous crystalline salt, KCN, which is often used in extracting gold and silver from ore. But it has been known to be used as a poison by killers or people with evil intentions," he finally said, as if it was difficult for him to say this at first.

Though I appreciated the long diatribe, which I thought was a scolding lesson than information, I felt most of what he said were unnecessary. He almost bored me to death with his in-depth explanation of the different types of potassium. It was good that he differentiated them but I was already aware of most of them. I could not have told him that, for fear of interrupting his long discourse, if you want to call it that. I still went ahead and listened, hoping it will make a good reading for my readers. As a journalist I always appreciated knowledge and didn't especially mind the long diatribe.

"Don't confuse sodium cyanide with potassium cyanide," he said, as if I wasn't there. But he knew I was listening and that I wanted to know. "Sodium cyanide is also a white deliquescent poisonous salt, used in electroplating fumigation.

As for potassium cyanide, any amount of it can kill a person instantly, whether it is 200mg (0.2grams) or even smaller. Though a dosage of 200mg will kill an individual quicker than a lesser dosage, any amount is enough to kill.

There are countless other poisons that are toxic and less efficient as potassium cyanide. Poisons like arsenic oxide, strychnine are such toxic poisons. What makes potassium cyanide a poison of choice is its fast action. Don't get me wrong, cyanides in general are fast acting poisons. Cyanides such as potassium cyanide, sodium cyanide and hydrogen cyanide, are such fast acting poisons in science.

Once, in a training camp in Mali, an Indian trainer had told us that rather than divulge any type of information to the enemies of Islam that it was okay to die with a teaspoon of cyanide, which he said we could dissolve in water and swallow. He said a teaspoon of potassium cyanide would be more than enough to kill. He said when swallowed, the cyanide could take effect within 30 seconds as one loses consciousness and collapses immediately afterward.

In case you are wondering about the smallest amount needed for any form of effect, a gram of potassium cyanide mixed with about 8oz of water could immediately induce consciousness within seconds, and death immediately afterward," he said, with that stoic expression he maintains when he discusses death.

I once covered a story about a terrorist who hijacked a commuter bus full of people returning home from work, and school children going to a playground to play basketball. The terrorist had been one of the passengers who had boarded the bus, but as the bus moved through the congested traffic, the terrorist had stood up and announced to the other passengers that the bus was being hijacked. As the hijacker made the announcement, he brought out an AK47 he had hidden inside his trench coat and waved it around.

When the passengers saw the gun, they immediately knew he was not playing, that he was serious. With the gun in one hand, and what looked like a hand grenade in the other, the jihadist was able to convince the passengers, including the driver, that he was not bluffing about bombing the bus, if need be. Seeing that he wouldn't hesitate to use the bomb, the passengers who had wanted to play heroes quickly stopped.

Something unusual had happened as the hijacker waved the gun around. A former marine who served in Iraq and Afghanistan, and who had been watching him very keenly quickly saw that the hijacker wasn't holding the gun properly. The way the hijacker was holding the gun informed the former marine that the hijacker did not know how to use the gun or the hand grenade. The former marine feared that the hijacker could accidently kill all of them with the grenade if it accidently discharged.

What the former marine did after that shocked the other passengers who did not see his action coming. Having carefully watched the hijacker, the former marine threw a small heavy metal object that looked like a golf ball at the passenger. The object knocked the AK47 off the hand of the hijacker. The hijacker made a feeble attempt to retrieve the gun, and as he did so, the hand grenade fell off his hand and rolled under the seats. It was then that the former marine suddenly lunged forward, knocking down the hijacker.

The hijacker fought back, hitting the former marine with a surprised uppercut that sent the former marine reeling backward, sending him to the floor. As the hijacker made a quick effort to retrieve his gun, the former marine kicked him hard in the groin, followed by another heavy kick on his liver, which made the hijacker double with pain.

Even with the pain, the hijacker was still able to hit the former marine with a swift kick that sent the former marine back to the floor of the bus. But the former marine quickly got up, rushed the hijacker, and wrestled him to the ground. With his right hand, the former marine pummeled the face of the hijacker until blood spurted from the mouth and forehead of the terrorist Seeing that the hijacker was subdued, the other passengers joined in the beating, kicking and hitting the now helpless hijacker who lay prone on the floor of the bus, bleeding.

Within minutes, police cars surrounded the bus as the driver pulled to the side of the road. The driver must have radioed for help. Bomb squads immediately boarded the bus with dogs, looking for the hand grenade. The passengers were immediately evacuated from the bus, as law enforcement agents searched the bus for more bombs. Not long after, the media arrived, with television cameras and reporters. I was one of the reporters who had arrived at the scene of the attempted hijack.

The hijacker was immediately handcuffed and taken away but as he was being led to a waiting police car, he slumped, fell to the ground and within seconds was pronounced dead. We learnt later that the hijacker was a jihadist with a notorious Chechen terrorist organization, with link to al-Qaeda. What really surprised me was when the medical examiner said the man had had a pill of cyanide in his mouth, which he had swallowed immediately he was arrested by the police.

But as he was dying, he punched a button on a small device that was sewed to the inner cuff of his shirt, blowing himself, the bus and law enforcement agents to smithereens. Luckily, the passengers had been rescued but a few of the passengers nearby were still injured. But all the law enforcement agents, their vehicles, and a few media vehicles were killed and destroyed in the explosion.

I had gone further to do some investigation into the background of the terrorist. I had used my influence with the FBI to find out the name of the hijacker, and with the name, I did a quick background check on the suspect and did not find anything. My contact in the FBI told me there was no record of the man ever being a U.S. legal resident or a citizen. But a half burnt passport found on the man had identified him as a Chechen terrorist, on the wanted list of the Russian FSB.

Further details revealed that the man had been smuggled into the U.S. through Mexico by the Mexican drug cartel, with link to the Chechen terrorist organization. A quick check with the

Mexican authorities confirmed that the terrorist had temporarily lived in Mexico before being smuggled through Texas, into the U.S. Mexican authorities and intelligence agents had put the terrorist on a watch list, and had even put a tail on him, until he slipped away.

Mexican secret agents believed the terrorist was heading to the U.S. and had been smuggled through the border by Mexican coyotes, with the help of the Mexican drug cartel. My story had led to another big story about the drug trade between the Chechen terrorist organization and the Mexican drug cartel. I also found out that the Russian mob was involved. The Chechen terrorist organization was selling drugs through the Mexican drug cartel, with the Russian mob involved, in helping to make sure the drug makes it to Mexico.

The money from the drug trafficking helps the Chechen terrorist organization to fund most of its activities. My investigation had also revealed that arms were being supplied by the Russian mob through the Chechen terrorist organization, through Mexico into the U.S. Somehow, the Chechen terrorist organization and the Russian mob were working together to sell arms and drugs. While the Russian FSB and soldiers are fighting the Chechen terrorist organizations and rebels, the Russian mob were secretly profiting from the insurgency and conflict.

The weapons being supplied to the Mexican drug cartel by the Chechen terrorists and rebels were Russian weapons, smuggled out of Russia by the mafia, and supplied to the Chechen terrorists, in a barter of drug for arms, which somehow finds its way to the U.S. through Mexico.

When my story had hit the airwave, it had shocked authorities on both sides of the border that so much illegal activities were occurring right around the border; that had escaped the attention of the border patrol, and law enforcement agents. Other media organizations in the U.S. and Mexico had also aired my story, which even brought the Interpol into the picture. The lack of oversight on both sides of the border had made the U.S. Congress to act immediately on ways to further tighten security to prevent terrorists from entering the U.S.

The attempted hijacker was linked to the Boston Marathon bombing, in which two brothers, Dzhokhar and Tamerlan

Tsarnaev, were identified as the bombers, who had used two pressure cooker bombs, to kill three people and injured over 264 others. The bomb was said to have exploded 13 seconds and 210 yards apart, near the finish line of the marathon, on Boylston Street.

My investigation had revealed that the hijacker was a member of the same Chechen terrorist organization that had radicalized the Boston Marathon bombers, in Massachusetts. When my story aired, other wannabe Chechen terrorists that tried to make their way to the U.S. were apprehended and arrested by a combined teach of both the U.S. and Mexican authorities.

Chapter 11

It was getting dark when I told the jihadist I was tired. I didn't want to leave to go back to my hotel. I was worried that the jihadist may not last the night. Or, better still, that he may be finished off by the overzealous Nigerian law enforcement agents who were anxious to show the nation of Nigeria that they were winning the war against Boko Haram. I had seen the look in their eyes and had known what they were capable of doing. I figured if I wanted to get my story or the full gist of the confession that I needed to hang around.

I pulled up a dirty, blood stained cot, whose collapsible frames had been damaged. It was still useful as a bed. With my state of fatigue, anything would have sufficed. It didn't matter that people may have died on the cot. I was ready to get some sleep and I was sure the jihadist was ready for some sleep also.

I slept fitfully, with one of my eyes opened, watching the gurney the jihadist lay on. I wanted to make sure one of the soldiers did not sneak in at night to kill the jihadist. I could tell by the demeanor of the soldiers that they were ready to finish off the jihadist, and move on to other members of Boko Haram. They did not feel it was necessary to waste too much time and resources on one member of Boko Haram.

The only luck I had was that the CIA commander was on my side. He wanted to get as much information, through me of course, as possible from the jihadist. I said the CIA commander was on my side, not exactly in a cordial way. He was interested in the information I was getting from the jihadist, and most especially, he wanted to know the next targets and plans of Boko Haram. Since the jihadist was a senior member of the sect, it was necessary for him to be on my side to get the jihadist talking. It was the only way he was going to get anything out of the jihadist. Torture was out of the question since the man was already dying. There was nothing to be done to a dying man, and he knew that.

The next day, I brushed my teeth with my emergency toothbrush that I always had with me, and washed my face with the dirty water that came out of the borehole outside the bungalow. Since there was no running, drinking water in Nigeria, Nigerians had improvised their own drinking water with boreholes. Even with that, only those who could afford boreholes had them. Others trek to the ponds and streams in the surrounding bushes for water. And the water was always wholly unhygienic and unsanitary.

The water always had mud and dust, sometimes with worms and gems. But the deprived Nigerian populace had little choices. It was nothing to them, even though the disease infested water they extracted from the ground was contaminated. I was lucky on that day because the bungalow had a borehole from which I fetched a bucket of water to wash my face and brush my teeth. The bucket was dirty, caked with mud and old dirt, with dried blood around the edges. But it was the only way I could get water. For a white man who was used to luxury and hygienic way of life, this was suicidal. But I didn't care. When in Rome, they say, one had to behave like a Roman. Since I was in Nigeria, I had to behave like a Nigerian if I were going to survive.

After I had finished brushing my teeth and washing my face, I went to the newspaper vendor at the gate of the bungalow and purchased several Nigeria newspapers. Some of them were printed on very poor newsprints that looked over recycled. But then, this was Nigeria, and of course Africa. Despite the reported upsurge in economic growth, the continent still looked ancient, like it belonged in a lost era. Nigeria especially appeared to still live in the stone-age, even with the country's enormous oil wealth. Corruption, embezzlement, greed, selfishness, had hindered progress and development in the country.

Roads across the country were potholed, waterlogged, and bad. Electricity was only available once a week. Even with that once a week, it was only available for a few hours. Most households used small generators and hurricane-lamps for lights. Several homes had been razed down by fire due to the use of generators and kerosene-fueled lamps. Fumes from the generators and kerosene lamps had killed so many Nigerians, but of course, this was Nigeria. Death hardly meant anything. As I said earlier, it was not uncommon to see dead bodies strewn everywhere, and being stepped over by pedestrians as they go about their daily business.

I took the newspapers to the bungalow, sat in the little cot that became my temporary bed and couch, and started to read them, as I chewed a chewing stick. I had to buy a chewing stick because the toothpaste was too harsh in the mouth. The newspaper vendor had advised me to use a chewing stick. I tried it, and alas, it was bad, but it was the best under the circumstance. It was still better than the toothpaste that I had unwittingly purchased from a store, not far from where the vendor was selling his newspapers.

As usual, the headlines were about Boko Haram and the latest coordinated attacks. As I began to read, I had forgotten about the chewing stick and the bloodstained cot. The news was as spellbinding and as appalling as the badly written English Language.

In Abuja, the capital of Nigeria, and at the Abuja National Mosque, 50 Boko Haram gunmen and suicide bombers walked into the mosque, and joined the worshippers for prayers on a Friday afternoon. Towards the end of the prayer, the 50 Boko Haram members went into action. First, the suicide bombers detonated the suicide vests and belts they were wearing, instantly killing a sizable number of worshippers in the mosque. Thirty gunmen, also part of the 50 Boko Haram terrorists, opened fire on those that tried to escape the bomb blast, killing all of them, as the thirty gunmen were also consumed by the explosion that killed their colleagues.

In north eastern state of Plateau State, Nigeria's twelfth largest state, and in another mosque in Konduga, 10 female members of Boko Haram, and two men joined a Friday afternoon prayer with the worshippers. Towards the end of the Friday afternoon prayers, in a coordinated attack, the female terrorists wearing black hijabs, detonated the suicide vests hidden in their clothing, instantly killing the majority of the worshippers. Those who tried to escape were gunned down by two male terrorists with automatic weapons. Five women, armed with automatic weapons, also joined in the shooting spree. No one escaped the attack, including the suicide bombers. The mosque was razed down.

Also, in the same coordinated attack, the palace of a prominent traditional ruler who had always spoken against Boko Haram, in the town of Damboa, in Plateau State, was bombed with a hand grenade, killing 10 members of the household of the traditional ruler. The main target of the attack, the traditional ruler, had escaped unscathed.

At the time the Nigerian law enforcement authorities realized a coordinated attack was being carried out across northeast

Nigeria, over 300 Muslims had been killed in mosques. To save lives, the military quickly deployed soldiers to the affected places, where they were met with tough, brutal resistance. In Damboa, the army tried in vain to repel the diehard jihadists who were bent on attacking more Muslim facilities such as the mosque in Damboa and the palace of the head of the district.

In the melee, in which Christians fought back, as the soldiers went on their own rampage against the Muslims and some unruly Christian teenagers, a state of anarchy ensued, following the deaths of over 1000 people on that Friday coordinated attack in Abuja and Plateau State.

A Nigerian military spokesperson said over 200 Boko Haram members were killed in the coordinated attacks. But a Boko Haram spokesperson said the army over exaggerated the number of Boko Haram members killed. According to Boko Haram, only five of its members were killed. The soldiers were said to have killed tens of innocent Christian teenagers who were trying to wade off the terrorists from their homes. Boko Haram challenged the Nigerian army to publish the names of those it claimed to have killed.

An assortment of weapons including rocket propelled grenades, 100 AK47s, machetes, axes, and daggers were displayed as weapons seized from the purportedly fleeing and dead Boko Haram members. Boko Haram debunked the claim, saying the weapons belonged to the army and not Boko Haram.

The following day, on a Saturday, around 2am, while the residents of Damboa slept, 100 Fulani members of Boko Haram affiliation, came back to the town, attacking the Christian residents of the town, and Muslims who had cooperated with the soldiers. Several homes were set ablaze after the throats of the residents had been slit in the attack. At the time the Fulani terrorists left the town, over 300 residents had been killed, with several homes razed down.

Chapter 12

The very next day, I was relieved to find that the jihadist was still alive and hadn't been killed. When he saw me, he smiled and said good morning. For the first time since I met him, I felt pleased to see him. In a weird way, he was right that it was a good morning. It was a good morning because he was still alive and I could continue with my story, which was his confession.

He must have sensed that I was happy that he was still alive. It didn't take long before my hatred of him took over my relief. The fact that he was a killer who had killed so many innocent people did not escape my mind. Though I was happy to see him the next morning, I was still subconsciously aware that he was an Islamic jihadist who believed in killing non-Muslims and Christians.

Any person who finds pleasure in killing women and children could not last in my good book. Matter of fact he was not even in my good book. It wasn't that I kept a bad book containing people that wronged, or did not agree with me. Mentally, I had a profound disdain for unconscionable people who enjoyed killing others, especially innocent children. I don't have children but one did not have to have children to have a soft spot for them. Children were the future, and by their innocence, were God's beloved children whom He expected everyone to love and cherish.

My mind riveted back to the confession and the carnage of the night by a group of Fulani members of Boko Haram. The images of dead several innocent lives went through my mind like a macabre. I shook and shuddered with the thought of those innocent lives that were wasted in the wee hours of the night. The cruelty of some sons of Lucifer was hard to comprehend as was the case with the carnage that occurred that Saturday night.

It took me a few minutes to recover and to concentrate on the matters at hand. I was still a journalist and had to maintain objectivity and fairness in my report. But it was hard to do so, sometimes, considering that innocent lives were still being taken by Islamic extremists on a daily basis. Boko Haram, it seems, had taken root as a terrorist organization like al-Shabab or al-Qaeda, in Nigeria, and continues to be emboldened by each terrorist act it commits. It appears the Nigerian army was no match for the terrorists as more soldiers continued to die in each attack.

Boko Haram had become so contemptuous of the Nigerian

soldiers that they now attack army bases and barracks, sometimes killing soldiers and their families. The Nigerian police had long been subdued by Boko Haram and Ansaru, with sophisticated weapons and planned attacks. Since the police had been counted out as a threat, Boko Haram no longer bothered about the police nor did they worry about the soldiers. I had covered stories where police had abandoned their posts and stations when Boko Haram Islamic jihadists started to operate.

Currently, Boko Haram operates from its three bases in the northeast of Nigeria. If the terrorists were not stopped, experts on terrorism believed that Boko Haram would spread its violence to the rest of the country, to places like Lagos, Ibadan, Ondo, Akure, Benin City, Warri, Enugu, Onitsha, Owerri, Auchi, and other parts of southern Nigeria. According to the expert I spoke with, it was just a matter of time before Boko Haram took over Nigeria and declares it an Islamic State, like Iran.

I looked, once again, at the jihadist lying on the gurney and wondered, for the umpteenth time, if I wasn't helping to promote his propaganda by reporting his confession. My journalistic instinct did not agree with me that I was helping to promote a jihad. As far as my journalistic instinct was concerned, I was doing a job, my job, which I was trained to do. If by error of commission or omission, I helped to promote the spiteful purpose of a jihadist's accursed objective, then it was pure coincidence.

"Your mind is playing tricks on you again," the jihadist said, as he looked worriedly at my face. I ignored him. But it wasn't for long as I knew I must soon talk to him to get him to talk more about his past misdeeds and evil. I didn't have to push him for long as he started soon enough.

"Sometimes, I feel some remorse about what I had done as a jihadist but since Allah had preapproved my actions, my remorse does not always last. In the holy Koran, Prophet Muhammad said it was a just fight, that which was fought on behalf of Allah. The thought that my actions were in line with what the Koran teaches, gives me solace but not enough to ease my worries.

When it first occurred to me that death was at the doorstep of my life, I began to feel remorse for my actions. Though my body was wasted and ready to give up the ghost, I could not rest until I had spoken to someone who would be patient enough to hear my confession. I had prayed to Allah for someone like you to come along who would be patient enough to listen. I had barely finished praying when you showed up, with that other American that looked like a killer himself," he said with a glint in his eyes.

I knew who he was referring to. He was referring to the CIA commander. And I also knew what he meant when he said the CIA commander looked like a killer. In a sense he was right about the CIA commander being a killer. Most CIA operatives were trained killers. Though their main job was stopping any form of espionage and terrorism; or the practice of spying or using spies to obtain information, their other duties included using any means necessary to stop terrorism, and any foreign country from invading the U.S., or stealing vital information that may hamper the interests of the U.S.

The operatives of the Central Intelligence Agency undergo the same trainings that regular army, air force, marines and navy undergo. They were trained tacticians in combat activities in the same way that soldiers were trained to fight wars. In some cases, CIA operatives fight their own wars to protect the U.S. without involving the U.S. military, and they always win such wars because of the clandestine nature of the wars they fight. The members of the intelligence agency do not generally fight a declared war as often fought between countries or in civil wars within countries.

As a journalist I had often followed the trail of a CIA operation, as I once did in Afghanistan when I had gone on a couple of operations against the Taliban in Kandahar and Kabul, against Taliban insurgence. In each of those operations, I had been made to sign a waiver that I was knowingly taking an obvious risk. It didn't bother me that much. Risk taking was part of the process of investigative journalism, or daredevil journalists like me.

I had seen a lot of my colleagues die in warzones while covering wars. In warzones, journalism was as dangerous as actually taking part in a war. I had gone on those dangerous assignments knowing the consequences, that death could very well be the end-result. Sometimes, the more dangerous the assignments were, the greater the glory when one cheated death. I had cheated deaths on numerous occasions. It was when one had cheated deaths unscathed that one really knows that he was in his divine-chosen profession.

I once had a very close call with death when I had unknowingly stepped on a landmine which was set as a booby trap for the enemy. The landmine would have exploded if I had had enough weight like soldiers' in full combat gears. I knew I had escaped death when a soldier in the same command I was with also made the same mistake. But alas his mistake turned deadly as the landmine exploded, killing him instantly. I only got a little piece of shrapnel that brushed past my bicep. But I was alright as it only left a small flesh wound. The other soldiers were not lucky as some of them sustained severe injuries, and later died.

Covering warzones as a journalist was a death-wish that every journalist was aware of. Believe it or not, the thrill of danger was what draws most journalists to warzones. The notion of dodging bullets and bombs had its own appeal. I will not lie and say I did not enjoy the excitement of toying with danger. Despite my love for dangerous assignments, I had often turned down assignments that I thought were too dangerous. As much as I loved danger and the thrills it brought, I also knew when to say no to death in the rare moments I was opportune to say no.

A person is not always opportune to say no to death but there were those moments when one knew his action may result in his untimely death. I guess my journalistic instinct warned me enough not to take any assignment that my sixth sense tells me was too dangerous. I once rejected an assignment in Aleppo in Syria when the rebels had first overpowered the Syrian troops to take over the town. My instinct had warned me against going to Aleppo and I didn't go because I knew the rebels were part members of al-Qaeda, and part members of the Free Syrian Army. There were too many factions fighting the Syrian troops, which made the town very dangerous.

Al-Qaeda operatives, in warzones, were more dangerous than al-Qaeda in Islamic Maghreb, and al-Qaeda in the Arabian Peninsula. The difference was that Islamic terrorists in those places only picked on select targets, whereas al-Qaeda operatives in a Syrian warzone did not play by the guidelines established by the Geneva Convention regarding wars and the treatment of the prisoners of war. With al-Qaeda in warzones, there were no rules of combat. Being aware of how al-Qaeda jihadists in warzones operated was enough to dissuade me from going to Aleppo. It was a good thing that I didn't go as a lot of my colleagues didn't survive in Aleppo.

After I had dwelled on the prospect of continuing with reporting the confession as truthfully as I could, I had wanted to call it a day and round up the story as concluded. Something told me the jihadist had not told me everything he knew. I knew there was still something he was holding back on. Or maybe he was not holding back but simply waiting for me to trigger his memory with a question.

My stomach was growling and churning like a growling thunder. I knew hunger was making my stomach make those hunger noises that stomachs often make when food had been denied it for too long. I was not hungry, but hungry, if you can understand my inference. Sometimes your stomach can crave food while your body resists the craving. Makes sense to you? It does to me because I had often gone a whole day without food and without feeling the urge to rush to the nearest restaurant for food. Don't get me wrong. I like food and you can almost tell by the size of my body and huge muscles. I weigh a solid 220lbs, all in muscles with hardly any fat. I eat very well but I was very selective of what I put in my mouth.

Having seen so many ghastly deaths in the last two days, I could understand the reason my appetite was nonexistent. Gory sights could do that to a healthy appetite like mine. Like I said earlier, I was used to seeing dead bodies in the streets of Nigeria, often left for days on end, uncollected by authorities. I once videoed a little boy jumping over a corpse as if it was nothing to him. I guess it would be to you too, if you were used to seeing corpses strewn everywhere unattended to, on a daily basis.

Nigeria, like most African nations, treats the dead like the living. What I am saying is that the dead are sometimes left to decompose in the streets while people go about their business as if the dead were not among them, in the streets. You see, where I came from in the western world, the dead was never knowingly allowed to decompose in the streets while people step over them. The dead, no matter what caused it, were often treated with respect, in the west.

I guess there was something special about the dead. The dead did not talk, someone once said. The notion that the dead was dead and could not talk was enough rationale to treat it with the last respect. I guess that was not a philosophy that was understood by every nation. If a dead body was left unattended to, and uncollected, in the western world, for days on end, the authorities involved would be under fire for such an unbecoming behavior. In Africa, and in Nigeria, seeing the dead unattended to, was sort of the norm, or so it seemed to me.

My mind reverted back to the issue of terrorism and how things had changed since terrorists took over the peace of mind that citizens of the world once enjoyed. Once upon a time, one could ride a train, an airplane or a bus, without fear of terrorism. All of that had changed. After the attempted bombing of a Northwest Airlines Flight 253 on December 25, 2009, with 290 passengers on board, by a 23 year old Nigerian, Umar Farouk Abdulmutallab, who had concealed a plastic explosive in his underwear, the joy of flying has been replaced with fear of terrorism in the air.

My Nigerian friend who retired from the Nigerian Television Authority (NTA) told me that as a child he used to walk around his neighborhood with his friends, having fun and eating suya, a shish kebab delicacy that was roasted or cooked on skewers. He said they would go to the movies to watch the latest Chinese or Indian movies at night, sometimes arriving home at 12 midnight or 1:00am. In those days, he said, there was never any fear of terrorism or of anti-robbery squad arresting teenage boys at night, coming from the movies. Armed robberies, he said, were not even as bad. What were common in those days, according to him, were highway robberies, in which traders coming from interstate markets or trades were robbed of their goods and cash.

He said kidnappings were unheard of then, in Nigeria. He also said there were more teenagers working then, than now. With jobs available for young people, kidnappings were uncommon, he said.

Somehow, I could relate to his observation. As a foreign journalist who lives in Nigeria, covering West Africa, with emphasis on Nigeria, I had covered stories about kidnappings of prominent Nigerians for ransoms. In some cases, the kidnappers would kill the victims after collecting the ransoms.

Though kidnapping was one of the oldest crimes in the history of mankind, dating back to the seventh century, it was never as common as it has become these days, in Nigeria. With unemployment said to be in the extreme high, around 50% among the youth, especially among the educated youth, sophisticated kidnapping has become the order of the day. Children of prominent crème de la crème wealthy Nigerians are now mostly targeted by kidnappers for ransoms.

To make matters worse, petty kidnappers had also joined the fray, robbing and kidnapping Nigerians in the Diaspora who often came home to visit their families and friends. It had gotten so bad that Nigerians who ventured to come home often visited incognito, living in hotels instead of homes, during their visits.

Kidnapping has become so lucrative for the unscrupulous that disgruntled family members now participate in the crime, by kidnapping their own siblings. There was a reported case of a Nigerian woman who had faked her kidnapping to test her husband's love for her, and to get some money from him, in the process. Since abductions and kidnappings were rampant in her area, and since law enforcement agents had largely been ineffective in combating the crime, she had felt safe to fake being kidnapped.

What had made the kidnapping ruse, or crime, if you like, suspicious was the paltry amount involved. The woman had used a trusted accomplice to carry out the crime, in which the sum of N 300,000.00 was demanded. The amount of ransom was what first triggered suspicion that it was the work of someone known to the family. Real kidnappers often demand millions of Naira, never small sums of Naira, as was the case in the crime.

Kidnapping is especially rife in southern Nigeria, in the oil producing Niger Delta area. In the Niger Delta, in the areas mostly controlled by militants, most of the kidnappings were often carried out by the militants who target foreign oil workers, mostly westerners, for ransoms. In the eastern parts, kidnapping was even worse. The crime had become so rife that the rich had their own armed bodyguards.

Kidnapping had become so lucrative that lots of Nigerian youths, both educated and uneducated, see the crime as their only way of getting a fair share of the national cake, and wealth. Most of the wealth from the oil in Nigeria was concentrated in a very few hands, resulting in some Nigerians becoming billionaires in hard currencies, at the expense of the downtrodden Nigerians in the slums of Niger Delta.

The Nigerian youth, or at least some of them, saw kidnapping and armed robberies of the rich as their own payback for the oil money stolen by the rich. Another target of kidnapping in Nigeria, were politicians who were said to be the most unconscionable thieves. Politicians like James Ibori, the former governor of Delta State, who stole and embezzled millions of dollars from his state's coffer, was one of the worst thieves in Nigeria's politics. Most of the money stolen and embezzled by Ibori were said to be slated for infrastructural development, creation of employment for the youth, and payment of workers' salaries.

In case you are wondering about the relevance of armed robberies and kidnappings to terrorism, I will explain. Youth unemployment and redundancy were said to be the engines of terrorism in developing countries. Countries like Nigeria and Yemen are haven for terrorism because of the prevalent poverty in those countries. In Nigeria's situation, the country makes enough money to eradicate poverty and lower youth unemployment. But the saddest situation about Nigeria's oil wealthy was that it was grossly and unevenly distributed, with the wealth mainly concentrated in the hands of a fraction of the population.

That fraction is less than one percent. In 2013, Nigeria fielded two billionaires on Forbes richest, one male, and the other female. For the male, his wealth stemmed from oil and cement. For the female, the bulk of her wealth stemmed from oil, about 99.9%, according to available data about the sources of her wealth.

When the details of such an enormous wealth in the hands of one person are examined, the dichotomy begins to emerge how the main axis of the Nigerian population forks into only two segments of the very rich and the very poor. In Nigeria, there was no middleclass. Economically, one was either very wealthy or very poor. There was no in-between economic class system between the upper class and the lower class. There was no traditional middleclass in Nigeria's socioeconomic structure.

Countries that allow unemployment to go unchecked often run the risks of high crimes. Again, in Nigeria's situation, adults who are employed sometimes do not get their salaries on a timely basis.

Most government departments and agencies perennially owe employee salaries, sometimes for months on end, without payments. Some government employees often go five months without their salaries and wages. Teachers sometimes do not go to classes to teach the students because of lack of payment of salaries. Most states often owe salaries in arrears of six to ten months at a time, making working for government in Nigeria, unenviable.

Though government employees do not get paid on a timely basis, lots of Nigerians still want to get those government jobs, even with the abysmal method of paying salaries. Now, you are beginning to see how terrorism and unemployment are related. A popular proverb states that an idle mind precipitates evil and becomes the devil's haven. An unemployed youth whose means of fulfillment is nonexistent will resort to any means to achieve any modicum of significance.

The successes of one youth in crimes such as kidnapping and armed robberies often lure others to the profession. Successful armed and pen robbers were known to often flaunt their ill-gotten wealth in parties, and in neighborhoods, with palatial buildings and expensive cars, making the business of crime attractive and lucrative.

In terms of terrorism, terrorist recruiters also exploit youth unemployment by providing monetary incentives and bonuses to potential recruits. African youths in Africa, and in the Diaspora, were often drawn to terrorism because of economic opportunities and fulfillments. The risk of death was usually secondary in the quest for economic fulfillment. Religious fulfillment, though said to be the drive that propels youth recruitment by terrorist recruiters, was often not the primary purpose for joining terrorist sects, for African youths. The primary drive and purpose was the search for economic significance and fulfillment.

Al-Shabab was said to be successful in luring Somali youths in the Diaspora because of the poverty that exists among such youths in countries such as the U.S. and Britain. Less than 30% of the reasons why Somali youths join al-Shabab had to do with religion, or Islam, if you like. So, even in advanced countries like Britain and the U.S., unemployment was a catalyst that drives youth involvement in terrorism. A gainfully employed or engaged youth will hardly be persuaded by religious brainwashing to kill himself in the name of Allah or jihad. In the same token, according to a recent poll, an unemployed youth will be likely susceptible to crime and terrorism, for economic and physiological fulfillment.

The same socioeconomic reason is responsible for Nigerian females, both young and the not so young, going overseas to countries like Spain, Italy, and France, for prostitutions due to lack of economic opportunities. I once covered a story where a couple had sold the house the wife inherited from her late father, to travel to Italy for prostitution. The initial plan was for the wife to make enough money from prostitution, then come back and take the husband so that he could be with her.

The wife successfully made it to Italy, and was able to make enough money from prostitution to pay back her sponsor who had helped to smuggle her into Italy. The wife had kept her side of the deal by sending money back home to take care of her husband, and to build a new home. Rather than use the money being sent, to build a house, the husband had started living a lavish lifestyle, wasting the money on young girls. He also bought and rode around in expensive cars, with the money.

During the process of running around with different women, the husband met and fell in love, with a young girl, and married her. Meanwhile, his first wife was still in Italy, working as a prostitute and sending money home. The man spent some of the money on a bride price, and on a wedding. The wife working in Italy, meanwhile kept sending money, thinking the husband was making good use of it, for a new home for them.

After five years of prostitution, the woman felt it was time for her to go back home to her husband. She made arrangements to return home. In the meantime, she did not know that her husband was married to another woman at home, in Nigeria, and living an extravagant lifestyle with her money. On the day she planned to return, she did not tell her husband that she was coming. She had wanted to surprise him.

Upon landing in Nigeria, the woman joyously went to the house address her husband had been using to receive mails and money, thinking that was the new house he had built with her money. She arrived at the house and was surprised that it wasn't as big as she had expected, despite the large sums of money she had sent to her husband over the years.

At the house address, there was no one at home and the flat was locked. Since she did not tell her husband that she was coming, she went to a hotel and rented a room, still hoping to surprise her him, even though disappointment was beginning to set in after seeing the house. She rested at the hotel, and later in the evening, decided to hire a cabbie to take her back to the same address.

Upon arriving back at the flat, she saw that there was a car parked outside the house and felt suspicious. Her husband had not told her he bought a car. Still hoping that things were half as she expected, she went to the door, and knocked, hoping to surprise her husband.

After knocking four to five times, a young mother, holding a baby in her hand, came to the door, with a face towel and breast pump, obviously breastfeeding the child. The woman began to wonder. Still not completely taken aback by the appearance of the young girl with the baby, the woman thought the girl was probably a visiting relative. She did not want to jump to conclusion at the sight of the girl and the baby.

The young wife had never met the wife in Italy and hadn't been told by her husband that he was already married to another woman. The girl greeted the woman at the door sweetly, as the baby in her arm giggled playfully at the woman. The woman smiled back and asked if a man called Okoro lived in that house. The young mother nodded, saying he was her husband and asked who the woman was.

At this time, nervous apprehension had set in, and there was a growing faintness in the woman as she introduced herself. "Really, I didn't know Okoro was married. Anyway, I am his cousin," the older wife said, not wanting to burst the girl's bubble. The young woman embraced the wife, invited her in, and said her husband would soon return home from work.

The older wife sat in a couch, and looked around the living room. She saw marriage photos framed on the wall, and a picture of the baptism of the baby the woman was holding, on the wall, surrounded by a priest, her husband and the young woman. She maintained her cool, and managed to keep a smiling face as she waited for her estranged husband to return.

Thirty minutes later, the husband returned, and was met at

the door by the young wife who quickly told him that he had a visitor. The man did not suspect that the visitor was his wife in Italy. He asked who the visitor was, and was told that it was a distant cousin. The husband nodded, went first to the bedroom, taking the side door, before reemerging in the living room, moments later, with his top agbada taken off, leaving a singlet on.

He came to the living room with smiles, hoping to meet the mysterious cousin. He got as far as the middle of the living room before he suddenly came to an abrupt stop as his face turned ashen. He was shocked beyond words, as he stood there, staring at the woman sitting in the couch, as if he had seen a ghost. He was lost for words. After a full one minute, he recovered and the first word that came to his lip was, "Fidelia!"

She looked at him with hatred in her eyes. "Who is this woman, Okoro? And is this the house you built with all the money I have been sending you?" She asked. The man stammered, lost for words. After a few minutes he said. "I didn't know you were in Nigeria or even coming to Nigeria," he said. Fidelia looked at him with contempt and anger in her eyes. "I didn't know I had to tell you that I was coming so you could hide all of this, and lied to me. I am glad that I didn't call to let you know I was coming.

Is this what you have been doing with all the money I have been sending you? I sold everything to go to Italy to make money for us and this is what you have been doing with my money!" Fidelia cried profusely.

The younger wife stood there, rooted to the spot she had been standing, like a tree, with a look of shock in her eyes. The whole thing was like a bad dream to her, and was as much a surprise to her as it was for Fidelia who was still crying.

After a few minutes the young wife said. "Is this your cousin or your girlfriend, Okoro? I want you to explain what is going on," she said, looking at Okoro. "Madam, this house belongs to my father and my husband is renting it from him. I don't know about a house being built for you, but this is my father's house," the young woman said. "Shut up, Esther!" Okoro said, trying to keep her quiet. But it was too late.

"So, Esther, is this your father's house?" Fidelia asked, and the young woman nodded. "Well, I am not surprised. I have been married to this useless man you call your husband for 10 years. In the past five years, I have been in Italy, working as a prostitute and sending money home to my supposed husband here, which he had obviously been using to live like this," she said, waving her hand around. "But don't worry, he is going to get me my money," she said storming out of the rented flat, and heading towards the taxicab that had brought her from the hotel.

She had wanted to teach her husband a lesson by physically hurting him with the pepper spray she carried in her purse. But she wanted him to suffer in a more profound way. Pepper spray will be too easy for him. Armed mobile police would be a whole lot better than using a simple pepper spray. She wanted revenge and blood. She wanted something lasting that would leave a permanent scar in his body as a memento of his betrayal of her love and trust.

First, he had to pay her back her money, with cash or his life. She did not care if the punishment resulted in death. The wages of his betrayal was death, she told herself. He has betrayed her by stealing her money and betraying her love. He has to pay, one way or the other. She was past caring about taking his life to pay for the betrayal of her love and trust. He has to pay, even if it was the last thing she did.

And he did pay, when one night as he slept with his young wife, five heavily armed police officers entered his rented flat and cut his throat as he slept in bed with his wife. His young wife was also killed, while the child was left unharmed. To make it look like a robbery, several items were taken. The killers had been police officers!

She did not once think about the consequence of taking her estranged husband's life. She reckoned if police officers were used in killing him that it would be perfectly legal and there would be no consequences. And she was right! Somehow, she was right in her assumption.

If he should die in the hands of the police, it would be a legally sanctioned death, as the police in Nigeria were beyond reproach. The police in Nigeria enjoyed enormous impunity. Killing, even if unjustified, often goes unpunished. After all, they were the last bastion of the law, whose authority was never questioned.

In most cases in Nigeria, the police often assist in committing crimes such as armed robberies, bank robberies, and assassinations of political opponents. One of the reasons that crimes had tremendously increased since politics returned in 1999 was because of the lawlessness often perpetrated by police and politicians.

Being a journalist, stationed in Nigeria, to report stories breaking out of sub-Saharan African countries, in West Africa, stories such as political assassinations often interested me as I am sure such stories interested my readers worldwide. The assassination of the Federal Minister of Justice and Attorney General of Nigeria, Bola Ige, was one of such bizarre situations that grabbed my attention the moment it happened in 2001. Such a thing could only happen in Africa.

An Attorney General and Minister of Justice, who had the police guarding his house at all hours of the day and night, being gunned down by assassins while the police were supposedly protecting him, defiles logic, one Nigerian Newspaper's editorial had said. It was odd that police officers guarding the former minster would be withdrawn right before his assassination. Though the complicity of the police was never proven, since it was impossible for the same police to implicate itself, the crime was never solved.

A lot of Nigerian journalists that I had discussed the death of Bola Ige with had implied that terrorism in Nigeria started with political assassinations of political opponents by Nigerian politicians. As politicians hired and trained thugs to carry out assassinations, once the elections were over, the same thugs often resorted to full time crimes such as kidnappings and armed robberies, and in some cases, terrorism.

Most of these thugs were said to have joined Boko Haram, in 2001, when the Islamic jihadist sect was formed. Mohammed Yusuf, the leader who founded Boko Haram, in 2002, was said to have first started his campaign of terror as an assassin, hired by some unscrupulous northern politicians, before he felt confident enough to establish Boko Haram, in northern Nigeria.

Notably, Bola Ige, as the Attorney General of Nigeria and Minister of Justice, had fought against the establishment of Sharia Law in northern Nigeria, right before his death. Bola Ige was assassinated in 2001, at the outset and formation of Boko Haram.

The death of Bola Ige, I once wrote, was the beginning of

lawlessness in Nigeria; which had endured and degenerated into terrorism and militancy in northern Nigeria and in the Niger Delta. With hardly any strong voice against violence, and with the advocates of law and order silenced forever, it didn't take long before anarchy followed. As was once reportedly said by some unscrupulous prominent northern politicians, Nigeria would be ungovernable if the north was not given the mandate to continue to rule Nigeria.

The same logic followed that northern Nigeria had for long been trying to impose Shara Law in northern Nigeria, for which Mohammed Yusuf was a strong advocate of. The same logic followed that Bola Ige was killed, coincidentally at the same time that he had arduously fought against the imposition of Sharia Law in northern Nigeria. The same year Bola Ige was killed, in 2001, was the year the former minister of justice refused the Sokoto State government the permission to execute the judgment of a verdict passed by a Gwadabawa Sharia Court that Safiya Hussaini be stoned to death for adultery.

It is no coincidence that since Bola Ige fought against Sharia Law that northern states were trying to impose in northern Nigeria, that Boko Haram would be formed the same year to fight for the promotion of, and establishment of Sharia Law in Nigeria.

Of course, the death of Bola Ige was blamed on the political squabbles in western Nigeria. Those arrested and accused of assassinating the former Minister had long been acquainted, and the killers, not unexpectedly, had never been brought to justice or found.

Chapter 13

A recent study also showed that young women now join terrorism to fulfill their own economic and physiological significance. Most unemployed young women in Nigeria often engaged in prostitution.

Recently, a boat carrying immigrants, mostly Africans, from Nigeria and Ghana, capsized near the Italian island of Lampedusa, south of Sicily, drowning more than 94 immigrants. These immigrants were traveling to Italy, looking for economic opportunities that did not exist in their countries, when they took the risk of traveling through unsafe waters in an unsafe method of transportation used by human smugglers.

The boat was said to have been carrying more than its legally required number of passengers of over 500 people which included women and children, when fire broke out in the boat's engine. With the boat submerging over 40 meters, only few immigrants escaped being drowned. When all was said and done, over 200 immigrants were never recovered, with over 94 confirmed dead.

Those Africans who risked their lives to seek economic opportunities in Europe did not know that they will be returning home in body bags or end up in the bottom of the ocean.

Despite the growing economic opportunities in Africa, corruption and embezzlement still undermine such economic growths. For years, Lampedusa has been the port of entry for many African immigrants seeking what the authorities called a backdoor entry into many European countries like Italy and Spain. Summer time provided calmer waters, across the Mediterranean Sea, for human smugglers to smuggle thousands of Africans through the dangerous 70 mile journey in small boats to their European destinations. Lampedusa was said to be the easiest backdoor entry for African immigrants, because of the nearness of the port to Malta and Tunisia.

For human traffickers who undertake these dangerous journeys, profits become the motives, with total disregard for the immigrant passengers. But for those poor Africans escaping famine and poverty in their countries, the risk was often well worth it. For them it was either hunger in their countries or death on the road to economic succor. For a lot of them, death at sea was a whole lot better than facing the humiliation of failure in their countries.

In an article I had written and published in a major newspaper in Britain, I had written that the same desperation that drives illegal immigration was also responsible for major crimes and terrorism in Nigeria. For a while, Nigeria had enjoyed an enormous degree of tranquility, with terrorism mainly existing in the Middle East and Asia, like Afghanistan and Pakistan. That changed when, as I said earlier, the civilians were handed over power in 1999.

Chapter 14

I stared at the jihadist, wondering if he had answers to any of the thoughts that had been floating through my mind. I knew he had been fed some liquid diet, which gave him some sort of energy to continue the confession. I figured I had given him enough time to relax and to collect his thoughts.

As I folded the newspaper in my hand, and thought it was time to start rounding up the confession, my small satellite phone, tucked under my armpit, rang. I didn't want to take any calls yet from my editor. I knew he was anxious to know that I was safe since I hadn't reported back to him in almost 24 hours. Not that he cared about my wellbeing. I doubted that he cared if I lived or died during my assignments. The story I was pursuing was more important to him than my life, obviously. In journalism, and as a journalist, you are always on your own. No one really cared about you but you, except maybe, a few colleagues who would mourn and celebrate your death if death should come untimely.

Musa, my guide, came looking for me, obviously wondering if things were going well. He had left the night before, to go home to his family. I did not object to his going home. After all, in these parts, people did not work 24/7, even in emergency situations as they did in the west. With them, there was no overtime. A twelve hour shift was a twelve hour work, no extra pay or anything like that. There was no labor law that was enforceable. Even if there was a labor law, no one obeys it.

Children from the ages of three years of age, hawk foods in the streets of Nigeria, without anyone in authority bothering to question the abuse of the children. In the west, authorities would have questioned or arrested the parents of such children for child abuse. But in a country where lawlessness was the order of the day, and where labor law was hardly enforced, if it even existed, no one cared about the children. Some parents thought it was normal to send their children to the dangerous streets where traffic laws were often not obeyed, where they do existed, to hawk cooked rice, pure water, bread and wares, to supplement their meager incomes.

As far as the parents were concerned, there was nothing wrong with sending their children to the lawless highways to hawk goods. After all, they themselves were abused by their own parents. It was a vicious cycle passed down from generation to generation that had become the norm in these parts.

Sometimes, the authorities and law enforcement agents who should care and know, would patronize the same children, buying banana or soda from them, as they drove on the highway, nonchalantly ignoring the abuse of the children

In most African countries, and in warzones, like Central African Republic, Somalia, Sudan, Niger, Chad, Mali, Algeria and Congo, child soldiers were common. Some African countries recruit children as soldiers. The rebels and insurgents in several of these African countries recruit children from the ages of seven, as soldiers, trained to fight and kill in war zones. At the time some of the children were eleven years old, they were already experienced in killing and fighting, with some of them becoming captains and colonels at the age of thirteen!

In Angola, during the civil war in that country, that lasted 27 years, which started immediately after the country gained its independence from Portugal in 1975, children were the warlords. Child soldiers existed in Angola prior to the country's independence in 1975. Before the civil war, which most Angolans called a decolonization conflict, or the Angolan War of Independence; children assisted in fighting the colonialists in a guerilla war, for independence. After independence, the power struggled that ensued were mostly a war of attrition between two former guerilla warlords of the People's Movement for the Liberation of Angola (MPLA) and the National Union for the Total Independence of Angola (UNITA).

Even the superpowers that took sides in the war did not acknowledge the ubiquitous presence of child soldiers in the ranks and file among the militants. The superpowers used the country's conflicts to fight their own cold war, with the Soviet Union backing the communists, and the United States backing those clamoring for democracy. In between, smaller players like Cuba, joined the fray, trying to establish a foothold in the conflict, while the child soldiers fought in the surrogate battleground and wars.

The MPLA and UNITA had their different grievances as to who had the right to rule the country that was rich in diamond and oil. Though both rebel sects shared a common interest in ending colonial rule, they had their own agenda as to how the country should be ruled. Out of greed and disregard for the children,

children were heavily recruited to fight the war. With the rebels choosing to have socialist-communist leanings, to get international backing, the so-called socialist warlords started branding themselves as Marxist-Leninists, to get the Soviets to arm and fund them.

Other rebels and guerilla warlords called themselves anticommunist freedom fighters, enlisting the backing of the U.S. in the process. But a third lesser known rebel group, National Front for the Liberation of Angola (FNLA), that fought with MPLA and UNITA, during the struggle for independence, would further worsen the post independence struggle, making the war a protracted bloody struggle, that would last two decades.

Also joining the fray was the Front for the Liberation of the Enclave of Cabinda (FLEC) which included disgruntled separatists from the other guerrilla war sects that had fought for the province of Cabinda, during the war, but later became a rebel group, with majority of its foot soldiers becoming child soldiers, strapped with Russian made AK47s and machetes. The colonial masters branded the freedom fighters as terrorists, until the superpower countries began using each side as pawns to fight their cold-war.

In Namibia, and the Republic of Congo, children fought along their peers as child soldiers, raping the women, and ravaging the villages and towns for spoils. In some cases, they chopped off limbs of those who refused to cooperate with them. The war was mostly fought on the basis of greed, avarice, and personality conflicts.

Some of the former child soldiers would later become terrorists in Somalia, joining al-Shabab and becoming part of al-Qaeda in the Maghreb and in Iraq. The exploitation and use of children as soldiers in hostilities in such roles as porters, spies, messengers, lookouts, and foot soldiers, created a tremendous advantage for the group that had the most child soldiers. Al-Shabab had, in recent years, continued with the recruitment of child soldiers in its Islamic jihad.

In Nigeria's Boko Haram, there were also reports of child soldiers but most of the child soldiers in the rank and file of Boko Haram were said to partially meet the requirements of the United Nations Convention on the Rights of the Child, Article 38, of 1989, which stated that parties in conflicts shall take necessary measures to make sure children who have not reached the age of 15 are not allowed to take part in conflicts. The reported child soldiers fighting for Boko Haram, were said to be 15, and under 18 years of age, as stipulated by the United Nations.

It was not that Boko Haram cares about meeting the requirements of the United Nations. I think their preference for children 15 years and above was probably due to religious reasons or for the sake of effectiveness in fighting the holy war of jihad. After all, Boko Haram disdained everything western, which the United Nations mainly embodies.

As I was reflecting upon how terrorism had taken root in Nigeria and across the world, I thought of a recent incident in which members of Boko Haram wore army uniforms and blocked a popular highway in the north, while waiting for motorists, in the wee hours of the morning. When the first vehicle had approached the roadblock, the driver was ordered to stop. Thinking he was obeying a legal roadblock, the driver of the eighteen wheeler truck had stopped, and was ordered out of the truck. His assistant was also ordered out of the truck at gunpoint.

Since Nigerian soldiers and police always point guns indiscriminately at passengers on the highways to force bribes from passengers, it didn't appear odd to the driver and his assistant when the soldiers pointed their guns at them. It was when they were ordered to lie on the ground that they started to think something was very wrong. Nigerian soldiers and police may point guns at you but they would never order you to lie on the ground facedown, unless they were about to shoot. Their fear soon manifested when one of the soldiers shot and killed them. As they lay dying, they realized they were dealing with terrorists. The terrorists dragged their bodies off the road and dumped them in the nearby bush, on the side of the road.

The next vehicle was a commercial bus, carrying about 60 passengers. Since it was dark and no street light, the unsuspecting driver did not know that his life was about to be snuffed as he obeyed the gun wielding terrorists whom he assumed were soldiers. As he approached the roadblock, his headlights picked up the dead bodies of the occupants of the 18-wheeler parked on the side of the road. The passengers in the commercial bus had also seen the dead bodies and had started to scream at the driver not to stop.

But it was too late as the bus driver had slowed down. As the bus driver tried to accelerate to increase speed, the 15 terrorists, armed with AK47s, and hunter knives, started shooting down the tires of the commercial bus, while at the same time shooting the driver and his assistant to death. The terrorists climbed aboard the bus and ordered all the passengers to come down. Like lambs being led to the slaughter, they all climbed down. Some attempted to run and were gunned down while those who did not run had their throats slit and were hacked to death with machetes.

One of the passengers, a pregnant woman, pregnant with triplets, pleaded with the terrorists to allow her to live, at least for the sake of the triplets she was pregnant with. As she pleaded for her life, a female member of the terrorist gang, hacked her head with the axe she had with her, killing the pregnant woman instantly. Somehow, the dying pregnant woman managed to give birth as she lay dying, on the ground. The three female terrorist members of the gang picked up the newborn babies and started caring for them, cutting off the umbilical cord.

Each passenger died either with a bullet wound or with a slit of the throat. It was a gory sight that was beyond the realm of reality. But it was Boko Haram in action, displaying the nature of the type of terrorism that had become the norm in northern Nigeria. In all, when the carnage ended, all 60 passengers in the bus were shot, hacked with axes, knifed or bludgeoned to death. Before he faced his own death, one of the passengers was able to call the Maiduguri-based joint task force that was supposedly enforcing the state of emergency, declared by the government of Jonathan.

In that wee hours of the morning when traders were heading to the markets and motorists were heading to their various destinations, through that popular road in Borno State, deaths visited over 150 passengers riding in cars, trucks, Lorries and buses, on that fateful day. Boko Haram quickly claimed responsibility when the news hit the airwave the next morning. In Nigeria, bad news travel fast.

Despite the state of emergency declared by the government of Jonathan, Boko Haram was able to kill that many people, under the watchful eye of the joint taskforce. It was another humiliation for the taskforce and government that claimed to be winning the war on terrorism.

After listening to the news about the carnage, in my satellite radio, I felt disgusted. It occurred to me that terrorists were winning in Africa because of lack of effective governance. In the west, a terrorist sect could not have operated with so much audacity and frequency as al-Shabab and Boko Haram had been operating in Africa.

In the case of al-Shabab, the terrorist sect controlled most of the country of Somalia, with only a small portion in the hands of the central government that partially controls a fraction of the capital of Mogadishu. As for Boko Haram, they mostly function in the northeast of Nigeria, with only a couple of towns serving as their havens.

In terms of resources, al-Shabab had more soldiers and military hardware than Boko Haram. But in boldness and aggression, both terrorist sects were known to carry out deadly attacks that often astounded law enforcement agents.

Al-Shabab on its part was a known affiliate of al-Qaeda while Boko Haram was said to have a link to al-Qaeda. Most of the members of Boko Haram were trained by Indian and Pakistani terrorists, while al-Shabab's trainers are mainly Chechen terrorists who were said to be as deadly as the members of al-Qaeda, if not deadlier. Chechen terrorists were also said to have links to al-Qaeda even though their methods were fundamentally different from that of al-Qaeda, Boko Haram and al-Shabab.

It was almost four hours later before I could have the opportunity to continue with the confession. Several people from both the Nigerian government and international community had come to check the jihadist and to examine him like a prized object. Somehow, words had gotten out that one of the Islamic extremists had survived, or had been captured alive. I don't know who leaked the information but my guess was that the other media outlets had published the news that the jihadist had survived and was captured.

The fact that the news was out did not bother me. After all, I was getting the scoop and they were getting the small scalps which were being provided by law enforcement agents. To my joy and relief, the jihadist would not talk to anyone. It was as if he was unable to talk whenever other news reporters visited, which pleased me tremendously. Somehow, he must have felt that he was only obligated to me, plus, he probably didn't want to go through another hours of narration and confession.

Whatever reason he had, not to talk to other news reporters was good for me. I wanted the scoop and I guess he felt he could trust me. If he chose to only talk to me out of trust, I can say he had done his homework. He must have known about my reputation, which essentially speaks for itself. I had been the West African bureau chief for my news organization for years, and through the years, I had built an enviable reputation of being a trustworthy reporter.

It had come to my notice that I was well known in Africa, especially in West Africa, which was the focus of my perennial media coverage. A journalist can become trustworthy when he reports fair and balanced news. Fair and balanced reports continued to be the nexus of my news report. I guess it was obvious enough that people in this part of the world appreciated my honest journalism.

Throughout the years, I had always believed in fair and honest journalism. It pays not to take sides, and to be objective, and not be biased. The fact that I was not biased may have been the reasons I was able to survive the West African tough terrain. The West African sub-region had gotten tougher with each passing year as terrorism grew with leaps and bounds. And thankfully, both sides in the conflicts knew that I would provide a fair and accurate coverage. And I did.

The enemies, as both sides liked to call each other, appreciated my fairness. The government had sometimes tried to bully me with their own brand of hard facts, which had always fallen on deaf ears as far as I was concerned. I had often made it clear to each side of a conflict in any warzone that I preferred to gather my own news than be fed with their own version of the truth. The government spokesman had not been happy when I had refused to let him tell me the number of casualties in one very bloody weekend conflict between Nigerian soldiers and Boko Haram.

As a seasoned journalist, I had learned to find good sources that were never biased. The best part of being a good and trustworthy journalist was that good and reliable sources always chased after you. In some cases, the best sources often come from each side of the conflict. In the west, they called such people whistleblowers because of their readiness to divulge secret information to the press, out of conscientiousness.

Every conflict always had a whistleblower that was not completely in agreement with the activities of his organization or country. Those types of whistleblowers were the breads and butters of every good journalist. They were invaluable to news gathering and reporting. They were always the conscionable members of any group who often felt differently than the rest of the group, about the actions of their groups. They were those that will secretly disagree with the aims and objectives of their organizations and will be ready to take their secrets and information to the media.

On the government side of the conflict, we had our sources, which some would call informants; that provided us with reliable information. If casualties occurred on any side and the numbers were exaggerated, the conscientious ones would always be the ones to provide us with the real number of casualties. Parties in conflicts often inflated casualty figures for reasons best known to them.

In the U.S., Edward Snowden and Bradley (now Chelsea) Manning represented such conscientious types that will take personal risks to voice out their feelings when faced with situations that they were unable to cope with. While the U.S. government may call such actions treasonable offences, and betrayal of sworn trusts, the whistleblowers often saw their actions differently, as patriotic rather than as traitors and treasonable offenses.

Musa, my guide, for some weird reason, started to really show an uncanny respect for me that I could see in his eyes. I used the word uncanny because it seemed odd, eerie and mysterious that he would even respect my style of journalism, considering I had on two occasions disagreed to follow his instructions on issues he had pointed out to me. You are probably wondering why a guide would be giving me an instruction but when you are dealing with a guide who had been assigned to you by your own embassy, who for all intent and purposes may be a spy, you begin to get the picture.

In a foreign hostile territory, a guide can be invaluable to your personal safety. They know the area very well, or claim to know the area. In my case, I was always given a guide as a form of protection by the embassies in the host countries where I often covered stories. As journalists we often had to register with the embassy when we travelled to foreign countries, and in hostile countries, the embassies always assigned guides to us. Though using such guides was optional, my media organization always insisted I go along with the embassies in order to be guaranteed protection, or in case of an emergency.

In the case of my guide in Nigeria, Musa, I had an instinctive dislike for his arrogance and ways, especially when he pretended to be a normal guide when it was obvious he was more than a guide. I knew people like Musa. Every embassy had a Musa. They often try everything to hide who they really are. Being a seasoned journalist that I am, it was very difficult for anyone to deceive me. It is not that I am saying Musa tried to deceive me.

My fear about Musa was that he was working for both the embassy and Boko Haram. I wasn't sure and wasn't about to find out. Since I did not take sides in conflicts I was not particularly concerned which sides he was sympathetic with. My first and foremost concerns were my safety and wellbeing. For all I cared, he might as well be the devil as long as he wasn't there to hurt me. Don't think for one second that I was not patriotic. I was, but my safety came before patriotism. Unlike most people, I did not put country first. I put my safety and wellbeing first, before the needs of my country. I guess you could call that selfish, but I saw it differently.

After I had made sure Musa was out of sight, and had wandered away from where I stood. I continued the question I had had in mind before the sudden appearance of Musa, on my side. If he was trying to eavesdrop on the discussion I was having with the jihadist, he wasn't doing a good job of it, as he was always walking around, as if he was restless. The night before, he had gone home to his family, leaving me, and a few of the soldiers there, in the bungalow. The CIA commander was there of course. Like me, the CIA commander had no need to go home, as he was far from home like I was.

In a sense we shared a commonality, which was that we were globetrotters. In my nature of work as a journalist, globetrotting came with the territory. On his part as a CIA operative, I was sure traveling also came with his job. Being a globetrotter turned me into a citizen of the world without any direct allegiance to any particular country, including my country of origin. Though I was largely a westerner, I never wore my superior race on my sleeve. Like I said earlier, when in Rome, one behaves as a Roman, if you know what I mean.

When I was in Nigeria, a place I was at very frequently because of my base there as a bureau chief, I often acted as a Nigerian. I did not try to make myself conspicuous for obvious reasons. Though I have Caucasian features, I always did everything I could to hide that fact. Like I mentioned earlier, in these days in Nigeria, it was not safe to be seen as a westerner because of the presence of terrorism in that country. I remember when it was fun to work around in shorts and visit the beach and other interesting places like upscale shopping centers and restaurants. But those luxuries are too dangerous now to indulge in, since Boko Haram and Ansaru took residence in the country.

Don't get me wrong, I still found a way to enjoy myself. I was not talking about sleeping with the local girls. I tried as much as possible to stay away from that habit. Most westerners, especially those in the oilfield, often slept around with the local girls. Not me. I couldn't afford to risk getting killed. No, the girls did not kill. I am talking about diseases like sexually transmitted diseases like HIV or Aids. Majority of the girls in Africa did not believe in the use of condoms. A lot of them did not believe that there was Aids, or that aids kills.

The current president of South Africa, Jacob Zuma, was once quoted saying he did not believe in the existence of aids. To prove his point, he was said to have slept with a woman with aids or HIV. As to whether he contracted aids or HIV, I do not know. Another thing was that I never did verify the truthfulness of that story. But lots of respectable newspapers published the story, but as always the case with me, I never touched the story. I did not want to ruffle any feather or be part of a conspiracy that tarnished the image of someone as important as Jacob Zuma. It was not that I was scared, no. Far be it from me, I was never afraid of anyone. But yellow journalism was not part of my calling.

If something could not be independently verified, I did not pursue it. I hated hearsays or third party rumor-mills. I liked to do my own investigations. But news about the then vice president of South Africa sleeping with someone with aids was hardly a newsworthy report that my editor would approve of. It was not particularly an interesting story. I was sure it would be more of an entertainment story for those media in the entertainment business. My business was to inform, not mislead. So I made it my job to stay away from any slander or libelous hearsays.

Journalism can be practiced safely if one chooses to. In my over two decades in journalism, I had never been sued or be party to a libel. I stayed away from controversial issues that had no foundation of truth. Now, if it was of international scope and could be verified, I wouldn't hesitate to go after the story. I did not chase fiction, or false stories, if you like. I had a natural ability to smell fiction when I saw one.

The same reason I did not chase falsity was the reason I did not chase fictitious news or what some would like to call disinformation. False information that some government agencies or military establishments would deliberately and covertly spread to influence public opinion or hide the truth, was not part of my type of journalism. I knew when I was being fed nonsense. That goes for both parties in a conflict, not just the government. I guess that was why I did not take sides.

Chapter 15

I had given the jihadist enough time to rest while I fact-checked some stories that I had been working on, prior to my encounter with the jihadist. I had also taken the opportunity to read about the stories I may have missed while I had been with the jihadist. In my business, I had to keep my ears and eyes opened and also stay informed about current affairs as they unfolded around the world.

Sometimes, I would call my sources around the world to see if anything had been going on that I missed, while I was sleeping or on an assignment. Some of my sources would call me if there was something newsworthy but I often called them before they had the chance to call me. It pays to stay on top of things. And by calling them as often and as regularly as I did, they felt empowered to be more resourceful. Some sources were like paparazzi because of the aggressive manner they pursued newsworthy stories that they knew would interest a reporter. Don't get me wrong, these sources were not paparazzi. They had the same aggressive attitude towards news gathering as paparazzi towards celebrities, for photographs.

These sources work for several media houses but over the years, I had managed to cultivate honesty and trust among my sources that made some of them very loyal to me. Some journalists were known to rip-off their sources by failing to pay them or even denying that they had received any newsworthy information. Just like in real life where you have unscrupulous individuals, so it was in journalism. There were a few unscrupulous journalists amongst us, and because of their attitudes toward their sources, they made my job much easier. Sounds ironic? You bet!

They made my job easier because of their unscrupulousness. When a journalist creates a bad reputation for cheating his sources, those journalists that did not cheat their sources become invaluable to those sources because they knew such journalists were reliable and would pay them. So, in my profession it pays to be honest and diligent in the pursuit of news. Sometimes, I didn't even have to worry where the next story would come from. My reliable sources often made sure that my well of stories never ran dry.

So, after I had reflected and cross-examined several stories I had been working on, and some that had escaped my notice since I devoted a great deal of my time to the confession of the jihadist, I decided to once again go back to the confession. Like I said earlier, time was running out for the jihadist. With each passing hour, he was getting weaker. His condition would sometimes look good, and other times would look bad. By the look of the only nurse taking care of him, I knew he wouldn't last long.

I reckoned I still had a few hours with him before he gave up the ghost. I hastened up whatever I had been reflecting on, to fully concentrate on him. He must have sensed my urgency because of the way he looked at me. I could tell he had read my mind when he smiled that hideous smile that had become part of his persona. There was no doubting the fact that the jihadist was an intelligent man, in an uncanny way. He could almost read my intentions, and sometimes my mind, before I even got a chance to open my mouth to say something. He was very good at it. As much as he surprised me with some certain things that he said before I had the chance to utter them, I had refused to acknowledge that he was good.

Like I said earlier, I had a grudging respect for the jihadist. He was intelligent but he was also an unconscionable killer, who killed without remorse or feeling. A cold-hearted killer will hardly be someone that would win my admiration, no matter how intelligent or insightful he was.

My face had remained stoic and deadpan throughout my encounter with the jihadist. Over the years, I had become the master of deadpan in collecting news and monitoring both my sources and my interviewees. Being deadpan during my news gathering gave me a perception of seriousness, which also made me appear professional. I guess you could say every journalist that was worth some salt was a master of deadpan or disguise. Like most professionals who make a living conducting serious businesses, journalists often had to put up an appearance or demeanor of deadpan in order to be taken serious.

I once interviewed a guerrilla warlord who was wanted by Interpol and law enforcement agents, and bounty-hunters around the world. A heavy bounty of $5million was placed on the head of the guerrilla warlord, which made him a target of even his own men. He could not trust anyone, not even the people around him. But he trusted me to grant me an interview. Matter of fact, he sought the interview.

One night I had come to my hotel room, late in the evening

and was tired after a long day in the streets, covering a story about an attempted coup d'etat of an unpopular military government. Somehow the news about the coup had leaked before it could be carried out. The military head of state and the military supreme council had summarily sentenced the coup planners to death by execution. The coup planners had been tied to stakes and prepared for execution. As was often the case with the military junta, the media was invited to witness the execution. I was one of those invited. I had stayed on the execution ground, interviewing the coup planners before their executions. Some of them were remorseful while some were unrepentant. One in particular was swearing at the head of state and military council, saying their days were numbered, that the people were fed up with their corruption and crookedness.

I had entered my room, tired and ready to hit the sack, when as I sauntered toward the light switch I heard a voice. "I wouldn't do that if I were you," the voice said with enough menace to send a chill down my spine. I quickly spun around towards the direction of the voice but in the semidarkness I could see the muzzle of the sub-nose of a semiautomatic that was pointing at me. I remained frozen to the spot. I know I had not offended anyone. But in journalism you never know. But as I inwardly said my last prayer, I realized that the man was not there to kill me. If he wanted to kill me he would have done so the moment I entered the room. He was there to talk and probably didn't want me to scream before he had a chance to talk.

"There is a story that I want you to get to the public and you are the only one I can trust," he said unapologetically. "You are right, I am not here to hurt you but I cannot take chances either," he said as if reading my mind. I relaxed, and waited for him to tell me what he wanted printed or aired. "I have some information complete with account numbers about the head of state and some members of his military council that I will like to get published. I have heard so much about you that I felt I could trust you," he said.

As a rule, I did not publish information that would hurt anyone if it was not verified. I told him so. He nodded, and I could see the outline of his head in the dark as he said the information was verifiable. He told me to verify the information, that he was telling the truth. At this time he had lowered his gun and had put the gun on his lap. I was not worried about the gun. Guns had been pointed at me before, and as a veteran of war, guns do not faze me easily. Once a soldier, one always remains a soldier, and soldiers were trained to accept death as inevitable at any time. That training was forever.

"From time to time, I will be giving you information that is verifiable. I know your reputation. I am not here to make you go against how you practice your profession. The information I will be giving you will be verifiable information but you cannot use my name as your source," he told me. I told him that as a rule I did not use the names of my sources in my stories. All my sources were always anonymous, I told him, as I took a couple of wrinkled folders from him.

He was satisfied with my answer, or appears to be. He got up, shook my hand and apologized for the inconvenience he had caused me. I told him I will take that kind of inconvenience any time, if it was going to benefit my media organization. He smiled, and I could see his gleaming white teeth in the dark. He seemed pleased with my answer.

As he left my room, I wanted to ask how he managed to get in the room when I had the key. I knew better to ask him such an absurd question. Men like the guerrilla warlord had a way with everything. After all, the man had managed to evade law enforcement agents across the world for decades. Stories abound that he goes around in the open, wearing different disguises. I wouldn't doubt that either.

Though I did not get to see the face of the guerrilla warlord, I had seen his pictures in different news outlets across the world. His was said to be the most wanted warlord in the world. The CIA and Mossad were said to have put a heavy bounty on his head. Even with all that bounty, no one had come forward, and he still continues to remain elusive.

There were reports that he uses black magic that gives him supernatural power over natural forces. There were rumors that he performs magic rites and incantations that gave him extraordinary power and influence, which allowed him to move around unnoticed, and resist bullets. The supernatural power also gave him the power of disappearance and the ability to cast spells and produce illusions by the sleight of his hand.

Witchdoctors and native healers were also said to be part of his guerilla army. There was a legend that he was once surrounded by a battalion of soldiers with artilleries, in the wee hours of the morning, and as they made an attempt to capture him, he disappeared right before their eyes. Another legend was that one of his soldiers had tried to behead him with an axe but as the soldier raised the axe to behead him, an invisible hand reached out and turned the axe on the soldier, beheading the soldier instead.

One particularly interesting legend about him was when he had entered a military base and singlehandedly killed a battalion of soldiers. It was said that the soldiers were shooting at him but that the bullets were bouncing and ricocheting off his body. Those who claimed to have seen him said he wears a magic charm around his neck that was prepared with human blood and flesh, with a human eye on the pendant.

I remember from a long time ago, how a villager had said on television that he had been face to face with the guerrilla warlord. The villager had said the warlord had bewitched and held him spellbound that he could not scream or say anything until the guerrilla warlord had magically disappeared, taking his crops with him. Among his many abilities included the power to charm, enchant and influence people with magic.

It was also said that he charms beautiful women that he fancies, to magically appear in his hideout, for sex. After having sex with any woman he chooses, rumor had it that he would often use charm to erase the memory of such encounters from the minds of the women, creating in them a sense of illusion and delusion.

Among his many sources of power included voodoo, sorcery, necromancy, witchcraft, devilry, diablerie, ensorcellment, bewitchment, conjuration, mojo, thaumaturgy, and natural herbs. These supernatural forces were also said to be part of the disguise that allowed him to change into any human form, sometimes as a beautiful woman.

One legend had it that he changed into a beautiful woman and then lured a military officer by magically appearing at the hotel the officer in charge of his case had lodged. He had enchanted the officer with magic and supernatural power, that the colonel became seduced. As the colonel took the beautiful woman to his room to have sex with her, he was stabbed in his heart. Before the colonel's men could understand what had happened, the beautiful woman was gone, as were the colonel's weapons. There were other legends but most of them were absurd.

After the guerrilla warlord had left, I could not sleep for the rest of the night. It was not that I was scared or anything, I was not. I was intrigued. Since it was morning in some European countries where I needed to verify the various account numbers the warlord gave me, I went straight to work. But it wasn't easy. At that time, Swiss authorities were not cooperating with Interpol and giving out names of their account holders. I had to contact a friend of a friend, who was very influential with Swiss bankers, to confirm and verify the accounts.

Every tip that the guerrilla warlord gave me was authentic and verified. I was impressed. The very next day I had sent the information to my editor who had also verified the information all over again to make sure I did not make a mistake. It wasn't that my editor did not trust me or anything like that. It was just the way we practiced journalism. It had nothing to do with trust. It was just fair and balanced journalism in action.

When the account numbers and the huge sums of money in them were published, three days later, a coup took place, overthrowing the military junta and president. Don't ask me how that was possible. Most military leaders often conducted a rigged election to reelect themselves to power soon after seizing power, to legitimize their government. And those who had stolen the money and whose accounts were published were sentenced to death by the new military supreme council, and executed. The cycle of viciousness had ensued, after my story.

I remember that I had felt guilty for months as I blamed myself for their deaths. It took time for me to convince myself that the men were crooks and murderers but I still couldn't justify the fact that they deserved to die. I knew they deserved to be punished but to me, death was too extreme. But then again, I had reminded myself that this was Africa, where human life had little value.

The guerilla warlord had been allegedly responsible for lots of kidnappings and drug trafficking in Africa, for a long time. A few of his men who had been captured by authorities had given unconfirmed information regarding some of the activities of the warlord. Some of that information included the fact that the warlord uses diabolical means to carry out crimes that he perpetrates, that it will be impossible for the authorities to apprehend him.

In the last few years, the warlord was said to have been responsible for the kidnappings of foreign oil workers in Nigeria, and in the West African sub-region which included Cameroun, Nigeria, and Ghana, among many other countries in the sub-region. He had also been, allegedly, involved in other criminal activities, according to unconfirmed rumor, such as oil bunkering, and piracies.

Though he had not been directly linked to terrorism such as the type of terrorism that Boko Haram and Ansaru were known to carry out in Nigeria, the warlord had been involved in a different kind of terrorism. One of such terrorism included the chopping off of the heads and limbs of those who had betrayed him, making the victims who did not get beheaded cook and eat their own limbs as a lesson to those who may want to betray him in the future.

Recently, four American oil workers, working in the Niger Delta region of Nigeria had been kidnapped by the warlord's men, who had mysteriously appeared in the rig that those four Americans had been working. Out of the 20 foreign oil workers in the rig, the kidnappers had specifically picked out those who were American citizens. The reason behind picking out only Americans to be kidnapped had not been given, but local law enforcement agents figured it might have had something to do with the recent U.S. bounty of $20million on the head of the warlord for his suspected involvement in another kidnapping of an American citizen who was later released after a bounty of $1million had been paid by the oil company.

Several bounties had been placed on the head of the warlord, including the EU's $5million, and the U.S.'s bounty of $5million, and lately $20million. Despite all of that, there was a growing fear that the warlord might stage his own fake capture to collect the money as he had done in the past with a lookalike scapegoat.

A few years ago, the warlord had used a lookalike to pose as himself including making sure that the man had the same tribal marks on his face. The man had been dressed in the same military uniform that the warlord was accustomed to wearing, and with a few additional disguise, he had had one of his men fake the capture, which had been handed over to the Nigerian authorities. The international and local law enforcement agencies had congratulated themselves for the capture of the wanted warlord, and had paid the bounty of $5million dollars, which had gone directly to the coffers of the warlord, unbeknownst to the authorities that the person captured was a perfect lookalike.

Since a DNA could not be done to ascertain the authenticity of the captured warlord, it took a long time before it was discovered that the authorities had been fooled. At the time they had found out, the money had been paid, with an April fool publication of the ruse. For months, the fake kidnapping had made the rounds of talk show hosts in the U.S. and other countries. It was embarrassing that a country as advanced, and as sophisticated as the U.S. could be fooled with such a ruse. Newspapers and online editorials had made mockeries of the foolery to no end. After that incident, a new foolproof method had been devised to verify the capture of future fugitives to make sure the same mistake was not repeated.

For a while, following the incident of the fake capture, years later the death of Osama Bin Laden had been doubted as another ruse. Many people doubted that a man as elusive as the al-Qaeda chief could be easily captured as reported by the media. If the same Navy Seal that purportedly captured and killed the al-Qaeda leader could not capture a less sophisticated al-Shabab leader in the Somali town of Baraawe, how was it possible for a well organized al-Qaeda founder and leader to be captured? To add to the doubts, since the body of Bin Laden was not publicized, the belief was that the al-Qaeda leader was still alive somewhere in the caves of Tora Bora. It didn't matter that Bin Laden's death occurred long before the attempted capture of the Somali warlord in Baraawe. The doubts still lingered.

Though other al-Qaeda members and leaders in the Maghreb and in the Arabian Peninsula had confirmed the death of their leader, skeptics still had their doubts that it was really Bin Laden that had been captured. After botching the supposed capture of the Somali warlord in Baraawe, that was widely publicized, skeptics remained doubtful.

I remember covering a meeting of the Free Syrian Army and the Syrian Government, in a border town between Turkey and Syria, where a man who boldly identified himself as a member of al-Qaeda boastfully told me that Bin Laden was alive and well, that the infidels in the west could never touch him. This was months after the capture and death of Bin Laden. I was not totally naïve to the game. I knew it was probably a propaganda plot by al-Qaeda to create confusion and doubts. It was probably concocted by al-Qaeda, knowing I was a reporter, thinking I would report the comment. But I did not report the comment since there was no way to confirm whether he was telling the truth or not.

As I said earlier, I knew how terrorists operated. I had been covering terrorist activities for decades, going back to the October 23, 1983 suicide bombing of over 299 Americans and French servicemen during the Lebanese Civil War when two trucks loaded with bombs had struck the buildings housing the U.S. and French military personnel who were members of the multinational forces (MNF) in Lebanon. A terrorist group called Islamic Jihad had claimed the responsibility for the carnage.

The death toll had been appalling as it had included 241 American military personnel which comprised 220 marines, 18 sailors and three soldiers. Over 128 Americans were also wounded in the blast. Thirteen of those wounded military personnel later died from their injuries. I also remember reporting that the explosives used in the attack were the equivalent of 9525kg or 21,000 pounds of TNT.

Islamic Jihad was, at that time, said to be the brainchild of Hezbollah but that was never confirmed, even though I had mentioned it in my coverage. I also remember writing that it was an unverified implication of Hezbollah as the sponsor of the barely known Islamic Jihad, which had just started its terrorist operation in the area, at the time.

Years later, it would be rumored that Osama Bin Laden had been a member of the Islamic Jihad, though this was never fully verified and confirmed. I have had doubts about the link between al-Qaeda and the Islamic Jihad because the latter was known to be active only in Lebanon where they operated along the Syrian and Turkish borders.

Chapter 16

The Jihadist felt abandoned and I could tell by his demeanor that he thought I was through with him. He was wrong about that. I had been waiting for him to recuperate from whatever was bothering and ailing him that made him seemed weak. But looking at him from the corner of my eyes and seeing the way he was looking at me strangely, as if bewildered, it had occurred to me that he was confused about my inaction towards him. I had given him a break but it looked as if he didn't want a break. He was anxious to get the confession over with. My distraction seemed to have bothered him a great deal.

Having sensed his mindset about my behavior, if you want to call it that, I decided to talk to him. "Is something wrong, sir, are you alright?" He smiled weakly, in a condescending way that almost made me feel as if I was being patronized. I ignored the obvious and let him have his way. "I am fine. I was just wondering about you because you appeared to have been gone, even though you were here," he said.

I knew what he meant. I had been thinking about things unrelated to the confession, including reviewing certain cases that I had covered. I had also been reflecting on some of the news report that I had read in some Nigerian newspapers. Since I had been preoccupied with covering the confession and taking notes from the jihadist, several events had been unfolding in the world. As a journalist, it was always my business to know what was happening around me, and around the world.

I hated to be behind on current affairs and events. And to make sure I did not miss anything, I stayed on top of things, including checking on my daily news alerts, and reading every piece of information and news that I could put my hands on. I generally started my day around 5am, by first reading the e-news on my tablets, before getting on my computer to read the news headlines from the Economist, New York Times, Chicago Tribune, London Mail, HuffPost, The Observer, CNN, and occasionally FOX news and al-Jazeera in English.

"As part of my confession, I want to tell you about the quest," he said pompously, as if the quest was something sacred. I was wondering what type of quest he was referring to. I was aware of a few quests and I didn't think he was thinking of the type of quest that I knew of. Of all the quests known to mankind, the most important and elusive was still the quest for the Holy Grail. But I didn't think he was referring to the proverbial quest which was as mysterious as its sacredness.

There was the chivalrous quest which goes back to medieval times that involved an enterprising and adventurous journey. But I didn't think he was referring to that either. But there was a part of Islam that involved a religious journey but then again that involved a long fasting period and observance of the five pillars. I didn't think that was what he had in mind either. I did a quick soul searching to second guess him, to make sure I understood him.

There was the quest of inquiry that people who leaned towards curiosity seek for answers about knowledge; but I also didn't think he was referring to that either. If he wasn't talking about a quest for the Holy Grail, then what could he be referring to? I wondered. I did what I normally do when I wanted clarification or answers to some troubling issues.

When he waited for me to say something and I didn't, he decided to go on with his explanation of what he meant by the quest he was referring to. "In Islam, we have what we Muslims of Sunni leaning called the quest for religious purity. The quest for religious purity includes first purging oneself of any impurities, before going on the quest for the salvation or rescue from the sins or impurities of life.

To a lot of people, Sharia Law limits the freedom of its adherents but that is not true. Sharia Law redefines the way its adherents should live their lives. It is for such a quest for purity that Muslims make the pilgrimage to Mecca during the Hajj period in the twelfth Muslim lunar month of Dhu al-Hijjah. As the birthplace of Prophet Muhammad and the site of Muhammad's first revelation of the existence of the Quran, in a cave, Mecca is considered the holiest city in the religion of Islam, that every Muslim must make a pilgrimage to, for the obligatory Hajj.

Don't get me wrong, the quest is not about making the pilgrimage to Mecca for Hajji, it is far deeper than that. Like I said, the quest is purging oneself of impurities. The process of such purging includes freeing oneself from moral and ceremonial defilement. It is like a medicine that purges toxins from the body. When a person has succeeded in purging himself by removing the undesirable and treacherous elements that causes that person to be disloyal to Islam, then that person is considered purged.

But the process goes a whole lot deeper, far deeper than I can possibly explain. Once the quest is completed, the person undergoing the purge receives an invisible hand, just a hand, in a vision that anoints the head of the purged, as part of the confirmation of a completed quest. That hand, my friend, is the hand of Allah. And for any Muslim to be pure enough to be honored by the visit of the invisible hand, that Muslim must have undergone the redefined journey of the purged.

Only a very few Muslims have accomplished the quest in their lifetimes. And there is something else that you must know. It is not every Muslim that is chosen to seek the quest. To be chosen, you must strive towards satisfying the five requirements of becoming pure, which itself is not easy. Those requirements include first becoming a soldier of Allah by being anointed by an imam who has not been tainted by sins or impurities. I said that because some imams have been known to backslide from their anointment as the prayer leader of the mosque. Remember, that an imam is a divinely appointed prayer leader who is expected to be sinless, infallible and a representative of Prophet Muhammad.

Some imams have been known to become sinners and backsliders and upon those imams be the curse of Allah, as they have been known to mislead many Muslims. Now, you can begin to see why the quest can be a difficult journey. The reason is because it is hard to find an infallible and sinless imam. Just like fake prophets in the Christian religion, so it is with Islam, regarding fake imams. For those imams that have fallen from their temporal leadership positions, any Muslim they touch becomes corrupted with sins.

The reason I am explaining this to you is for you to know the origin of radicalism in Islam. A lot of people, alas, including me, had been misled by the radicalism of a backslide imam who, rather than purify me, made me more impure than I had been before my quest.

I was lucky enough, or I thought I was, to have recognized my impurity early enough. Or it could be I never got started or even knew if I was in the right direction because of the misdirection I got early on, in my search for enlightenment in Islam.

Enlightenment and the quest, go hand in hand, as both are intertwined. To seek the quest is to seek enlightenment in Islam, and that enlightenment is part and parcel of purity of the soul and mind.

Regarding the anointment that I mentioned earlier, a true imam is divinely anointed with a holy oil from a sacred bowl that is administered as part of a religious consecration, in Islam. Once an imam is anointed, and he is divinely purified, he is then gifted with the power of foresight and healing. Like a true prophet or holy man, an anointed imam is able to lead the way of purity for a Muslim willing to go for the quest.

For years I have been searching, and my search for the right quest had led me from one mosque to another. I received several instructions from several imams in different mosques. I watched videos and movies of jihadists before me and how they supposedly achieved the quest, and were able to peacefully make their way to paradise. Along the way, I may have missed the point of the quest, because as you can see, my friend, I did not achieve the quest, despite all my efforts," the jihadist said, with sadness in his eyes.

As the jihadist rested for a while after his long speech, I started to think. Perhaps, I told myself, I have just discovered the root cause of radicalism in Islam. If there were impure and pure imams, it means the impure imams were the ones brainwashing their flocks with radicalism, while the pure ones were the ones preaching peaceful religious worship in Islam. I was not sure if my understanding was correct. I felt the need for further clarification about this quest. So I waited for him to continue. It didn't take long before he continued. He started from where he had stopped, like a man with a renewed vigor, on a mission to finish what he had started.

"The truth, if you must know, is that the quest is, like I said earlier, searching for the Holy Grail. It is very difficult to achieve the quest in Islam. Finding a pure and an infallible imam is like looking for the Holy Grail itself. Most imams claim to be infallible, but the proof, like they say, is in the pudding," he said, almost breathlessly.

I was a little bit confused by his words. I couldn't understand him when he said the "proof is in the pudding." I thought of asking him to explain the comparison between the proof being in the pudding and the quest in Islam. After thinking about it for a while, I gave up the idea of asking him. It was not necessary, I told myself. There were other issues I would like to ask him, but the 'proof-in-the-pudding,' wasn't one of them.

The quest for the Holy Grail has been interpreted to mean so many things by scholars, but the comparison of the quest in Islam to the Holy Grail, was in my mind, most extreme. The Holy Grail, as I understood it, was more mysterious and sacred than the quest in Islam.

To a lot of people, the Holy Grail was some kind of cup that was an integral part of the Arthurian mythology. In the Arthurian narration, the Holy Grail was said to be a mystical myth, akin to the earthly Golden Fleece, in a dragon-guarded grove that was said to have been recovered by the Argonauts. The difference was that, the mysticism surrounding the Holy Grail was buried in a myth that dates back to the unfinished romance of Chretien de Troyes.

The Chretien's story and interpretations of the 12th and 13th centuries mysticism, and Wolfram von Eschenbach's contribution to the mysticism of the Grail as a supposedly precious stone that fell from the sky, was another version of the myth that was still unfathomable, even to this day.

In essence, the interpretation of the Grail as a legend has transcended time and tide, and somewhat interwoven with the legends of the Holy Chalice, which was used as a vessel to serve wine in the Last Supper. But the interpretation of the Grail goes deeper, unlike the quest in Islam. There was the other myth involving the Joseph of Arimathea. The myth continues with the last Supper and the crucifixion of Christ.

In the case of Joseph of Arimathea and his receiving the Grail from the apparition of Jesus, and the Arthurian connection, the mysticism becomes even more mystifying. The Holy Communion, which is said to be a representative of Christ's blood and body, is said to also have some significance and connection to the Holy Grail, as the Grail was said to have been used to preserve the blood of Christ in England. The cauldron, also known as the vessel or the Grail, was said to have some divine power of healing.

My understanding of the Holy Grail ends in England where the Arthurian Legend originated. The trail of the Grail also died in England, depending on the interpreter. But on the question of the quest in Islam, as carefully explained by the Jihadist, I could not find the link between the Holy Grail and the quest in Islam, which was simply a search for spirituality in Islam.

"Let me shed some more light on the subject," the jihadist continued, as if reading my mind as he had always done. I remained quiet and waited for him to continue. I was too confused to even argue. Even though I had never argued with him, nor had the desire to do so. Like I said earlier, I was there to listen and record the confession, not to judge or argue with him. Occasionally though, I would analyze what he had told me in the interim of his rest.

"In case you are still confused about the quest, I will give you an example of a typical quest in Islam. When you hear about some American citizens joining al-Shabab, the reason those young Americans join the jihadist sect is for the quest, based on what they had heard in the mosques back home in the U.S. They had been told about the wonderful paradise that awaits the faithful, and felt obligated to search the path to the mystical paradise.

Sometimes, in their search for the pathway to paradise, which is the quest, they join the only known point of entry, which is the society of fellow seekers. Those fellow seekers are the foot soldiers in Islam, who fight daily to protect the religion of Islam. The infidels are always against Muslims because of their fear that Islam would dominate the world as the most visible and dominant religion. It is their fear that is driving their persecution of Muslims around the world.

To earn the quest, most imams often tell their flocks that they have to first fight the holy war to protect the religion of Islam, for Allah to approve their quests. We believe everything that imams say to us. We have no reason to doubt the words from their mouths because of their divine association with Allah and Prophet Muhammad. Like Prophets in the bible, imams can also be real and unreal. I used the word 'unreal' loosely, in the context of those imams lacking any element of reality, substance, credibility, genuineness and originality in Islam. In other words, the word fake, describes those imams.

The reason those imams may be fake is because some of them may be self-appointed, without Allah's anointment and blessing. If an imam is anointed and blessed, the chances of that imam misleading anyone in the name of Allah becomes very slim. The quest has to follow the direction and instructions of the imam. Achieving the quest will depend on whether the person was lucky enough to have associated with a genuine imam," he said, with that faraway look on his face as if he was listening to an inner voice.

I was tempted to ask him if he had received his instructions from a genuine imam or whether he was on the right path to achieving the quest. Since he was in the throes of death, I also wanted to ask if he succeeded in his quest to achieve paradise. I almost answered my own question, knowing that he had earlier answered the question. I wanted more explanation that wasn't forthcoming but I figured it was worth trying to ask. If he had succeeded, he wouldn't have had the need for the confession. But then again, this may not be a confession at all. It may be part of the propaganda to leave a lasting legacy about the success of his quest.

I didn't know. And because I didn't know, I kept quiet. I figured it would be safe for me to find out the answers to my unasked questions on my own. Sometimes, I had learned, you can almost decipher facts on your own. It may take time, but when you think harder about the matter, the answers always come rushing to you, as it had happened to me on countless occasions.

"If it is true that achieving the quest can be a daunting task, how come a lot of people still embark on it?" I asked, trying to figure out the reason people try at all if they were not sure if the quest was right or wrong or even achievable. I wasn't surprised when he answered in a condescending manner that gave me the impression that he saw me as an infidel.

It was not that I cared how he saw me. His answers came flowing like cascading streams of water. "A lot of people do things because they believe in it. For instance a peanut hawker will hawk peanuts because he believes people will buy it, and that he will make enough money to pay back those he owed for the peanuts, or make a profit to meet his basic needs. In the same token, a trader goes to the market to buy goods, hoping that customers will come and buy those goods. If the aforementioned people have enough faith to believe that their actions will produce a result, why then should I worry about the rightness or wrongness of my quest. I guess what it all boils down to is faith and belief.

If a man believes in what he does, he will worry less about

results and work harder to achieve the objective of his mission. In the same token, when a person gets behind the wheel of a car, it is always with the faith that the car will crank up and get him to his destination without any obstacle," he said, without mincing or sugarcoating words.

I saw immediately that I was not getting anywhere with trying to lure him into more discussions about the quest, so I decided it was time to get him to confess to another issue that might be of interest and intrigue. As always, like a psychic whose lots rest in his craft, he came out with it in a torrent.

"Concerning rituals and using human sacrifice, is it true that jihadists often use their victims' blood for sacrifice?" I asked, half expecting him to be angry about the question. I had used the question to lure him into discussing the matter of rituals and human blood among Islamic radicals and extremists.

"Jihadists believe only in Allah and do not have the need for human sacrifice. In my years as a foot soldier of the holy war, I never participated or knew anyone in the Islamic faith who participated in any form or shade of human sacrifice in the name of Islam. It is an abomination for any Muslim, let alone an Islamic Jihadist to participate in any sacrifice that involved human blood. The actions and beliefs of Islamic radicals and jihadists are as prescribed by Islam, and in accordance with the laws divinely made visible to Holy Prophet Muhammad, upon who be peace and blessings of Allah," he said with anger as if I had said a taboo.

I immediately spotted a discrepancy in his comments about using human blood for rituals and sacrifice. He must have forgotten that he had earlier told me about using the blood of a virgin, and beheading a Christian as a form of initiation ritual. But I kept quiet. I thought about peace in Islam and how things had changed from the way Muhammad had intended, if the book of Islam was to be believed.

"In the early days of Prophet Muhammad, the religion of Islam was peacefully preached and spread to unbelievers without any violence. It was when the prophet saw the way his spread of Islam was being perceived that he declared the holy war against those who did not want the religion of Islam to exist. At the initial stage, what the prophet wanted was to preach Islam as an option to those who did not believe in Christianity. But the Christians saw his actions as an affront to Christianity and preempted the persecution of Islam and its adherents.

Prophet Muhammad was chosen by Allah to promote the religion of Islam, and like I said earlier, the assignment was intended to be peaceful until Christians turned it into a war, which Muhammad later christened a holy war, following the declaration of war by the Christian leaders of his time.

You have to understand that Prophet Muhammad was chosen to be a religious, as well as a military leader from Mecca, with the assignment to unify Muslims. As a messenger and prophet of Allah, Muhammad was seen by all Muslims as the last Prophet sent by Allah to redeem the religion of Islam, and to some extent, bring an alternative religious understanding to people of religious faith. Another thing you should know was that Prophet Muhammad was sent to restore order, and most of all, to reintroduce monotheistic faith in Islamic religion.

Another thing you should know was that Muhammad was born in the 570 CE, in the era of religious strife in the world. Recall that I mentioned earlier that he was born in the holy city of Mecca, where he was orphaned at a very early age. Having been brought up by his uncle, Abu Talib, he became a skillful merchant and a shepherd before he received the divine call, while he was first married at the ripe age of 25.

In those early times, the prophet was known to often retreat to a cave in the mountains for several nights for seclusion and prayers. It was in the cave, during one of the retreats in the mountains that he received his revelation at the advanced age of 40, from Allah. The revelation from Allah was for him to start preaching what he had been told by Allah, to redeem and preach to unbelievers about the goodness of Allah and the need to believe in Him.

During those early times, Muhammad met resistance and was only able to gain few followers to believe in Islam. Realizing that he could not do it alone, he sent his followers to several lands such as Abyssinia and Medina, to preach, around 622. At that time, like now, Muhammad met resistance from unbelievers in Mecca, Medina and Abyssinia, and these unbelievers were determined to stop Muhammad by every means necessary. At the same time, Muhammad's followers had also grown in strength and size, and he was able to take control of Mecca after years of fighting.

This is how the holy war started. It was not initiated by Muhammad. The enemies of Islam started the war against the peaceful preaching of Prophet Muhammad. You have to understand that those who resisted him in Mecca and elsewhere in the region were mostly pagans who were afraid that the religion of Islam was going to take over their religion.

In 632, when Muhammad returned from a farewell pilgrimage to Mecca, he had fallen ill and died, leaving a legacy that was largely continuous and unfinished. Before his death, Muhammad had succeeded in converting many pagans who once resisted Islam, to believe in Islam. To this day and time, the signs of Allah or the Ayah, that Muhammad received before his death is still visible among the genuine imams who are touched by the holy hands of the Prophet Muhammad," the jihadist said. I started to think of what he had said. From what I knew about the religion, I had a feeling he was right, to some degree. He continued after a short break.

"Apart from the Koran, there are things Muslims uphold, especially jihadists who still adhere to the old tradition of the holy war, such as *sira* and *sunnah* which are considered the vanguards of Sharia Law. In Islam, and among Muslims, the revelation that Prophet Muhammad received from Allah is taken with reverence by believers. The mere reference to his name among jihadists with traditional understanding of Islam, during prayers and discussions, saw him as the only and direct messenger of Allah. The genuine imams of today are known to carry the touch of the Holy Prophet Muhammad," the jihadist said, as if he was lecturing me about the life and time of the prophet.

Chapter 17

Musa, my guide, approached me with candor, telling me that I had used up more time than I was originally given, to speak with the jihadist. I didn't know how to answer him. Rather than tell him what I wanted to, I kept quiet. I didn't want to add fuel to the already blazing flame. I knew some of them were upset with me for trying to protect the jihadist from death, to enable me get the confession from him.

Musa was patient with me, realizing that it was important that I completed the confession. Despite that, he still told me what he wanted to tell me, without sugarcoating the facts. "You know he is alive because of you. The Nigerian soldiers and even the CIA commander wanted to finish him off, and move on," he said.

I clearly understood him. He was my guide and was probably told to tell me that. I didn't believe him that the CIA commander was among those who wanted to finish off the jihadist. I knew men like the commander. If he wanted the jihadist dead, he would have not bothered to even use Musa to achieve his goal. I had the feeling that it was the Nigerian soldiers and secret service agents who wanted the jihadist finished off. The CIA commander had vested interest in keeping the jihadist alive. He was as interested as I am, in what the jihadist had to say.

When Musa saw that he could not get me to agree with him to let the jihadist be taken away, he smiled. I couldn't tell if he was smiling because of my stubbornness or because he agreed with me that the jihadist be kept alive. After all, he was a Muslim like the jihadist. I didn't know if he shared the same extremist beliefs as the jihadist. I will hope not. If he shared the same extremist beliefs, then I am in trouble, as he was my guide.

I didn't think he was a jihadist or even a sympathizer himself. But then again, you never know with Muslims. Sometimes you can think they are on your side when they are actually with the enemy. Major Nidal Malik Hasan was an army major and a psychiatrist who took an oath to serve and protect the U.S., counseling returning soldiers from battlegrounds and treating them with psychiatric therapy, when he was secretly sympathizing with the terrorists, Taliban, and insurgents in Iraq and Afghanistan.

The major could not hold it any longer when he took up arms and shot 13 fellow soldiers to death, injuring many others. So when it comes to Muslim soldiers, one never knows when they can turn on you. Even in Afghanistan where Muslim sympathizers were recruited to serve in their country's police force and armed forces, they sometimes turn the guns they are training with, on their American trainers, killing them.

So, with Musa, I didn't know whose side he was on, even though he worked for the U.S. embassy. Most of these Muslims operate as double agents, working for both camps, and exploiting the gains and spoils from such double dealings. Everyone, including me, knew that working with Muslims had its inherent dangers but in some cases, you had to take what you could get, especially in hostile Muslim countries where the need to use Muslim agents were crucial and critical to an operation.

The CIA had to often use Muslims in the war against terrorism. If it had not been for the reliable information provided by a Pakistani doctor, Bin Laden would not have been captured. The subsequent prosecution of the Pakistani doctor, Shakil Afridi, for helping the CIA during the mission to find Bin Laden was a case in point. For years, the Pakistani authorities claimed to be helping the U.S. to find Bin Laden, when they were actually harboring him in their country. The evidence of their double dealing came to light when the Pakistani doctor who had helped to track Bin Laden was sentenced to 33 years in jail on charges of treason.

One wonders how much cooperation the U.S. was actually getting from Pakistan when the man the CIA was looking for, was living openly in a well protected compound, near a military base in Abbottabad, Pakistan. To make matters worse, the Pakistani authorities accused, arrested, charged and convicted the doctor (of treason), that helped the CIA to run a fake vaccination campaign with which he supposedly collected the DNA samples of Bin Laden and his family; that helped the CIA to track down the terrorist leader in a Pakistani town of Abbottabad.

Though the al-Qaeda chieftain lived openly in Abbottabad for years, the Pakistani authorities did not inform the CIA. They pretended to be helping in the war against the Taliban and Bin Laden while actually providing protection to the terrorist leader. This was the time the U.S. was pouring billions of dollars into the coffers of the Pakistani military to buy military hardware as an incentive to help fight the war against terrorism.

As I mentioned earlier, it is difficult to really trust a Muslim when it comes to the war on terrorism. Too many double dealings had taken place in Iraq and Afghanistan among Muslims who were supposedly working for the U.S. military and the CIA. With my knowledge and understanding of how Muslims work, I decided to keep my eyes opened, in case things go awry.

Don't get me wrong, not all Muslims are double-crossers when it comes to fighting terrorism and extremists. Some Muslims were genuine in their condemnation of terrorism among Muslim extremists. But a good majority of Muslims sympathize with radical Islamic extremists, and there are proofs of such sympathies in the news coming out of Afghanistan and Iraq, about how Muslims working with the CIA turn against their trainers, sometimes abandon their uniforms and run away with weapons from the armory of the CIA.

The jihadist fell asleep or maybe he pretended to have fallen asleep but I was still alarmed. In his condition, and with his wounds, any unusual behavior could be alarming. I immediately called the nurse and as I did so, he opened his eyes, and smiled. I was too overwhelmed with relief to be angry. But soon after, I smiled, realizing he had just played a fast one on me. I knew what he was doing. It was his way of getting my attention, which in a way was gratifying because I do sometimes get carried away.

"I know you like to analyze everything I say but you have to focus on what I am saying before doing a mental analysis. When I have finished my entire confession, and you have asked all the questions you want to ask, then be free to analyze all you want to analyze. But right now, in my present condition, you need to hurry up and finish because I am dying, my friend. When I say I am dying, I mean it.

In my consciousness I see angels pulling me toward a white gate. The gate looks heavenly and unearthly. I know it is the gate of hereafter. As the angels pull me, I see myself resisting it, and sometimes I feel I am succeeding. A few minutes ago, I shook my head and said I was not ready, and believe it or not, they said they will give me enough time to finish my confession to you.

I don't know if you have ever been in the throes of death as I am currently. It is a defining moment that brings you closer to your mortal presence on earth. If you haven't experienced death, it will be hard for me to explain it. In my current state, death is constantly beckoning me to come, and I have been able to resist it with my willpower but I don't know how long that willpower will last. I am sure you know that death has a superior power over mankind and that when your time comes, death will swoop down and take you.

But in a strange way, I have been able to overcome the grief of dying, knowing that my usefulness in this life has been overspent, with a past due notice on my door of life. In case you don't know, I am currently holding that past due notice in my left hand. I know you cannot see it but I can see it. And just in case you are thinking that my mind is becoming unstable and bedeviled by hallucination, come here and hold my hand and you will experience my state of mind," he said, waiting for me to try it.

I resisted the urge to play the mysterious hand of death. Though I was skeptical about what he was saying, I couldn't bring myself to try holding his hand. Something inside me, which I sometimes called my instinct and intuition, told me to stay away from such experiment. I was not usually given to superstition and supernatural beliefs but I knew when to draw the line. And right now, I felt the need to draw the line.

He smiled, realizing that I was not willing to play the game of death. Even though there was no immediate danger in my touching his hand, I still didn't want to do it. He knew I was afraid, if you want to call it that. And at that moment, I didn't mind him calling me a coward, if that was what he felt I was. But he didn't call me a coward. My reluctance, and well, refusal to touch him, confirmed his belief that he was right all along that he could inspire revelation and insight, by anyone touching him.

"I don't think you are afraid. I just think you are not willing to dabble with the unknown. I do understand that perfectly," he said, reading my mind as he always did, with uncanny accuracies. I let him have his moment, without a care about him reading my mind. As far as I was concerned he could be a fortune-teller or a crystal gazer, and I wouldn't care. As long as I was not dabbling with death, I was fine with whatever he wanted to think.

"The forces of the afterlife are very powerful. I once had a conversation with my deceased grandparents who died decades ago, in my conscious state of mind, with my eyes opened, telling me bedtime stories, as if I was a baby that needed to be put to bed. It was as I was trying to understand how a grown man could be sang to by his deceased grandparents in order for him to go to bed, that I realized that someone was already carrying me in her belly, and that I was about to be delivered to earth again as a newborn.

While I was in someone's belly, in my afterlife, I experienced several movements that I had no power to control. And then from time to time I would hear voices from everywhere and nowhere, as if they were in my head. They were not in my head because I knew what were in my head. I could see things clearly but I could not utter anything, as if I was watching a motion picture that had a life of its own without words.

It was during these moments of revelation that I realized that death was at my doorstep. I knew the moment my grandmother puts to bed in the afterlife that I will be dead in this life and be reborn in the afterlife. What surprised me was not so much about being reborn in the afterlife; it was my grandmother and grandfather becoming my parents in the afterlife.

I was disturbed in that revelation that my grandparents were very poor in the afterlife, where they were beggars, begging for alms from street to street, without a home they could call their own. It soon dawned on me that they were in hell in the afterlife, which made me rethink how I was living my life here on earth. Even if I could change things, I realized it was too late. I was already expected in the afterlife and couldn't do anything about it. The life I had lived here on earth had already determined my afterlife, I realized," he said, with what I thought were tears welling up in his eyes.

True enough, they were tears. I am not good with tears. I turned my head and waited for him to go through his moments. I was not about to add to it, even though I did not have any sympathy or empathy for him. In my holier than thou state of mind, it was very hard for me to show any empathy for a man who lived his life killing others for their beliefs. So many had tasted untimely deaths in his hand and I wasn't about to waste my sympathies on such a person. Like I said earlier, I am not in the business of being judgmental. But then again, I am still human.

"My grandparents were good people. They loved and showered me with affection while they were alive. They were well off, and didn't have problem with money. I don't know the sins they committed to have inherited such a great deal of suffering in their afterlife. Though I was a child when they passed on, my memory of them were of good ones. I don't think they ever hurt anyone in their earthly dwelling here, before their transition at a ripe age, well after their golden years," he said, still with sadness in his eyes.

Sometimes, it was easy for anyone to say their grandparents were nice people when they were actually coldblooded murderers. I knew a man once, who was a highly respected Islamic cleric, who was secretly a supporter of terrorism. He was like a Dr. Jekyll and Mr. Hyde. The cleric would secretly fund and support terrorism while openly condemning terrorism and purportedly working with law enforcement authorities to curb terrorism.

One day, an Islamic student who was a mole in the mosque where the cleric lectures, saw some odd looking men in the backroom of the mosque, leaving with the cleric and started following him. It was while he was tailing him that he saw the cleric drop off his son at a school, entered his van and drove to a storefront where he changed vehicles, and then drove to another deserted part of the city limit in a car with tinted windows. The mole followed him discreetly, without him suspecting anything.

After driving for five miles outside the city limit, the cleric turned off the main highway, entered a small dirt road that seemed covered with bushes and shrubs. Not wanting to arouse his suspicion, the mole used a long-distant eavesdropping device that was also a tracking device to track him. Using an inbuilt monitoring device built in his car, the mole was able to monitor the cleric enter a small hut, where he met with five suspicious looking characters. He held a meeting with five men in white Muslim robes, gave them a thick white envelope and quickly left the hut, and drove back the same way he had come.

The mole did not go after him, realizing he was probably heading back to his van, where he would probably change vehicles. Rather than follow the cleric again, the mole went toward the hut, on foot, where he found the small clearing where the hut was located. At first glance, the hut appeared like a small wooden cabin, and then as it became visible, the mole saw that it was actually a hut. He saw that the hut neither had electricity nor any form of heating. He reckoned it was a safe house where Muslim outlaws and fugitives often hide.

It was well hidden from view. If he had not been looking for it, he would have missed it as the hut was designed with green materials to make it merge with the greenness of the forest trees. He was impressed by the look of the hut, and obvious trouble the builders went through to hide the hut from view.

He observed from afar, the five men talking in hushed voices in old Arabic dialect that he could not understand. Rather than tried to figure out the dialect, he used his eavesdropping device to record the conversation which he later took to his CIA contact, for translation. After that, he had discreetly tipped me about the cleric, giving me the least details possible, enough for me to do my own investigation. And it was with that, that I started watching the cleric in my own way, without raising suspicion.

With the limited spending funds provided me by my editor, I was able to hire a private investigator that I always use for matters of such importance in the area. After a couple of weeks of hard digging, the PI called me one day with excitement about his findings, telling me to meet him at a designated location, to provide me a full report.

I had gone to the meeting place, where the PI gave me pictures and tapes containing evidence that the cleric was also working for al-Shabab and al-Qaeda, as a recruiter and a spy for the terrorist network. I had taken the photos of the cleric, with the terrorists, and published it, along with details of his association. Before publishing the story, I had asked for, and received the nod to do so, from the mole as I did not want to jeopardize the CIA investigation. But I needn't have worried as the CIA had already gotten enough evidence to go after their target.

Since the cleric was no longer of interest to the CIA, I published the story, which was carried by my television station, the sister-print media affiliate, and several other media outlets. It was also carried by other foreign media. It was a couple of days later that I found out that the cleric had committed suicide with a handgun, when the story had been published.

I don't know if the cleric had actually committed suicide or had been killed by the Islamic jihadist sect he worked for. I knew for a fact that terrorist sects like al-Qaeda does not tolerate carelessness and mistakes. Once they found out that he had blown his cover, he would have become useless to them, and to make sure he did not reveal whatever he may know, they could have killed him, to make it look like suicide. I don't know for sure but that is my theory, based on what I know of Islamic terror groups.

I do know for sure that terrorist sects do not like their information getting leaked. They would rather kill the source of the information than risk law enforcement agents getting hold of the information. Like every secret organization, which includes intelligence agencies, terrorist organizations often take out those they thought had become a liability to them, no matter the importance of that person to the organization.

The cleric's death was made to look like suicide. The so-called suicide smacked of murder. As an investigative journalist, I could smell it was murder a mile away. Whoever had killed the cleric had hurriedly planted the handgun in the palm of his hand, without a suicide note. Usually, every suicide has a note. It was seldom that you find a suicide without a note. The fact that there was no note was the first clue. The second clue was that Muslims do not believe in suicides, unless it was an attack on others. And even with a suicide attack, it was always deemed a selfless sacrifice, never something that was done with guilt. Suicide attacks were often carried out with bravado and vengeance.

The murder was too obvious for me to ignore. Though the significance of the death of the cleric was irrelevant, it did occur to me that a follow-up story might interest my readers, so I went ahead and published the suicide as well as my analysis and theory about the so-called suicide.

So, I was aware of double dealing when it comes to people who led secret lives. His grandparents may have led secret lives that he wasn't aware of. But that was hardly of great importance. The important thing to me was getting the gist of his confession. So I urged him to tell me something I didn't already know. I searched my mental notes to see if there was something relevant that I could ask him to tell me that I hadn't already known. My mind went to the recent use of a five year old boy by the Taliban to carry a small explosive package to a group of newly recruited Afghan police officers, who were bombed while being addressed by an Afghan police chief. The Taliban had detonated the bomb, killing the boy and the officers.

Last year, a boy of seven who was hawking oranges in the streets of Kandahar was given a small letter by one of his customers, a Taliban member, to deliver to a group of police officers. The boy did as he was told after the Taliban had reportedly given him a few Afghani notes, in addition to buying his entire tray of oranges. Relieved that he wouldn't have to spend additional hours hawking the oranges on the tray in his head, the boy gladly took the package to the police station, where several police officers were listening to the instructions of their police chief.

The boy had stood there, watching the police officers who typically ignored him as an innocent bystander, as they usually did with boys that age. In Afghanistan, it was not uncommon for kids that age to stand, watching police officers as they paraded and practiced, before being dispatched to their various posts. After the boy had reportedly watched the police officers for what seemed like thirty minutes, he approached one of the officers and gave the officer the package, which was addressed to the police chief.

Since boys that age were never considered threats to anyone at the time, the police officer who received the small package from the boy did not think twice that the boy might be carrying a bomb. And what was so cruel about it was that the boy did not know that he was carrying an explosive that could possibly kill him. The poor boy had waited, still mesmerized by the uniform and parade of the police officers.

Unbeknownst to the boy that the Taliban militant who had given him the package was going to detonate the bomb, a few yards away, in a small uncompleted building, the boy had waited, not knowing that death was about to take him to the afterlife. As the police officer who had received the package handed over the small package to the police chief, who was standing in a small makeshift podium and lectern, addressing the police officers, the explosives went off, following the detonation, instantly killing the 20 newly recruited officers, and the boy.

It was one of the most daring attacks that had taken place since the U.S. invasion of Afghanistan over a decade ago. The attack was meant to destabilize and derail the effectiveness of the newly formed Afghan law enforcement agents who would be replacing the U.S. security personnel in the country. The Taliban claimed responsibility, saying that Afghanistan would be ungovernable as long as the U.S. continues to spread its western influence in the country. A Taliban spokesperson, Shahidullah Shahid, was quoted saying that the only accepted police force in Afghanistan were Islamic Sharia Police Force, and not a U.S. created police force.

Apart from the cruel use of a very young boy to carry an explosive, I also wanted to hear about the importance of Hakimullah Mehsud, an alleged Taliban leader, who was killed in a CIA drone strike recently. I knew that as a senior Boko Haram operative that the jihadist would know especially as the jihadist had confessed to me that he had often traveled to Taliban strongholds in Afghanistan and Pakistan to receive training on weaponry and explosives.

"Yes, Hakimullah was martyred, and it was with joy that he was considered important enough to have been martyred. For years now, the U.S. had claimed victory in Afghanistan but we members of the Islamic jihad community knew better. The Taliban was still in power in Afghanistan, with Sharia Law, as the only acceptable law in the very many towns and cities controlled by the Taliban. Despite claims that there was a central government in Kabul, the U.S. appointed and imposed government was only governing a portion of Kabul and Kandahar, with the protection of U.S. forces.

And without U.S. forces to protect the so-called president, he would have been dead in minutes, long ago, after he was made president. If he was truly a legitimate president, how come he had U.S. and NATO forces protecting him, morning, noon and night, 24/7? A legitimate government would have its own trusted regular army, an air force, a navy and its own administration, not a handful of so-called provincial governors who operate from hideouts. They knew if they came out in the open to declare their authority that they would be killed. And the Taliban has done that on numerous occasions.

The only legitimate authority in Afghanistan and some parts of Pakistan was the Taliban, which controlled more towns and cities than the so-called central government of Hamid Karzai who was supposedly the president of the Islamic Republic of Afghanistan. If Hamid Karzai was truly a legitimate president, how come he never travels around the countryside to campaign during the sham elections that was supposedly held a couple of times, since the U.S. forces invaded the country and imposed him as the president?" he asked, looking at me.

I couldn't give him any answer to that question. I knew that Hamid Karzai was the legitimate president of Afghanistan. Though I did not know how many parts of Afghanistan he controlled, I knew there were state governors and local governments that govern the states, while Karzai governs the central government, with the headquarters in Kabul.

I knew Islamic jihadists liked to exaggerate their importance and relevance. I was not sold on the propaganda that Taliban still controls Afghanistan. The Taliban rule ended in 2001, following U.S. invasion of Afghanistan. And even while the Taliban was in power in the country, only a handful of countries recognized the Taliban as a legitimate government. Only countries like Pakistan, Saudi Arabia, and the United Arab Emirates, recognized the Taliban as a legitimate government between September 1996 and December 2001, with Kandahar as the country's capital. Mohammed Omar had continued to serve as the spiritual leader of the Taliban, a position he has held since 1994.

Like Boko Haram, Ansaru, al-Shabab and al-Qaeda, the Taliban operates its own strict interpretation of the Sharia Law, which includes the brutal suppression and treatment of women as second class citizens. Though the Taliban was feared by adherents, most of the militants were mostly Pashtun tribesmen who had been influenced by the instructions and teachings of Deobandi fundamentalism, in a social and cultural doctrine called Pashtunwali.

The Taliban was said to have its own allies, which the west alleged, supported and funded the insurgency movement. In its continued terror campaign to destabilize the Karzai administration and the U.S. led NATO forces in Afghanistan; the Taliban often uses terrorism to further their ideological and political aspirations and fundamentalism. Those who had resisted the Sharia Law imposed on Afghans living under the areas it controlled had often been dealt with, with amputations, and instant beheadings.

While the central stronghold of the Taliban had moved from Kandahar to Quetta in Pakistan, which served as the base of the

Quetta Shura, the umbrella organization of the Taliban, a lot of towns and villages along the Afghan-Pakistani border were said to be under the control of the Taliban. It was said that the Taliban had two different types of administrations in both Afghanistan and Pakistan, where it still controls several cities and towns. The Pakistani Taliban was said to be fundamentally different from the Afghan Taliban, though they both operated under the Quetta Shura fundamentalism, in Quetta, in the Balochistan province of Pakistan.

I had to think of a new strategy since the confession was going in the direction that I did not like. To make sure the confession goes the way I preferred, I deliberately set the tone for a different discussion that, I hoped, would lead him to confess to additional jihadist activities he may have participated in. Don't get me wrong, I was not trying to get him to talk about the carnages he had been involved in, or participated in. I was basically trying to understand how far Islamic extremists would go in their holy war.

"The Benghazi attack of the U.S. diplomatic mission in Benghazi, in Libya, on September 11, 2012, by heavily armed terrorists, resulted in the death of Ambassador Chris Stevens. The attack was carried out to mark the anniversary of the September 11, 2001 attack of the World Trade Center. The local Libyan police officers left the annex, right before the attack. Why do you think the Libyan police evacuated the annex, before the attack?" I asked, hoping he would elucidate more on the deadly attack. As usual, he did not mince words in his explanations.

"First, let me state that the attack was carried out by members of al-Qaeda operating in Libya. Those al-Qaeda operatives were part of the militia contingent that had fought against Muammar Gaddafi in Libya. The al-Qaeda operatives, in Libya, see themselves as the main reason Gaddafi was toppled. And they were the same people that had killed Gaddafi to prevent any trial that would have revealed their strong presence in Libya and Mali.

Al-Qaeda operatives are the largest group of militia operating in Libya. They are the police force, as well as the armed forces. They were the same militia men and women who had forcefully taken the Libyan Prime Minister, Ali Zeidan, from his hotel where his office was located, for several hours, before he was finally released, after purportedly answering questions about his involvement and knowledge about the CIA-led Navy seal and Special Forces that had arrested Abu Anas Al-Libi, an al-Qaeda operative wanted for 15 years, from his home in Tripoli.

Now, to answer your question, let me point out that the attack on the U.S. consulate in Benghazi was planned months before it actually happened. The boldness of the plan was that the same al-Qaeda militants that planned the attack before it took place, had secretly and deliberately leaked information about the attack, to let the U.S. know that it cannot be stopped. And to prove their point, their intended target was hit, as well as the CIA operatives that were supposed to fortify the compound.

A lot of people in the so-called Libyan government, including the Prime Minister, Ali Zeidan, knew about the attack, days before it occurred. They were warned that providing any form of security for the annex during the attack would mean a direct confrontation with al-Qaeda. The Prime Minister was told to keep the unarmed police officers away from the building during the hours of the attack.

An hour before the attack, the police officers that were protecting the annex quietly drove off, as the Libyan based al-Qaeda operatives arrived at the compound. The al-Qaeda operatives came with rocket propelled grenades, missiles, and explosives that they had effectively used in the attack, with very little resistance that they had quickly suppressed. They had anticipated a weak and feeble resistance.

Another thing you have to know was that it was the Libyan government officials that had informed al-Qaeda operatives and militia men, in Benghazi, that the U.S. ambassador was going to be in Benghazi on the fateful day of the attack. The original plan was to destroy the consulate and its staff, to create the same carnage that had occurred in East Africa when two U.S. embassies were bombed in Nairobi and Tanzania in 1998, which had led to the death of 212 people in the attack.

The magnitude of the attack was intended to be as good as the East African attack. The presence of the U.S. ambassador in Benghazi was an added bonus which gave the attack more significance than the East African embassies' attacks. The whole idea of the attack was to make the U.S. know that al-Qaeda was still potent and strong in the world, especially in Africa, Yemen,

Iraq and Afghanistan, despite the death of Bin Laden.

The attack was condemned by the Libyan government, as they had told the al-Qaeda operatives in Libya they would, to look good and unsuspected in the eye of the world. The Libyan authorities had also pretended by playing double in their role of cooperating with the U.S. while working with the militias who still controlled the country. Al-Qaeda felt betrayed by the Prime Minister, Ali Zeidan, who had known about the proposed snatching of Al-Libi. It was the utmost betrayal of al-Qaeda loyalty by the Libyan authorities. The loyalty that al-Qaeda had had for the government in protecting it, and also in helping to topple Gaddafi, was said to have been betrayed by the government. As far as the al-Qaeda operatives were concerned, it was a slap in the face, that the government they had helped create and establish would cooperate with the enemy, to capture their leader, al-Libi.

About the attack itself, it began at night, on the eve of the 9/11 anniversary, and ended in the early morning of the next day, in which the CIA annex in another compound was also attacked. The coordinated attacks of the consulate was planned to make sure enough carnages and casualties were created.

Another show of diplomacy that the Libyan government embarked on, which they had earlier taken permission from al-Qaeda, for, was to announce that they were disbanding the militia groups in the country as well as getting rid of al-Qaeda operatives. It was necessary for al-Qaeda to approve the show of diplomacy so that the weak Libyan government could continue to get funds to operate the government, from the U.S.

If the Prime Minister had openly taken sides with the militia, it would have led to the U.S. cutting off diplomatic relations with the Libyan government and labeling it as a sponsor of terrorism like Gaddafi had been labeled, which would have made it impossible for al-Qaeda to effectively operate in the country. It was necessary to draw the enemy closer so that it could be vulnerable and unprepared. It would be grossly unwise to let the U.S. classify Libya as an axis of evil, and concentrate its forces and missiles in the country. It would be counterproductive and bad for al-Qaeda.

The reason that al-Qaeda in Iraq, Afghanistan, Pakistan and in the Maghreb had been very successful was because these countries had diplomatic relations with the U.S., which makes the U.S. a good target because of their vulnerability in supposedly friendly countries. Though the militia leader, Ahmed Abu Khattala, was said to be a wanted terrorist with a huge bounty on his head, he was living openly in Libya, protected by the same government that was also working with the U.S. to fight terrorism with *words*, since that was all they could do. After all, al-Qaeda militia men were the armed forces and the police in Libya.

Just like Pakistan paid lip service to the U.S. during the hunt for Osama Bin Laden in Pakistan, while secretly harboring the al-Qaeda leader, and using the same funds provided by the U.S. to fund Bin Laden and his family, the Libyan government was doing the same thing. The funds provided by the U.S. to support the new Libyan government also pays the salaries of the militia men and women who are also members of al-Qaeda. You see, the war on terrorism was really being won by al-Qaeda.

Whether the U.S. knew it or not, the funds al-Qaeda uses for its operations are indirectly provided by the U.S. and its taxpayers. The reason I say this is because the same governments in Pakistan, Libya and Afghanistan that the U.S. funds, also use the same funds to support and arm al-Qaeda, against the U.S. whom both countries secretly loath," he said, wiping sweat from his face.

I knew what the jihadist was saying. It was not the first time that I had heard that the arms and ammunitions provided by the U.S. to other countries often ended up in the hands of al-Qaeda. A lot of policymakers were aware that most of the funds that go to weak countries like Yemen, Afghanistan, Pakistan and Libya, often ended up in the hands of al-Qaeda. In Yemen for instance, the al-Qaeda in the Arabian Peninsula was said to be very strong that it controls a fraction of the government. A government that was supposedly an ally of the U.S. in the fight against terrorism was also double dealing with the enemy. The same goes for other countries where the war on terrorism was ongoing.

Chapter 18

The day was sunny and windy but cool, and the temperature was less oppressive as it had been a couple of months before. A few of the soldiers said it was cold but to me, it was still warm. I realized it was the period of dust-laden wind from the Atlantic coast of Africa at this time of the year. I was a little restless, and was ready to conclude whatever it was the jihadist had to say. I was tired, hungry, and thirsty. I didn't want to risk drinking the so-called pure water that street hawkers were selling. Rather than drink the unfiltered water, I resorted to drinking coke and orange soda.

I knew I couldn't drink soda forever. I had to drink water at some point. Being holed up in the bungalow, getting down the confession, I knew it would be hard for me to get a filtered water to drink. The only way to get back to my routine was to finish as quickly as possible. But each time I thought I was about to finish, the jihadist would come up with something else, as if trying to delay me. He must have known that I was the reason he was still alive.

As much as his confession was important to me, I was tired and ready to call it a day. It had been a daunting task to get him to talk, even though the original idea was his own. Let me correct that, he had been talking, but the constant digression to less important matters had made the whole thing lengthy and laborious. I was used to cutting to the chase and getting the gist of any report without delay. But this was a different situation. There was a question of life and death at play that I couldn't rush, if wanted to. I had to be patient even though I was losing my composure.

As I said earlier, patience comes with my training. I was trained to have the patience of Job, but it is hard to maintain that stance sometimes. Over the years I had taught myself to be open-minded in my approach to issues, without the traditional impatience that often dictated the work of most journalists. Even though patience comes with the training that most journalists like me received in school, it was hard to maintain that training sometimes. It was not that the training goes out the window in real life, no, that is not the case. It was just that certain situations dictated the level of one's patience.

A long time ago, I was in Sarajevo, during the war, in

Yugoslavia, to remove the then president of Yugoslavia, who was bent on ethnically cleansing his own people from Yugoslavia. When Bush 41 had U.S. soldiers to topple the dictator, I was one of those journalists that were allowed to go in the battlefield with the soldiers. It was an experience that had stayed with me to this day. For a while the experience pervaded my senses in such a way that I suffered post traumatic stress disorder, even though I was not directly engaged in the battle to free the Baltic country.

Even though I had overcome the PTSD that I had suffered at the time, during the war, I didn't let that stop me when operation desert storm came around, when Saddam Hussein had invaded Kuwait to take that country's lucrative oil field. Again, as was the case in Bosnia and Panama, Bush 41 did not hesitate to send U.S. soldiers to liberate Kuwait from the menace of Saddam Hussein, who was determined to run over the country of Kuwait.

Just like his war with Iran, Saddam Hussein had miscalculated. He did not factor in, the possibility of a U.S. intervention in the proposed annexation of Kuwait. He was surprised when his soldiers retreated and gave up arms to the superior firepower and Air Force of the U.S. military. I was there when Saddam Hussein regrouped his soldiers, and even chopped off the limbs of the soldiers who had abandoned their weapons at the sight of the invading U.S. army.

As if bent on proving his was still in charge, Saddam continued his ethnic cleansing of the Kurds in his country, again trying to force out the Kurds in order to annex the oil region, within the Kurds' territory. With the help of Bush 41, that effort failed. Saddam Hussein was furious and wanted to silence Bush 41 privately, in his own way. He had sent a group of world-class assassins out to find, and assassinate Bush 41. With members of his own secret service involved, the contract was signed, sealed and delivered for Bush 41 as the mark to be eliminated.

Again, as was the miscalculated invasion of Kuwait, and the attempted ethnic cleansing of the Kurds, Saddam Hussein was in for a surprise. Bush 41 was more than ready for such feeble attempts on his life. Having been a fighter pilot and the director of the CIA, in addition to his stint in espionage, Bush would summon the final death knell that finally ended the dictator. Saddam Hussein would, once again, fail in his stark underestimation of

Bush 41.

I remember doing an in-depth investigation of the attempted assassination of Bush 41 by Saddam Hussein. Like most people in the west who had heard about the attempted assassination of the 41st U.S. president, I didn't believe that Saddam Hussein was that naïve to think he could easily get Bush 41 assassinated. Though he was a known callous dictator who was hard-hearted enough to chop off the limbs of any Iraqi who disagreed or went against his regime, I didn't know he was also that stupid to think he could get away with it if he succeeded.

And though he didn't succeed, he didn't get away with the attempted assassination. Bush 43rd, the son of Bush 41, did not forget, and was bent on finishing what his father had started during operation desert storm. The event of September 11, 2001 was the perfect excuse for Bush 43 to go after Saddam Hussein; even though the Iraqi president had nothing to do with the terrorist attack of the World Trade Center and the Pentagon, of September 11, 2001.

The first excuse that Bush 43 came up with to carry out his vengeance was to accuse Saddam Hussein of possessing weapons of mass destruction that the dictator purportedly planned to use on the Kurds and his people. Since the U.S. had formally declared war on terrorism, and Afghanistan had been invaded in 2001, immediately after the 9/11 attack, to take out the Taliban in Afghanistan that was said to be harboring Bin Laden, Bush 43 had used the opportunity to get the international community to go along with him to invade Iraq, with the intention of getting rid of Saddam Hussein.

With the British Intelligence (M15) and the CIA on his side, Bush 43 said he had evidence that Saddam Hussein had acquired weapons of mass destruction that he was not only planning to use on his people but on the world. The gullible international community, with the U.N, in tow, bought the story, hook, line and sinker. But not Kofi Annan, the then U.N. Secretary General of the United Nations, who felt the U.S. should wait until there was a concrete evidence that Saddam Hussein had amassed weapons of mass destruction. Mr. Anna's reluctance to go along with the U.S. to invade Iraq, on the pretext of Iraq possessing weapons of mass destruction immediately put the U.N envoy in the disfavor of the

U.S., a country that had been instrumental in his ascension to the post of Secretary General of the U.N., in the first place.

In my report the following year, after it had been determined that Saddam Hussein did not posses weapons of mass destruction, after the fall and death of Saddam Hussein, I wrote that Bush 43 confessed to making a mistake in assuming that Saddam Hussein had weapons of mass destruction. I also included in my report at the time, that the then Secretary of State, Collin Powell had admitted his mistake about Saddam possessing weapons of mass destruction. The Secretary of State had blamed his intelligence on the report provided by British intelligence.

I guess the reason I had gone into this long narration was to point out that I had a very long experience with the issue of patience and how to exercise it. Even with that mindset, I had often found myself struggling with impatience. I know no human can ever surpass the patience of Job, but the virtue of having enough patience to get what I want has always been part of my own practice of journalism.

"There is something else that I wish to confess to, that I have not mentioned before," the jihadist said, after he had closed his eyes and opened them again. I had become used to his antics of closing his eyes. But I could tell by his demeanor that all was not well with him. I couldn't tell whether he was really in pain or going through some sort of personal issue. All I knew was that something was a little amiss.

I listened to him as I had done since meeting him, and waited for him to continue. "In my early years as a jihadist, there was an incident on campus that I hadn't mentioned earlier. As a freshman, and well into my sophomore at the university, I had to choose a side to belong to, sort of like a fraternity. If you were thinking it was a cult, you were probably right. But it was promoted like a fraternity, for reasons best known to the members.

Before coming to the university, my notion of a fraternity had been a sort of male student organization that was mainly concerned with social gatherings, with secret rites for scholastic and extracurricular activities where debates and other social functions often occurred. But it turns out I was wrong. The fraternity I was lured into joining was, like I said earlier, a cult with dangerous secret rites. The dangerous rites involved initiation processes which included the use of human blood.

To be fully accepted, even if lured into the cult by the cult recruiters, included using the blood of someone the cult member loves or had affection for. In a sense it had to be someone whose affection had been obtained and or returned in a carnal form. At that time I was gradually transforming in my views and perceptions as a Muslim. It was at the same time I was traveling to Yemen, Mali, Somalia and Pakistan that I was also being initiated into a cult on the campus, at the university. I know I said earlier that I never participated in any form of human sacrifice but this was totally different.

At first I didn't know which was more daring and venturesome, whether it was the Muslim faith or the fraternity at school. To complete the initiation process as a campus cult member, I had to cajole my girlfriend at the time, a Christian, to submit to a blood swap of love, which was a pretext to take her blood. Thinking I was in love with her and wanted a long lasting relationship, she had gladly submitted to the blood swap which I had taken to the cult meeting for the initiation. To this day, I still don't understand the significance of the blood swap. At the time it had seemed to me like a meaningless rite.

If you knew anything about campus initiation process you will understand that there was nothing meaningless in their rites and actions. Every action was well articulated and planned. And don't think they were playing or having fun. They were dead serious. Any member that betrayed the oath of initiation was often penalized with the consequence of death. So, as you can see, there was nothing frivolous about the practice of cult on campus.

Now, about my initiation, I was asked to join a group of five members which included three boys and two girls to rob a local bank. The success of that operation, I was told, would confirm my initiation process into the cult.

For weeks we had watched the targeted bank, inside and outside, checking out the employees' routines to make sure everything was in order. It was a very daunting process. We had to make sure the timing was right for the robbery. On the day of the robbery, we had first gone to the police station in the area, shot out the station, killing six unarmed police officers while the others ran into the bush. The next move we had made was to mount a roadblock on both ends of the street where the bank was located before starting the operation.

While we were at the police station, we took every item that was important, which included weapons, ammunitions, and bulletproof vests, before setting the station ablaze. After demobilizing the police, we robbed the bank with laxity, without a worry in the world. If you had seen us, you would have thought there was no law in the state. If you think about it, there was no law in Nigeria. We were the law and order. The police was taken out of action, and that made us the law.

We ransacked the bank's vault, taking as much money as we could carry. Since the money was very weighty because of its continuous devaluation, we had to basically use a police pickup truck to take the money. The whole operation lasted four hours. You would have thought that police reinforcement would have arrived to challenge us. Wrong, no police reinforcement came. We operated with total impunity, taking over N300 million. For a group of students, that was a lot of money.

We bought cars for ourselves, took care of our girlfriends and lived lavishly. Some of the cult members paid for their grades. The lecturers that did not comply or cooperate were punished with death. The law that existed in our campus was only the law written by the cult. And we were the only cult. Anyone who chose not to join the cult was made to serve members of the cult. No one, including male and female students, dared refused us.

With so much money to spend, it was easy for me to go on my various trips to Yemen, Pakistan and Somalia, without financial worries. Though I needn't have worried for money because of my father's wealth, I didn't want my father to know most of what I was doing on campus, and with my Islamic faith. As far as he was concerned, I was on campus reading my books and working towards my medical degree. As long as my grades were high and in good standing, there was no need for him to be concerned about me.

Though a lot of the cult members bought their grades, I never participated in the purchase of grades. I wanted to have a real education. I did not want to leave the university as stupid as I was when I first came in. I wanted to be smart and intelligently educated, and that was what I did. I read my books. Most of my fellow cult members didn't like the fact that I was constantly reading my books and attending lectures. Once, a lecturer had approached me, praising me for my studious diligence, assiduity and good grades. I had thanked him without comments. He knew better than to criticize my fellow cult members. He had given his compliments and moved on. I had secretly appreciated the compliment even though it did not show on my face. It was good to know that I was not perceived as bad as my fellow cult members. It was not that it mattered. I never cared or bothered with others' opinions and perceptions of me.

On campus back then, we were highly respected by everyone. No one dared go against us. We were like kings and queens living in our own palaces with our own rules. It was fun, as those who liked women could have any woman they desired without worries. I loved women but my Islamic religion forbade me to indulge in certain practices. I knew a lot of people did not understand this, but in Islam, any form of careless indulgence with women was heavily frowned upon. There was a moral code of conduct, even though it was often hard for non-Muslims to know and understand the practice," the jihadist said.

I profoundly disagreed with him that Muslims had restrictions when it comes to women. A lot of Muslims practiced polygamy whereby some of the men marry more than one woman. I remember asking an imam in Nigeria if it was religious for Muslims to marry several women while claiming to be religious. I remember him telling me that in Islam Muslim men were allowed to marry more than one wife as long as they could take care of them.

I had also asked the imam if women could be allowed to marry more than one husband since the men were permitted to marry more than one wife. The imam had laughed, saying it was unacceptable for women to be married to more than one man. I recall telling the imam that polygamy entails a man or woman marrying more than one mate. The imam had laughed so hard that tears came to his eyes, as he explained that it was fornication for a woman to be married to more than one man, in Islam.

To me it was a double standard that Islam does not permit women to enjoy, if you call it enjoyment, the privilege of multiple mates like men. I had explained to the imam in details that polyandry, like polygamy, means women could have more than one husband or males at one time.

While polygamy is a practice that allows me to have more than one mate or spouse at one time, polyandry allows women to also do the same. I told him about polygyny and how it means men could have multiple mates. He nodded his head and said that was how it should be. He did not like the practice of polyandry among women and said no man should allow such a practice in Islam, especially as the religion forbids it, he said.

In ancient Hindu, and according to the epic legend of Hindu, beautiful Agnijyotsna or Krysna draupadi, who was said to be the daughter of King Drupada of Panchala, was the wife of five Pandavas or husbands. Though born with darker complexion and was fondly referred to as Krishnaa because of her dark complexion, her beauty was unsurpassable by any woman of her era. Later when she became the queen of Indraprastha, she was said to still practice polyandry.

In Saudi Arabia and other Muslim countries, according to Islam and Sharia Law, men were allowed to take up to four wives as long as the women were treated equally. In Saudi Arabia especially, polyandry was not even an option as women did not have the same rights as men. Women of course were not allowed to drive, participate in government and matters of importance in the kingdom.

Not too long ago, in the 21st century, a woman was convicted, to be stoned to death, for fornication, when her male counterparts could arbitrarily practice polygamy without restrictions. Like Krysna, the woman accused of fornication should have been allowed to also practice polyandry without restrictions, if egalitarian privilege existed for women in the Arab world.

I do not think it would bother me if a girl that I was intimate with decided to date other men; but I do not know about marrying a woman who was already married to other men. But in reality, several men in modern times do sleep with married women. Though not popular, polyandry is very common among women who cheat on their husbands or have multiple partners at the same time. If a woman cheats on her husband with another man, she is essentially practicing polyandry.

Unlike Krysna who was epically married to five husbands, a

lot of women in the 21st century, and centuries before, have been known to maintain multiple male partners at one time, for a long period of time. Though generally frowned upon as prostitution and fornication, a lot of women in the western world often engage in sex with multiple partners at the same time, without the implicit definition of polyandry but still with the practice of polyandry.

I thought of asking the jihadist about polyandry in Sharia Law, and how he felt about it. After weighing the significance of asking him, and whether it was relevant, I decided it was necessary to get his point of view on the subject.

"I was curious about your feeling about polyandry and whether Boko Haram agrees with it, since it hates western influence," I asked him. He looked at me as if he didn't understand what I meant by polyandry. But I was wrong. He understood. After all, he was a learned medical doctor, with a strong worldview.

"Polyandry is forbidden in Islam and in Sharia Law. Women who practice polyandry are harlots and prostitutes who have no place in Islam. I do not know of any Muslim country that will allow polyandry. It is a taboo in Islam for women to have more than one husband or mate. In Boko Haram's Nigeria, any woman caught practicing polyandry would be stoned to death.

Western countries allow disturbing practices like polyandry, homosexuality and all sorts of societal dysfunctions and ills, but not in Islam and in the Muslim community. By the special grace of Allah, when Boko Haram succeeds in establishing Sharia Law in Nigeria as a whole, you will see how moral conduct will become the norm in Nigeria.

Right now, in Nigeria, corruption has become very prevalent so much so that the country's economic growth has been seriously hampered. Under Boko Haram, Nigeria will only conduct business with Muslim countries. Western countries will be forbidden to have their embassies in Nigeria and to conduct businesses. Oil companies with western influence will be driven out of Nigeria," he said.

For a man who was trying to confess to his sins in order to have a smooth transition to the world beyond, he had spunk, I told myself. His double standards and words were sometimes disturbing that I felt I was being used to promote an agenda. I felt the need to call my editor in chief to ask his opinion about the relevance of pursuing the confession. As soon as the thought entered my mind, I realized it would be futile to get my editor to agree with me. He had already said he was looking forward to the story in its entirety. To say now that I was changing my mind would be counterproductive, considering the great expense that I had encountered in the process.

I let sleeping dogs lie, if you know what I mean, and left the matter alone. After all, I already knew who I was dealing with. The jihadist was a killer, a man without any conscience. There was no reason I should believe him when he said he was trying to cleanse his soul so he could have peace in the hereafter. If what I knew about jihadists is anything to go by, I do know that they fervently believe in going to paradise in the hereafter.

Since I already knew that there was a tremendous double standard among Muslims when it comes to the practice of Islam, I decided to leave the matter alone. After all, in Christianity, there was also double standard and misinterpretation of the bible to serve the needs of the church. In an era when ordained priests allegedly molest little boys entrusted to them, it was hard to really accuse Muslim clerics of double standard and hypocrisy when it also happens in other religions.

And if I might add, hypocrisy started a long time ago in various religions. In Christianity and in the times of Christ, the messiah warned of false prophets. The reason, I suspect, Christ warned Christians of false prophets was because of those who may come in the name of the lord to deceive Christians with false prophesies and pretense. And in today's environment, it was happening everywhere. There were more self ordained prophets and pastors in the world than ever before, even much more than in the times of Christ.

If falsity had become the norm in Christendom then it would be unfair to accuse Muslim clerics of the same misrepresentation when such a practice had been ongoing before Prophet Muhammad's time. In fairness to Christians, brainwashing adherents to harm others was not part of their religious practice. Some Muslim clerics on the other hand have often used their positions of influence in Islam to lure unsuspecting youths into the sect, to commit crimes against humanity in the name of Islam.

Recruiting naïve and gullible Muslim youth to kill innocent

people, mainly Christians, in suicide attacks is evil and a crime against humanity. As the voice of Islam, some imams have been known to recruit impressionable Muslims to join the holy war and jihad against unbelievers of the Islamic faith.

Not too long ago, I had written a story in a popular newspaper that angered the Zionists when I had supported intifada as a legitimate fight for the freedom of oppressed Palestinians in the Gaza Strip and West Bank. I had written the article when Yasser Arafat was still alive and was being harassed and intimidated with bulldozers by Israeli soldiers who had threatened to bulldoze his compound where he was basically helmed in. This was before he was poisoned and killed, in Ramallah.

Like everybody else, I was angered by the unfair bulldozing of Yasser Arafat's compound. Though my article did not call for a new intifada, I did make it clear that it was time for Palestinians to take up arms and fight for their rights.

My article was not an incitement but a wakeup call to arms. I don't think anyone likes oppression, least of all the Jews who suffered in the hands of Hitler during the period of Hitler's ethnic cleansing of Jews in Germany. When I had interviewed Israelis for the story, a lot of Jews did not like the fact that Yasser Arafat was being intimidated and threatened in his compound by Israeli soldiers.

During the periods of intifada against the Israeli occupation of the West Bank and Gaza Strip, a lot of Palestinians were told that fighting for their freedom was worth dying for, if need be. And in fairness to the Palestinians, intifada helped the Palestinian cause as their plight became more international than ever. Uprisings and rebellions or intifada may have some justification since it was mainly to get attention to a people being oppressed by a superior power like the Israeli government.

Though intifada was seen as a form of terrorism by Israeli authority, with Hamas being mostly blamed for the uprising, and branded a terrorist organization, a lot of people, including me, did not agree that Hamas was a terrorist organization.

Before you start asking about the relevance of intifada and Hamas to terrorism, let me explain. Hamas, to the uninitiated, is a Sunni Islamic Resistance Movement with a military or jihadist wing, in the Palestinian territories. In the beginning of the fight against Israeli occupation of the Gaza Strip and West Bank, Hamas essentially used suicide attacks and intifada against Israel, and Yasser Arafat was branded a terrorist, until late in the 20th century when things began to change in favor of Yasser Arafat-led Palestinian territories.

That change came in a tremendous fashion in June of 2007 when Hamas won most of the seats in the Palestinian Parliament in the 2006 Parliamentary elections. With Fatah defeated and renewed violent clashes, Hamas would later be branded, again, as a terrorist organization by the west, including Japan.

I remember also writing that the plight of the Palestinians may have started jihadist attacks in the Arab World. Islamic fundamentalism gained momentum in the periods of intifada which had first been initiated by the Muslim Brotherhood, who felt the west was with Israel in suppressing and oppressing Palestinians in their territories.

Though the original cofounder of Hamas, Sheik Ahmed Yassin, emphatically stated that Hamas was created to champion the liberation of Palestinians from Israeli occupation, and to establish a Palestinian State (Islamic State) in Gaza Strip and West Bank, those who disagreed with the Hamas Charter and purpose saw the organization as a terrorist organization that was against the state of Israel.

I also remember writing an article at that time in which I stated that Khaled Meshal, the then political bureau chief of Hamas, was ready to work with Israel to end the conflict if both parties could come to an agreement that included a Palestinian State. I reiterated the demands of Meshal, that as long as Palestinian refugees could return to Israel and Jerusalem was divided between the two sides that he was ready to make a deal.

My article had irked several Israeli leaders who had pointed out that Hamas was not ready for peace since they continued to launch rocket attacks and use suicide bombings against Israelis. I also pointed out that it will be difficult for both sides to reach an agreement as long as Hamas continues to use suicide bombers to attack Israeli outposts and soldiers.

Now you can see the point I am making. That point again is that a lot of jihadists often refer to the oppression of Palestinians as the main reason for their jihad against the west. Bin Laden, the late modern chief jihadist, who was recently killed in his hideout in Pakistan by the CIA-led Navy Seal clandestine operation, was once quoted as saying the main reason he took up arms, against the U.S., was because of U.S. support for Israel against the Palestinians.

Chapter 19

On the third day of being holed up in the bungalow, taking notes and recording as much information as I could record about the jihadist's confession, I had just about had it. I was exhausted, hungry, thirsty and bored. I was not bored of doing my job, no, that would never happen. I was just bored of the whole situation with the confession. I felt I was wasting my time, that I should be pursuing other headlining stories. As much as I wanted to call it quits and pack my things and get out of Maiduguri as quickly as I could, I knew my editor would be highly upset if I gave it up after all the time and expense I had put into getting the confession.

To ease the boredom, I would read the Nigerian dailies for anything newsworthy. If you have ever read a Nigerian newspaper, you would find that most of the news, when you opened the newspapers, was about local politicians and the discords they were having in their political parties. Other items you would probably find in those papers will be accidents on the potholed and waterlogged roads that crisscrossed the country of Nigeria. As I said earlier, all the roads in Nigeria were bad, very bad and accident prone.

Frequent road accidents were not the only issues besetting the nation of Nigeria. Terrorism and Boko Haram were the next headlining, newsworthy stories in Nigeria. Since 2009, Boko Haram has killed thousands of innocent people, and attacked schools, churches, mosques, markets, police stations and military facilities, in the group's quest for an Islamic state in northeastern Nigeria, and Nigeria as a whole.

Though the Nigerian government declared a state of emergency in three northern states where Boko Haram essentially operates from, and uses as its stronghold, no significant impact has been made with the so-called military offensive against the sect. As I said earlier, the military had also reportedly contributed to the plights of the citizens of northern Nigeria by constantly burning villages and indiscriminately killing innocent youth who were not even affiliated with Boko Haram; and displaying dead bodies as the bodies of the members of the sect.

The military claimed to be defeating Boko Haram by constantly displaying dead bodies of supposedly defeated Boko Haram members. The spokesman for the sect had continually rebuffed such claims as false. Eyewitness reports had also corroborated eyewitness accounts about the military killings of innocent people not affiliated with the sect, in order to appear to be winning the war against terrorism. My sources told me that some of the reported deaths committed by Boko Haram were also part of the deaths caused by military offensive against innocent bystanders and villagers.

I had initially written that not much was known about the intentions of Boko Haram other than the fact that they want to establish an Islamic state in Nigeria. My sources in Nigeria confirmed what I already knew that the leaders of the sect live a lavish western lifestyles, while openly condemning western education and lifestyles. So, with the double talk and standards, little was known about the motivation of the sect. If it was to get rid of western influence in Nigeria, why were the leaders of the sect enjoying the perks associated with western education and influence?

Since establishing my bureau in Abuja, Nigeria, to cover Africa, I have often traveled to Johannesburg where it was more peaceful and safe to broadcast my story via a sister satellite network. I had covered Boko Haram activities and the havoc and carnage the group continues to create in Nigeria.

As I said earlier, Boko Haram is a religious organization with a motive that was difficult to discern because of its political interest in the country. I said political interest because of the reported infiltration of the group by disgruntled northern Nigerian politicians who were bent on destabilizing the government of Jonathan who is a southerner.

Reliable and influential sources that I had spoken to in northern and southern Nigeria had told me that Boko Haram became more active after the death of former President Yar'Adua who died of cancer, in May 2010. According to the source, when a northerner could not take over the reins of government, Boko Haram took up arms to destabilize the country of Nigeria, under the pretext of wanting to establish an Islamic state and Sharia law.

Though Boko Haram was established in 2001, in Maiduguri, in Borno State, long before Jonathan came along, the group's activities had increased to include other northern states where it continues to carry out its jihad and holy war against non-Muslims

233

and Muslims. The reported disdain for western education and corruption in Nigerian government, among government functionaries, continue to be the reported motivation of the sect.

To worsen the already bad situation created by Boko Haram in northern Nigeria, alternative schools had also been established by the sect where it teaches children and young adults about Sharia Law and the bad influence of western education. My sources had informed me that the Islamic schools were being used to recruit children and women as suicide bombers and jihadists.

Since the death of its flamboyant and lavish spending leader, Mohammed Yusuf, who was killed in police custody in 2009, the group was said to have reportedly increased its violent attacks on police stations, mosques, churches, military facilities, and government infrastructures. Other sources told me the violence increased because of the infiltration of northern politicians rather that the death of Mohammed Yusuf.

The year before, I had written a detailed, thoroughly researched article about the people mostly targeted by Boko Haram. During one of my investigations, I had found out that more Muslims had died in the hands of Boko Haram than Christians. Though Christian religious institutions had constantly been attacked, such as churches, the majority of the children and women killed had been in the four northern states where the group has targeted churches and mosques. In my article I had written that Boko Haram was not only targeting Christians and churches but Muslims and mosques as well.

The issue of Boko Haram and its attacks had long surpassed the earlier notion that it was a Christian-Muslim feud, which had earlier been reported as the motive of the group. While it can be said that the creation of Boko Haram may have been as a result of high unemployment among the youth in northern Nigeria, a lot of the people I interviewed said the original members of Boko Haram joined because they felt disenfranchised and cut off from the wealth and resources of Nigeria.

Boko Haram, according to my investigation, was part the creation of disgruntled northern politicians for whom Yusuf Mohammed worked as the leader of a bodyguard group, formed by northern politicians, for protection against political foes. It was said that Yusu branched off as the leader of a group of bodyguards to launch Boko Haram, with funds from some northern politicians. Boko Haram was, based on my investigation, initially started as a death squad to take out political opponents, before the group metamorphosed into a terrorist organization, following the death of Yar'Adua and the ascension and imposition of Jonathan as president.

My investigation had also found out that some of the security agents or Nigerian secret service personnel were also members of the sect, which makes the war on terrorism by the Nigerian government a tough and unwinnable war. The funds from the Nigerian government often find its way into the coffers of the sect, thanks to some corrupt security personnel who often use part of the funds earmarked to fight terrorism, to aid terrorism.

Another reason, I found out, that Boko Haram has been a difficult target for the Nigerian military was not only because of the corruption of a few security personnel but also the fact that the group had splintered into many subgroups which included Ansaru and some lesser known fractions.

As Boko Haram had splintered into armed robbery gangs, and kidnappers, so had a section of the sect ventured into politics, with some of its sponsors in high places in government who often used the sect to get rid of their political opponents, under the cloak of terrorism.

Boko Haram has so far taken over the northeast of Nigeria, despite the state of emergency declared by the government of Jonathan. To add to the already skeptical impact of the soldiers stationed in the three northeastern states to protect the residents and school students, within a month of the state of emergency, over 50 college students were killed as they slept in their hostels in the wee hours of the morning, by Islamic terrorists dressed as Nigerian soldiers. The suspected terrorists came to the campus with sophisticated machine guns, AK47s, machetes, and daggers that they had used in the attacks.

The Islamic terrorists chose the right time to arrive at the campus for the mayhem, as students slept in their dormitories, in the cloak of night. In my report to my editor the day after the attack on the school campus, I wrote that some of the shrouded bodies were hard to identify because of the nature of mutilation and level of decomposition of the bodies, days after the attack.

As I have earlier written, it was not unusual for dead bodies to be left in the streets for days, uncollected, as was the case with the bodies of the slain college students in Gubja, Nigeria. Though the attack was said to be the work of Boko Haram, a lot of the students that survived the attack by running into the bush believed the Nigerian soldiers carried out the attack, especially since the victims were mostly Muslims.

In my analysis of the attack, I opined that if the state was locked down as part of the areas declared by the government as a state of emergency, how did the Islamic terrorists get to the campus? The answer lies in the already known fact that soldiers sometimes carry out their own carnage, while blaming it on Islamic extremists.

My source told me that the soldiers involved in the attack may be part of the campaign to make sure Jonathan did not run for another election when his term expires in 2015. Since most of the northern politicians eyeing the presidency were already saying that Jonathan should not think of running for reelection, the rumor was that those politicians were trying to make sure an actual state of anarchy and insecurity was created to make sure Jonathan was not allowed to run for another term.

There were several indications that the military was involved in the attack on the college campus, based on the attackers' knowledge of the layout of the campus, and where students were likely to be. Since the campus was being protected at the time, and soldiers were the only ones likely to have a clear knowledge of the campus layout, the belief was that the soldiers carried out the attack, not Boko Haram.

The military style of the operation, in which some of the students were woken up, gathered outside their dormitories, and gunned down, explained why some of the students did not at first attempt to run as they believed the soldiers were there to protect them, and not to kill them. According to an eyewitness account, the gathered students were gunned down one after the other, as they were still clad in their pajamas.

Though the siege took place around 1 a.m. in rural Gujba, where the campus was located, the attack confirmed what most citizens of northeast Nigeria had been saying that Boko Haram was not the only terrorists killing them. The soldiers were also killing them, under the pretext of protecting them.

I had asked the jihadist if he knew anything about the attack. He shook his head vigorously. "Contrary to what people think, Boko Haram is not the only Islamic jihadist movement in Nigeria. There are other jihadists too, even though everything is always blamed on Boko Haram. Don't get me wrong, we are always in the forefront of the holy war but we are not the only ones killing people in the northeast of Nigeria. As I told you before, we always acknowledge every attack we are involved in. We believe in taking responsibilities for our attacks.

The attack at the Yobe State College of Agriculture was not carried out by our men. Our trademark was very simple. We do not hide under the cloak of nights to carry out attacks. If we were going to attack a campus, we would do it in the daytime when students were in their classrooms, studying. Remember that we hate western influence, which included western education. To make our point, we would have entered the classrooms during the day, to kill the teachers and students rather than attack at night," the jihadist said, without mincing words.

In a sense I agreed with him. Boko Haram would have attacked the students during the day to make a statement, while also killing the teachers in the process. The teachers would be their first target since the teachers or lecturers were the source of the western knowledge that the students get at the school.

Though Boko Haram had been known to kill both Muslims and Christians, they did not purposively target Muslim students, unless of course those Muslim students were being westernized with western influence and education. If that was the case, then the Muslim students at the Yobe College of Agriculture would be the type of targets that Boko Haram would have preferred to kill. As I thought about the western influence angle, I began to suspect that Boko Haram might in fact be responsible for the attack, even though they did not immediately take responsibility for it.

While the Nigerian military had been known to slowly react to attacks carried out by Boko Haram, I did not think they would be bold enough to kill those they had sworn to protect. The military uniforms may have been stolen from military facilities. In recent times, Boko Haram has been attacking military barracks, stealing military uniforms and weapons, and sometimes killing soldiers and their families.

Another reason soldiers were suspected of carrying out the carnage was because the female hostels were spared from the carnage. If Boko Haram had been responsible, they would not have spared the women. Boko Haram members often attacked women and children as they had done on numerous occasions, without reservations or a second thought. This may be an unlikely possibility. I decided to ask the jihadist for his opinion one more time.

"Based on what you know, and I know you know a lot of things, do you think Boko Haram will succeed in its campaign to establish Sharia Law in Nigeria?" I asked him, half knowing what his answer would be. He didn't hesitate with his answer.

"Boko Haram will not succeed in establishing Sharia Law in Nigeria because of the demographics of Nigeria and because of the population of Christians in Nigeria, which as you know, is almost as much as the population of Muslims. Boko Haram knows that it cannot succeed in establishing Sharia Law, but its motive, as I said earlier, was to create enough carnage and disturbance that a lot of people, especially those in the north, would propose the idea of a secession which would give us the opportunity we are looking for, to establish Sharia Law.

If the idea of secession should come from the north, Boko Haram would have succeeded in its campaign to establish Sharia Law. But if the idea comes from the south, the end result would still be the same, which means Boko Haram would still have succeeded in its goal to establish Sharia Law. The whole purpose of the increased violence was twofold. The first motive was to create a state of anarchy that would make the north, and a part of the south, ungovernable. The second motive was to create a guerrilla war atmosphere in the country with enough violence to warrant public outcry, and request for a new administration, at the central level.

Right now, a lot of people are fed up with the government of Jonathan. They think he is weak and unable to control the situation in the north. There are those who think that he is not taking the Boko Haram violent-campaign seriously enough. Critics have often said that because the south is not affected by the type of violence in the north, that the government of Jonathan is merely giving lip service to the war against Boko Haram.

If the war spreads to the seat of power in Abuja and violence spreads to most parts of the south, such chaos would have been enough to stir Jonathan to action. The type of trouble that can be stirred in the south includes insecurity and fear, as currently exists in the north. To make that happen, what was basically needed was to carry out a major attack that would baffle and shake the south, and then the country.

The type of attack I am talking about is like the Westgate Mall attack in Nairobi or the terrorist attack on the World Trade Center and the Pentagon. That is the nature of attack that I am referring to, something baffling and astounding enough to shake the seat of power and to create panic in the country.

But I have to be honest with you, the original objective of Boko Haram was to create enough strife and fear that the military would be forced to intervene, as recently occurred in Egypt when the government of Mohammed Morsi was toppled by the Egyptian military. If such a thing should happen in Nigeria, an interim government would of course be imposed, which would allow a new election to take place. A new election would invariably favor the north, which would usher in the possibility of Sharia Law, or even worse, the type of government that would lean towards the establishment of Sharia Law in the country.

What I am talking about is pretty much like what happened in Egypt when the Muslim Brotherhood won the election that swept Mohammed Morsi into power. Or like the Islamic Republic of Iran where Sharia Law was the only known law. If the situation leads to a revolution like the Arab Spring or the Iranian revolution that led to the ouster of the Shah of Iran, then the objective of Boko Haram would have been met," he said.

I was astounded by the information. I had known some of the information that he provided. I knew a long time ago that Boko Haram was attempting to create mayhem and fear, so that some kind of revolution, like the one led by the Ayatollah Khomeini in Iran in 1980, could take place in Nigeria. But the problem with that equation was that Nigeria was too diverse and fragmented for an Islamic revolution. An Islamic government would immediately lead to a civil war that would surpass the Biafrian secession.

Somehow, based on the explanation given by the jihadist, I

had the impression he was right. A civil war would tremendously benefit Boko Haram, as that could lead to the division of the country, as happened in Sudan when the country was split into north and south. If there should be a southern and northern Nigeria division, as occurred in Sudan, Boko Haram would most certainly have succeeded in establishing Sharia Law, especially as northern leaders had once advocated the idea of Sharia Law in the north.

And of course, there was also the theory that Boko Haram was nurturing the idea of having its own elected president; again, like the Muslim Brotherhood in Egypt, with its own president, from its own rank and file, like the ousted Egyptian President, Mohammed Morsi. Since the oil that contributes about 90% of the GDP of Nigeria comes from the south, it would be virtually impossible for the north to function and survive without the oil money from the south.

The north would be ungovernable and unmanageable without the oil from the south to run its government. Agricultural produce that the north had been mainly known for was no longer adequate or functioning, especially since the advent of Boko Haram, which had mainly swept out and destroyed the farming in the north. With the north bereft of foreign currency to manage a sovereign state, and with no sustainable foreign exchange earner, the north would be unable to function without the south. And the dependence on foreign aid would be inevitable, something that Boko Haram was against.

In theory, the north would predominantly live on foreign aids if it were to secede from Nigeria, or vice versa. The answer to the equation would be to have a one Nigeria that would be under an Islamic rule, which would create a permanent divide, and a continuous unrest that would make the country too hostile for foreign investment. Without foreign investment, and foreign oil workers to extract oil from the rocks and deep seas, Nigeria would earnestly be a failed state. Under the current dispensation, oil exploration and extraction was getting harder to get, due to incessant kidnappings of oil workers in the south by MEND insurgents, and the other insurgents in the Niger Delta. Eventually, Nigeria would essentially collapse from terrorism and insurgencies.

A collapsed Nigeria would of course benefit Boko Haram.

Terrorist organizations thrive more during strife and chaos as currently exists in Somalia, Mali, Libya, Syria, Central African Republic, Sudan, and Egypt. If there was no reliable central government, the opportunity will exist for terrorism and the flourishing of militia groups as currently happening in Libya, Mali and Somalia.

"So, tell me, how is confession going to accelerate your entry into paradise?" I asked him, again for the umpteenth time, trying to get a proper explanation about his intentions. I knew he was going to give me the same answer he had given me before. Somehow, unlike the past when I didn't challenge him with questions, my plan was to basically check the facts in his confession to make sure he wasn't feeding me with a cock and bull story. I knew a lot about terrorism and jihad, maybe not as much as he did. I intended to use my knowledge to steer him when he finally tells me the whole story, instead of piecemeal confessions.

"If Boko Haram succeeds in establishing an Islamic state in Nigeria, which it will, the first thing would be to introduce a new currency that would be totally different from the current naira – the Nigerian currency. The new Islamic bills will come in five denominations. The small denominations would have the face of Mohammed Yusuf while the bigger denominations will have the face of Prophet Muhammad," he said, with a hideous smile on his face. That contradicted his earlier assertions that Boko Haram was not trying to establish Sharia Law in Nigeria, only in the north. I was confused again. I left the topic alone, to pursue other theories.

I was curious about the name that would be given to the new Islamic bills. It seemed interesting that the extremists would like to have the face of their late founder, Mohammed Yusuf, on their proposed bills. It wasn't that I believed they would succeed in establishing an Islamic state in Nigeria. No, I don't think they will succeed. There were numerous reasons why they would not succeed. I think I explained some of them earlier.

If the reality of an Islamic state should come to fruition, it would be extremely difficult for such a country to exist among nations. For one thing, the United Nations will not recognize it as a legitimate country. Only countries that traditionally object to anything western would recognize such a country.

Though Boko Haram had officially been recognized as a

foreign terrorist organization by the United States, and the west, it had finally gained the recognition it had long sought. How this recognition would benefit the sect in the long run remains to be seen. In the quest to gain recognition, Boko Haram had killed and maimed thousands of innocent people, and the general notion was that it would finally come to an end.

Killing, I have come to realize, gives significance to a terrorist organization. The more lives Islamic radicals take, the greater the publicity they get. In this age of daily terrorism in the world, the death of five to ten people was no longer news. What makes news these days is when 50 or more people die. The ideal target of any terrorist organization was a football or soccer stadium where thousands of fans often gathered. Such carnage would put any terrorist organization in the spotlight as occurred with Chechen terrorist organization in Moscow, several years ago, when Islamic terrorists took over a theater packed with hundreds of children, men and women.

The enormity and monstrosity of the attack included 40 to 50 armed Chechens who reportedly claimed allegiance to the Islamic militant separatist movement in Chechnya. The Nord-Ost siege as it was called, took place on October 23, 2002, which resulted in over 850 hostages being held hostage by the Chechen Islamic terrorists. The terrorists had demanded that Russian forces withdraw from Chechnya and an unconditional end to the Chechnya war.

In my coverage of the hostage crisis, I had written that the extremists were led by Movsar Barayev, the nephew of the notorious Chechen warlord, Arbi Barayev, who was reportedly an FSB operative-turned-warlord, and who was killed in 2001.

The two day siege had ended when the Russian Alpha Group forces pumped chemical weapons into the building's ventilation system before raiding the building. Though Alpha forces had killed all 50 terrorists, its action had also resulted in the death of all 150 hostages who had died due to adverse reactions to the gas poisoning that the Alpha forces had used. The toxicity of the substance that was pumped into the theater had subdued and killed the militants, as well as the hostages.

Though the extremists did not kill the hostages but their actions resulted in their deaths. While the rest of the world condemned the Russian government for using chemical weapons to solve the attack, the terrorists claimed victory as it brought their cause to the attention of the world, which was their original intention in the first place. The effect of the chemical known as naloxone was so much that Russian authorities adamantly refused to disclose the name of the chemical.

Extremists generally like attention, especially the type that draws worldwide media coverage, as was the case with the Moscow theater hostage crisis. Though the terrorists had lost over 50 members of their group, to them it was a victory that was beyond their expectation. Russian authorities had played into their hands by using chemical weapons against the terrorists which drew the ire and condemnation of leaders across the world.

Chapter 20

I heard the sound of an ambulance in the distance. Since we were in the middle of a deserted area, I sensed the ambulance was coming to the building. I began to get worried that the ambulance was there for the jihadist. It had been almost 48 hours since the siege and attempted rescue by the CIA and M15. Dead bodies were still strewn everywhere in the compound. I knew Nigerian soldiers had been trying to remove the bodies, but as I said earlier, in these parts of the world, things move very slowly.

Here in Nigeria, bodies often decompose before getting picked up. I had basically given up wondering why authorities were slow to do their jobs here. I realized this was Africa, where priorities were often dictated by the amount of bribery given and received; and if one was willing to pay to make things go faster. The norm here was to wait endlessly for a simple task of getting papers signed by a senior official. Until money exchanged hands, things can be painfully slow. In some cases, if bribery was not involved, it even takes longer.

Sometimes, soldiers and or the police often carry out the grim task of picking up dead bodies in the streets. Since there was no emergency response unit or first responders, the Red Cross often handles emergency situations. If someone were dying, a relative would either rush that person to the hospital in a bike or by any local means available. Red Cross was only available in some areas, and even in areas where it was available, it was not 24hours as most emergency responders. After all, this was Africa where human lives meant very little.

If it would have been possible to have emergency responders, the ineffectiveness of the electricity system would have rendered it unworkable. To have an effective 24hours first responders or emergency units, there had to be a reliable power supply, 24/7. Another problem was that the phone systems must work and be reliable. It was not. Though mobile phones had made telecommunication ubiquitous, it was still a prepaid system. The mobile phone business has not advanced to where individuals could be trusted with contracts or monthly payments.

In Africa, and especially in Nigeria, individuals could only use the cell phones through a prepaid system, meaning you had to buy as many minutes as you needed; and when the minutes ran out, you buy more minutes. The reliability of the cell phones was another story. Most times, there was no network or signal, meaning the phones seldom work. I remember not being able to use my phone for a whole week even though I had purchased enough minutes to last a whole month on the phone. I had resorted to my emergency satellite phone.

There was a period when every cell phone needed to be registered to prevent kidnappers from being effective. The registration of individual SIM card was so poorly handled that many phones were disabled for weeks on end until they were all registered. I had registered my SIM card at a local bank as was instructed but even with that, it still didn't work.

The SIM card registration was another painful process. The process entailed waiting in line, in a bank lobby, for hours on end to be registered. In each bank location that I visited, only one person was given the responsibility to register the multitude of people thronging the designated banks for registrations.

The process was so horrible that I almost gave up having a cell phone. First, one had to supply all his personal information, including a fingerprint and other vital information that were laughably ridiculous. The process was not amusing by any means, but then again this was Africa, where things often take a painfully long time to accomplish. Though I had my satellite phone, I still needed my local number to be active.

I was still thinking about the slow processes of getting things done when I heard the sound of the ambulance as the sirens seemed closer and closer. I didn't need to be told that the ambulance was coming to the bungalow. My only fear was whether it was coming to take the jihadist away. Since I was not privy to any official information exchange, I was basically on my own, save for Musa, who would sometimes tell me something he deemed important enough for me to know.

Occasionally, the CIA commander would tell me something he felt I should know. I still did not consider him a friend, even though we were both westerners. He never acted or treated me as if we were on the same side. If anything he talked and acted towards me as if I was the enemy. Maybe being stoic and unfriendly comes with his training. It could be he was not trained to be friendly. In a sense I don't blame him. It was hard to be friendly in a hostile environment where trust was a forgone word. In Africa, to survive, one had to learn to only trust himself.

Though I respected the fact that he was a secret agent even though he did everything he could to hide that fact from me, I still felt there should be some kind of camaraderie of some sort between us since we were both Caucasians working in this Dark Continent where citizens were often told to turn in, early in the evening.

Anyway, as the siren got closer, I began to nurture a sense of forebode, that the confession was about to end. Over the years, I had learned to trust my instincts, even though my nerves and patience had been tested very badly in the last few days. And because of my bruised patience and nerve, I sort of didn't trust my instinct as I used to. In ordinary times, and under a normal situation and circumstance, I would trust my instinct. But not now, when I had been sleeping on this hard-surface cot for hours, night and day. It was hard for me to trust anything, least of all my instinct, as it had been shaken by unfathomable events.

I saw the same nurse with tribal marks on her face, walking briskly towards the gurney the jihadist lay on, and not long after, I saw the doctor that had shaken the wits out of the jihadist the day before. The commotion confirmed my worst fears that something very bad was amiss. As the sirens got closer and closer, I began to think of anything that I hadn't asked the jihadist, to make sure I had covered the bases.

The jihadist saw the alarm in my eyes and smiled. The smile was that same cynical smile that seemed to defy all worries. I had seen that cynical smile before. It was the same hideous but cynical smile he had on his face when I first met him. Though he was more apologetic and remorseful then than now, I couldn't help noticing the gradual changes that had occurred in his demeanor since then.

To me it was a kiss of death, that he had somewhat changed. With him, dying signifies that he was beyond caring about this world. He knew his time was very near, that it was useless for him to care about anything. Somehow I didn't blame him. If I were in his shoes I would probably act like that. Don't get me wrong, I was not showing any sympathy for him. As far as I was concerned he deserved what he had coming to him. It was hard for me to commiserate with a person who had spent his life killing people.

But despite my contempt for the life he had lived, I still couldn't help noticing how he had used the religion of Islam to hide his atrocities. Now, he may not be a natural born killer who loves to kill. The fact that he loves to kill others may have come from his Islamic belief that paradise awaits those who had sacrificed their lives for the holy war, jihad.

Leaving that mindset aside, I hurriedly asked him about the downing of the Dana Air plane that had crashed into a heavily populated Lagos neighborhood in Lagos, Nigeria, that had killed all 153 passengers that were aboard the plane, and 10 people on the ground.

"I was waiting for you to ask me that question. The downing of that plane was supposed to launch our heaviest casualties, or the mother of all casualties. Somehow, the Nigerian government successfully blocked the fact that Boko Haram was behind the downing of the plane. Two of our men were aboard the plane, and had successfully used the latest underwear explosives that al-Asiri had recently produced. Both men were wearing the underwear explosives, to make sure it was successful. And the mission was successful.

After the botching of the Christmas day attack that resulted in that Nigerian jihadist unsuccessfully detonating the bomb in his underwear, we were not taking any chances. Rather than send one jihadist, we sent two. And from the evidence of the carnage, we knew the underwear explosives had successfully detonated," he said with a proud smile.

I couldn't believe that the McDonnell Douglas MD-83 plane had been downed by suicide bombers. For one thing, Boko Haram spokesperson did not come out to take responsibility for the crash, and for another, the Nigerian aviation authorities had said it was due to bad weather. The funny thing about that assertion was that the weather on that day was good and sunny. In my opinion, Mother Nature did not play a part in the crash.

The confession of the jihadist, claiming that Boko Haram was responsible for the crash, stunned me beyond words and belief. I couldn't understand how it was possible for the crime to have been covered up. I could only think of one reason why the government would want to cover up such an atrocity and carnage. The only reason that came to my mind was that such a revelation would undermine the country's effort on the war on terrorism. Another reason that I could think of was that the government didn't want to make it look like the commercial airliners were susceptible to terrorist attacks, since so many foreigners had died in that crash, mostly westerners.

And there was that mayday call from the pilot of the plane that the plane was having trouble, minutes before it crashed. If the plane was having trouble minutes before the fatal crash, it means the plane went down because of mechanical failure rather than suicide bombing. As I thought about what the jihadist said, it began to make sense when you really think about it. The information about the pilot radioing that the plane was having problems came from the Nigerian government. No one else was privy to the source of that information. There was no black box to prove that the pilot had actually radioed that the plane was having problems.

If the pilot knew the plane was having problems and was able to radio the information, he could easily have been able to safely crash land the plane anywhere to reduce the amount of casualties and damage that later resulted from the crash. Every hypothesis zeroed in on the fact that the purportedly radioed information was made up, to cover up the actual crime.

It didn't make sense but then again nothing makes sense about terrorism and what goes on in Nigeria. It doesn't make sense that Nigeria has one of the highest unemployment and poverty rates in the world, when the country has enough oil resources to bring the poverty rates to the barest minimum. Rather than use the enormous oil wealth to modernize the country, the leaders would rather embezzle and steal the resources to amass their personal wealth. With three Nigerians in the list of the world's richest people, and with a vast majority of the sources of such wealth coming from oil, it didn't make sense that wealth should be concentrated in very few hands.

What didn't make sense was how a country with so much potential could allow its wealth to drift away into the pockets of a few thieves. Rather than use the wealth to develop the country's infrastructure, the embezzlers who were mainly government functionaries would prefer to take that money overseas to countries that were already wealthy, to build homes and enrich personal fortunes. A recent survey had showed that over 50% of Nigeria's foreign exchange earning end up in foreign countries.

If the current trends continue at a time most countries in the west are producing their own oil, and finding alternative energy to replace oil and natural gas, Nigeria may end up getting deeper into more debts with the Paris club and IMF, and the bottom of the world's poorest nations, unless development commences immediately. Nigeria already belongs to the club of the world's poorest countries by default. Such a poverty default could have been averted if the country's leaders, since independence, had focused on developing the country with the country's resources rather than lining their pockets with the wealth of the nation.

The downing of the Nigeria's Dana Air, was a tragedy that could have been avoided if the country uses its resources adequately to create world-standard security, and better aviation management equipment.

Though the aircraft had had a bad history of its own, it was still senseless to have exposed so many passengers to such a tragedy.

Though tragedy can occur anywhere in the world, regardless of the sophistication of the pilots and planes, the case of Dana Air was totally different. It was senseless. The plane was piloted by two experienced pilots. The captain was an experienced American pilot, while his copilot was an Indian, both experienced. It didn't make sense that a 45minutes flight would meet with such a tragedy.

As I analyzed the crash, it began to dawn on me that the jihadist's confession that the crash had been caused by the underwear explosives, that its operatives detonated while aboard the aircraft, posing as passengers, may have been right. What didn't make sense though was why the Nigerian government covered up the facts that the crash was caused by terrorism. It may very well be that the government did not know that explosives had been responsible for the crash. Another theory could be that the government did not want the international community to know that terrorists had infiltrated its commercial planes.

When I spoke to my source about the incident, he had informed me that if Boko Haram had been responsible that they would have claimed responsibility. Another source told me that since Boko Haram was an attention seeking sect that the group would have immediately claimed responsibility if it were responsible. None of the arguments made sense but what the jihadist said made a little sense that there was a tremendous amount of cover up involved especially as so many nationalities from different countries in the west, had died in the crash.

I couldn't quite resolve the question of who was responsible for the crash but one thing that lingered in my mind was that Abuja was a known Boko Haram hotbed, where the group had bombed a police station, a U.N building and churches in the past. The plane had departed from Abuja for Lagos when the crash occurred, as it was nearing its destination. It began somewhat to point to terrorism since Abuja was a known haven for terrorists.

If the plane had departed Lagos for Abuja, the chances of terrorism being associated with the crash would have been slim. Though this reasoning is feeble, it still makes sense that terrorism may have played a part in the crash. I had researched the history of the plane and found that it had a checkered past, with past problems of engine malfunction, and other mechanical issues. I learned a long time ago that the Nigerian aviation industry often uses planes that had been ruled unsafe by the rest of the world, because such planes were often cheap for leasing and purchasing.

I turned back to the jihadist who appeared to be sleeping. I knew the trick and feigned a cough to get his attention. It didn't take long before he got the hint. He flipped his eyes open, and looked at me, with a smile playing on his lips.

"It won't be long now. I can see the angels already beckoning me, and trying to grab me. They are trying to grab and pull me with them to the beyond, but somehow I have been able to resist them. I also see them laughing at me as if they are making fun of my feeble effort to resist them. I don't know exactly what it is that they are laughing at but it seems to me they are mocking me," he said incoherently.

In my mind I was thinking it was probably the agents of Lucifer that were pulling him rather than real angels, unless of course the angels were the angels of death. It defied all reasons that angels would be reaching out to pull someone who had lived his life killing and maiming people. I didn't believe for a second that the angels of God were trying to grab him. It was possible they were trying to grab him to toss him into hell where he belongs.

Or the devil may have put on the white robes of angels to deceive him he was going to paradise so that he could willingly surrender. Whether the dreamy forces that were trying to grab him were from God or Lucifer, I didn't care. It was not worth dwelling on.

"You don't believe me, do you?" The jihadist asked as if reading the disbelief on my face. In the past, since I started recording his confession, he had been able to read my mind. I was not sure he was entirely correct this time when he said he could read disbelief on my face. I may have disbelieved the fact that angels appeared in his vision, but I wasn't entirely disbelieving the fact that the agents of Lucifer were the forces that appeared in his vision.

The siren was getting closer than ever and by the look on the nurse's face and her body language, I knew it spelt a bad omen for the jihadist. Though the jihadist had accepted death as a necessary end for him, I was not ready to let him go, just yet. I still had things to work out with him. He was after all, the source of information concerning the insidious nature of terrorism in Nigeria. I eyed the commotion with suspicion, knowing that something was amiss, and about to transpire.

I could see in the eye of the jihadist that he was thinking what I was thinking, that doomsday was very near, nearer than ever. Though we suspected that the siren was bringing a bad omen, we were not entirely sure that the siren was coming to take the jihadist away. But the bungalow was the only house in the area. I told myself that they may have found more people who were not entirely dead in the surrounding bushes, following the aftermath of the botched rescue. Since I was not entirely a member of the law enforcement community, I knew they would not share information of any kind with me. If I had not stumbled on the dying jihadist when I did, this story about the jihadist and his confession would not have be written.

I had to think of something relevant as quickly as possible to make sure that every aspect of the story was covered. I thought of what I should ask that would lead the confession back to where it should be.

"Remember that when I met you that I was actually covering

the story about the kidnapping of five westerners by Ansaru, and how the CIA and M15 had managed to botch the rescue? How did Boko Haram get involved? I thought Boko Haram and Ansaru members did not work together or see eye to eye?" I asked. He looked at me as if I said something that was totally off the wall. But I maintained my stoic expression, not wanting to betray any emotion.

"You are wrong, like most people who think Boko Haram and Ansaru are sworn enemies. They are not. Members of Ansaru are former members of Boko Haram. They did not leave Boko Haram because of disagreement or infighting or anything of that nature. The members of Boko Haram that left to form Ansaru did so for a different style of holy war that was different from the type practiced by Boko Haram. Even with that, from time to time, Ansaru and Boko Haram would work together to share information and to carry out an assignment.

Don't get me wrong, Boko Haram and Ansaru are different in the way each work but they share the same ideology of establishing Sharia Law in northern Nigeria, and in Nigeria as a whole. The goal of both organizations is to see the whole of Nigeria under an Islamic rule, like the type currently in place in Iran.

The kidnapping of five westerners was first hatched by Boko Haram and given to Ansaru to execute. Even with that, the jihadists involved in the kidnapping were a combination of Boko Haram and Ansaru foot soldiers who had trained together for the assignment, before carrying it out.

The reason things went awry was that someone within the ranks of Boko Haram had sold out and given the information about the place the five kidnapped westerners were hidden, to authorities. I think someone in government that was probably playing double, sold out. I said so because a lot of people knew a lot about the proposed kidnapping before it was actually carried out," he said, with a thoughtful look on his face.

I was surprised when he said someone within the Boko Haram ranks had tipped the law enforcement agents about the hideout of the hostages. When he said that, the first thing that came to my mind was whether someone in government who was also a sponsor of the sect was trying to clear himself of any association by first selling out the group's proposed plan to make him look like an infiltrator, getting information for the government in which he was a major player.

Another theory that came to mind was that Boko Haram may have set up Ansaru to destroy the organization since Ansaru exists as a splinter group of Boko Haram. The latter theory seemed to appeal more than the former. Since the government of Jonathan had been focusing on those in government working with Boko Haram, those already under suspicion may be trying to clear themselves of such suspicion by becoming informants for the government, while also playing the role of informant for Boko Haram.

Using Ansaru to carry out the kidnapping may have been a ploy to get the government to refocus its attention on Ansaru instead of Boko Haram. If that was the case, and it seems to be the case, then it was a good ploy as the government had reduced its focus on Boko haram to once again focus on Ansaru. Especially since Ansaru had become a deadly splinter group.

Another theory may be that the plan was hatched by both Boko Haram and Ansaru to create confusion in the minds of the planner of the war against terrorism. Creating confusion in the minds of the planner of the war on terrorism, the government of Jonathan and the military will become ineffective. And the plan appears to be working.

The success of the plan was confirmed when the U.S. recognized Boko Haram as a terrorist organization, leaving out Ansaru. The recent recognition by the United States, of Boko Haram, as a terrorist organization confirmed the suspicion that Boko Haram had always sought recognition for its actions from the international community.

Before you start to wonder about the relevance of the recognition and the use of Ansaru to carry out the kidnapping of the five westerners, I will tell you. After the much publicized kidnapping of the five westerners, it became apparent to the west that terrorism was in Africa to stay, that the African brand of terrorism was no longer an offshoot of al-Qaeda. Rather than continuing to link terrorism in Africa with al-Qaeda in the Maghreb or in the Arabian Peninsula, it became crucial to recognize the only visible terrorist group in Nigeria, Boko Haram.

With al-Shabab having been recognized as a terrorist organization, and with Boko Haram creating more havoc and carnage in Africa than al-Shabab, it became urgent to recognize Boko Haram so that the international community could begin to focus on the Nigerian sect, Boko Haram, before it becomes an international problem rather than a Nigerian problem. So far, it is a Nigerian problem but the group's recent attack of a U.N building in Abuja points to the group's growing fierceness and viciousness.

For the CIA and M15, if Boko Haram was left to be handled by the Nigerian government, it could soon become a bigger problem for the world, especially as it appears the Nigerian government was unable to deal with the problem. With the recognition also came seizures of the assets of those who sponsor the group. The recognition includes the seizure of any known assets of the sect in foreign countries. Now you begin to get the picture, I hope.

As I was analyzing some of what the jihadist had said, an idea occurred to me. I had read in a recent Nigerian newspaper that the son of the governor of Kano State was sponsoring terrorism, by using his construction company to funnel money to the terrorist sect. I was not particularly surprised by the accusation since most northern politicians were said to be backing Boko Haram in its campaign of terror.

I wanted confirmation from the jihadist, who seemed to know everything by virtue of his position as a senior operative, in the rank and file of Boko Haram. As usually the case with the jihadist, he spoke as honestly as he could, that most politicians do work with Boko Haram and Ansaru.

"Without the backing and sponsorship of politicians in the north, Boko Haram and Ansaru will not have the funds or the influence to bring arms into Nigeria. Though they sponsor us, we also provide a service for them. From time to time, we would kill or derail political opponents of our sponsors, as a token repayment for the funds they provide for our sect.

As a rule we do not go soliciting funds from politicians. They usually come to us with a proposal, which we often verify for authenticity. You have to understand that we do not encourage politicians to sponsor or help us, as most of those politicians are known to enjoy western spoils and perks, that we in the Boko

Haram sect abhors. As a rule, we disagree with the way of life of our sponsors but because they believe in what we do, or at least pretended they did, we often allowed them to sponsor us.

We did not entirely depend on politicians for funds. We had well-wishers from every nook and cranny of the Arab world. We did not entirely starve for funds but we did not reject funds as well. If someone wanted to fund our programs and we could authenticate him as a genuine person who actually believes in our cause, we would accept such a donation. In return, we would carry out their wishes, if they had one. There were those who believed in us and for that reason, supported us with money.

We had Muslims in the west that constantly sent money for our operations. Some of them would send money directly to some of our members on the pretext of sending money back home to their relatives. And of course, there were those who lived in our strongholds that would send us money for protection.

The people that sent us money for protection did so because of fear that we would attack them. When a family or a business would send us money for protection, we would provide them protection. In some cases, those that asked us for protection would not get such a protection if they did not believe in our cause. We would take the money and still kill them if they said they did not believe in Islam or our cause. We did not reject anyone's money, and we did not solicit people for money either. Those that sent us money did so for reasons best known to them.

We would accept all kinds of donations or sponsorship without vetting the sources. But if someone comes upfront to us for any kind of help, we would vet the person to make sure he was not a setup by the government. We knew we had moles amongst us, but there was nothing we could do about that. A lot of organizations had moles amongst them, no matter how high or low they were, that provided information to the enemies. Even the great Satan, the U.S., had moles within its government that provides information to its enemies. Apart from those that come out publicly to admit that they were moles, like Edward Snowden and Chelsea Manning, there were those in Congress and in the Pentagon that were moles, providing secrets to the enemies.

We are no different from other organizations. We are only different by design and ideology. Our ideology is unique and compelling because we believe in it. We believe that part of the reason Nigeria was still backward after 52 years of independence was because of corruption and western influence which brought such crookedness as 419fraudsters, homosexuality and drug addiction.

Before the advent of western influence in Nigeria, our people traded by bartering their goods with others, without the need for money. But the influx of western goods also brought its bad influence which included the use of money. Money brought evil to Nigeria, and that evil has kept the country backward and retrogressive, while the perpetrators of the evil that bedeviled the country are out there calling the continent of Africa, a dark and an underdeveloped continent.

Now they are saying aids and HIV started in Africa, when they were the ones that brought the disease to Africa. For decades, Africans never needed condoms because there was no need for them. We were natural people that trusted one another. Our women never needed protection against diseases until westerners came to Africa with their evil and corruption.

Sleeping with animals started in the west, where the source of aids and HIV first started. Africans never befriended animals the way westerners did, until they brought that impure influence to Africa. The reason Boko Haram insists on getting rid of western influence in Nigeria is to make the country pure again so that development can start. Right now, there is no development because of the evil of money. Our people have left the farms for the cities because of the attraction of money that the west brought to Africa.

A long time ago, Africa produced, and exported food to the rest of the world. But since the advent of western influence, Africans now import food. Agriculture that used to provide food for everyone is now barely touched, thanks to western influence. Our kids now run away from their countries to overseas because of the attractions of the evil of the west. This has to stop. It needs to stop if Africa, and most especially Nigeria, is to forge ahead and be respected among nations. Africa cannot continue to languish behind western countries. The continent has enough mineral resources to be self sufficient and be respected. And the only way for Africa to be respected and be counted among nations on equal basis, is for Africa to go back to its roots.

It was the envious root of cultivation and agricultural produce that attracted the west in the first place. Africa can use its resources to surpass the rest of the world and be mighty, if it chooses to, and Boko Haram is doing its part to make sure Africa realizes its mistakes of the past, and present addiction to western influence," the jihadist said, as if he had had all of this pent up inside him for so long.

Somehow, I began to see his point. Don't get me wrong, I still did not agree with him, that killing others was the best way to make them believe in you, and change towards your direction. Jihad, for whatever reasons, has never been a successful quest for its practitioners. I believe if jihad was practiced as a peaceful holy war that it would probably achieve its objective better and more effectively. People generally do not respond very well to intimidation and coercion. The best way to change a people is not to kill and maim them. Intelligent persuasion is still the most effective way to change a people. Violence hardly achieves anything, I said to myself.

I turned to the jihadist who appears to be having trouble breathing. It suddenly occurred to me that he may have given his last confession. Death, it appears, was at his doorstep. He was shaking violently, as if taken by seizures, and then the sound of the siren got very close, as if the imminence of the jihadist's death had been timed. For the first time, I drew nearer to the gurney he had been lying on, and attempted to give him some comfort. It was no use. The man was shaking so violently, with his mouth foamy, that I began to really fear for him. It was uncharacteristic of me to fear for anyone, having been around death for too long. But the sight of the jihadist dying worried me to no end that I began to sob without realizing it.

This was a man I had come to hate for his actions. I could not understand the tears that were streaming down my cheeks. I had heard from people that the longer a person spends with another person, the sooner empathy crawls into the equation. It must have been the case with me, as I realized that my long held emotion was beginning to overwhelm me.

They said death was a gradual transition that gradually wears its victim down until the transition was complete. There were deaths that occur very suddenly, and before the victims were conscious of it, they were consumed and taken away untimely, without a formal notice. And then there was the death that comes while a person was peacefully asleep. Death exists in various fashions but death as is known, is the cessation of vital organs in a person. Though the most common form of death was through the phenomena of biological aging, there were other forms of death such as death by hunger, diseases like aids, cancer, heart disease, stroke, and of course murder in the hands of others.

In the case of the jihadist, senescence was not the cause of his encroaching death. If death had come to him in a natural order, it would be different. That would have been a death well earned. It was not that death was ever an earned cessation or accomplishment. No. Death was morbid, and a painful cessation that sometimes comes suddenly, without warning and notice. With the jihadist, the warning had been predated as if the weight of his earthly sins had accelerated the timeline of his life.

As I looked at the jihadist, I could see paleness already beginning to envelope his being, as if the substance of life had been sapped from his body. One thing I could see visibly was the gradual reduction in his body temperature as he continued to shiver and quiver. I knew his shivering was not due to fear as he was not afraid of dying. He had long craved and accepted death, long before it actually came.

As the trembling reduces, I could see his body stiffening in a sudden jerk, as if the time had come. His eyes opened just then as if to give a final farewell. His eyes were dilated as if empty of life. But it was not readily empty of life as there was still something lingering there that resembles life.

The irony of death was that life quickly transitions to death within seconds of death's final arrival, as was the case with the jihadist. Right before my eyes, I saw him fighting a losing battle with death. His eyes were closing and opening, as if he was trying to tell me he was fighting the inevitable. I could tell he was losing consciousness fast. I knew by just looking at him that his last breath was within seconds. As his final moment came, he gave one final effort but the cold hands of death were too powerful for him this time as they snuffed the remaining life out of him. His hands went limp, and his head rolled to one side, and it was then I knew he was gone, gone from this world, to the world unknown where speculations exist about hell, heaven and paradise.

This was death in its natural habitat where only the invited are granted passes. I could see that the jihadist's pass had been issued long before he knew he had a pass to enter the dark gloom of death's habitat. I shook my head, wondering if he would make it to paradise as he had been promised by the harbingers of his Islamic faith. I collected the few things I had brought with me, as the Yoruba nurse came to cover his face. She looked at me with sadness in her eyes. I didn't know if the sadness was for me or for the dead man. I didn't wait to find out as I left with Musa, into the dying sunset.

About the Author

Adrian Davieson is the author of several self published books which include: *Nemesis; The Hunt for a Notorious Terrorist; Identity Thieves and Swindlers; A Poetry of Contemporary Times; Twisted Intentions; Deadly Odyssey;* and *Management in Troubled Times.* All books are available at Barnes&Nobles.com and Amazon.com, including all online bookstores.

Inquiries about this above books can be sent to *adavieson@aol.com* or through the author at: 281-250-2480

36918905R00152

Made in the USA
Lexington, KY
11 November 2014